Illustrated Holy Scriptures

a biblical show and tell

Winston C. Fraser

1225 rue Bellevue
Saint-Lazare, QC J7T 2L9
438-969-2510
wcfraser@sympatico.ca

Layout: Winston Fraser and Jim Fraser
Cover design: Winston Fraser
Cover page photo: Winston Fraser

Dedication page photos: left: Ron Planche; right: Wikipedia.org

Section opener photos: istockphoto enhanced by author

Scripture quotations: All Scripture quotations, unless otherwise indicated, are taken from the Holy Bible, New International Version®, NIV®. Copyright ©1973, 1978, 1984, 2011 by Biblica, Inc.® Used by permission of Zondervan. All rights reserved worldwide. www.zondervan.com The "NIV" and "New International Version" are trademarks registered in the United States Patent and Trademark Office by Biblica, Inc.®

Back cover photos:
Top: Winston Fraser
Bottom: Fraser family archive

Printed and bound in Canada by:
Katari Imaging
282 Elgin St.
Ottawa, ON K2P 1M3
613-233-1999
www.katariimaging.com

Printed and bound in USA by:
Ingram Spark (www.ingramspark.com) and others.

ISBN: 978-1-7771308-7-9

Dedication

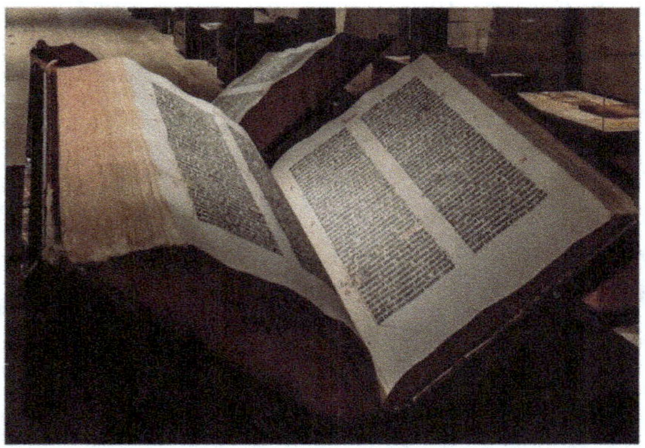

Gutenberg Bible at Yale University

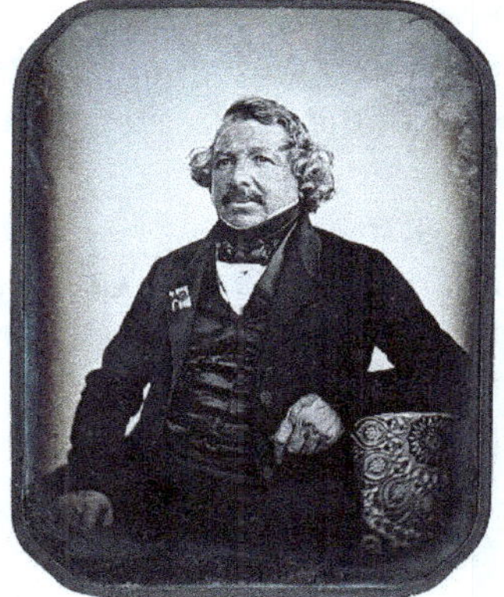

Louis Daguerre

Deciding to whom this book should be dedicated was a difficult challenge. There were so many individuals — past and present — who played important roles in allowing me to bring this project to fruition. But, after much reflection, I have decided to dedicate the book to two historical figures whose inventions had enormous and lasting impacts on the world and essentially laid the groundwork for this book. German Johannes Gutenberg invented a printing process that produced the Gutenberg Bible in 1455. Frenchman Louis Daguerre invented the daguerreotype, the first form of modern photography in 1839.

Acknowledgements

I wish to acknowledge the assistance of family, friends and others who provided photographs, acted as book reviewers or contributed in any other way to the realization of this book.

To all the following I extend my sincere thanks: Barbara Challies, Bill Ivy, Bruce Allen, Elaine Fraser, Greg Bailey, Greg Beck, Jody Robinson, Kira-Marie Lazda, Laurel Parson, Leslie Nutbrown, Linda Hoy, Pat Ivy, Phyllis Nesbitt, Ron Planche, Sharron Rothney, Susan Nutbrown and Warren Fraser. To any who have been inadvertently omitted, I offer my apologies.

Finally, a special word of appreciation to my brother Jim for his invaluable assistance with photo retouching, layout and production.

Table of Contents

Foreword

Do you long for God to speak to you? Have you ever thought, "God doesn't speak to me the way he does to others"? If those thoughts have crossed your mind, then cheer up, my friends. This is a book about how God spoke in the past and how he still speaks today. Maybe you thought that dreams, visions, and hearing God's voice were just for biblical times. Not so, my brothers and sisters! In fact, Hebrews 13: 8 (NIV) plainly says that God is the same yesterday and today and forever. He is still speaking through Scripture, dreams, visions, and the Holy Spirit.

In the preface to **Illustrated Holy Scriptures,** Winston shares with the reader how God spoke to him in a dream which culminated in the birth of what became a national enterprise called Proclamation — the reading aloud of Scripture without commentary or explanation. The power of reading God's word out loud has a formidable impact on all who participate, whether reading or listening. God's word always produces fruit when we act in obedience and for this initiative a debt of gratitude is due Winston.

Whether it was Frederick R. Barnard or Confucius who first said "A picture is worth a thousand words" is beside the point in this fascinating work by Winston Fraser. He has combined his God-given writing and photography skills to give the reader a veritable feast for the eyes and food for the spirit. As I read the Scriptures and appreciated the accompanying illustrations, it stimulated my remembrance of how those same verses have impacted my life and continue to do so. Through photos and Scripture, I find that this book speaks with compassion to where we all live and move and have our being.

The Christian life is a life of joy. We are not in this race alone, for we run with our Teacher. With his assistance we realize truth more strongly and see things more clearly. We run with others of like-mindedness. But this is not a race of constant activity. It must have times of pausing — times of contemplation, times of solitude, times of prayer. This is the prize the reader receives from Winston's timely work, **Illustrated Holy Scriptures.** It is meant to stir our hearts and to open our spirits to hear God and then to act in obedience to what we hear. As you read, take time to think, to see, to taste, and to know that the Lord is good. Allow the Lord to use this work as a resource in your spiritual formation.

In the Good News version of the Bible, a profound verse from Ecclesiastes 7:29 says, *This is all I have learned: God made us plain and simple, but we have made ourselves very complicated.* In this book, Winston has not complicated what God says in his Word or what He has done in nature but has plainly and simply combined the two so that the reader can rejoice over how great our Lord really is.

Winston states in the Preface his desire for this book: "May the fruit of my endeavour bring the reader hope, encouragement, and a sense of reassurance in these troubled times. And may these biblical appetizers provide motivation for the further exploration of God's lifechanging Word." I believe that this has been accomplished — and so much more.

— Phyllis M. Nesbitt

Preface

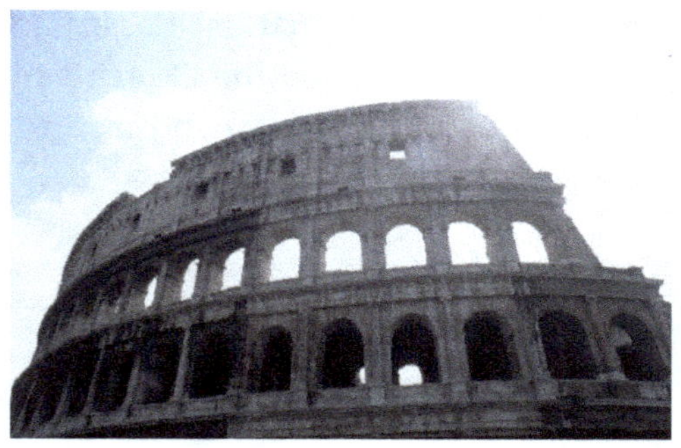

Colosseum, Rome

"Rome wasn't built in a day." Nor was the idea for this biblical "show and tell" book hatched overnight. Rather, it was conceived and realized over a period of more than 70 years – threescore-years-and-ten that were marked with several important milestones relative to both its show and tell aspects.

St. Peter's Sunday School

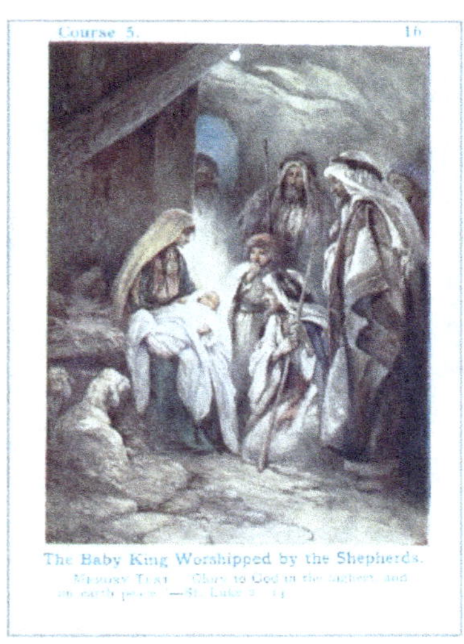

Sunday School memory verse card (Anglican Church archives)

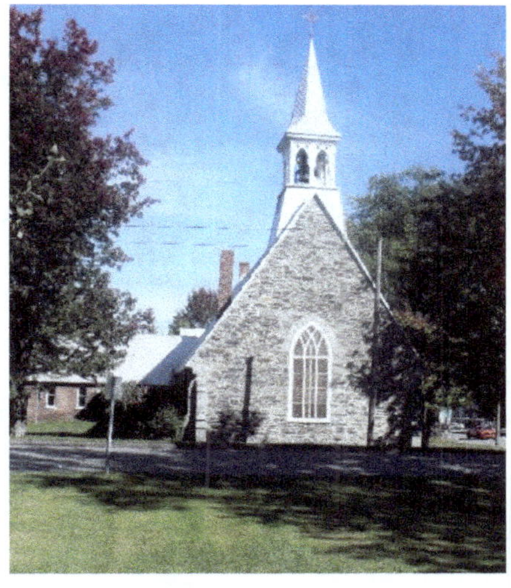

St. Peter's Church, Cookshire, Que. *(author)*

My first exposure to the Bible dates back to 1950 when, at the age of six, I began attending Sunday School at St. Peter's Anglican Church in Cookshire (Quebec). My Mom's diary entry for Sunday October 8 begins: "Very nice sunshiny day. Marina, Malcolm [my older siblings] & Winston went to S.S." What I remember most about Sunday School were the colour illustrated take-home cards containing a Bible verse relating to the day's lesson. Dressed in our

Sunday best, my siblings and I attended every Sunday, never missing a week unless we were sick. In June, we wrote Sunday School exams to test our retention of the year's instruction and received an official certificate if we passed. Around the age of 13, we attended Confirmation classes in preparation for the Bishop's visit where we formally joined the Church and took responsibility for the promises made on our behalf at our baptism.

Cookshire High School

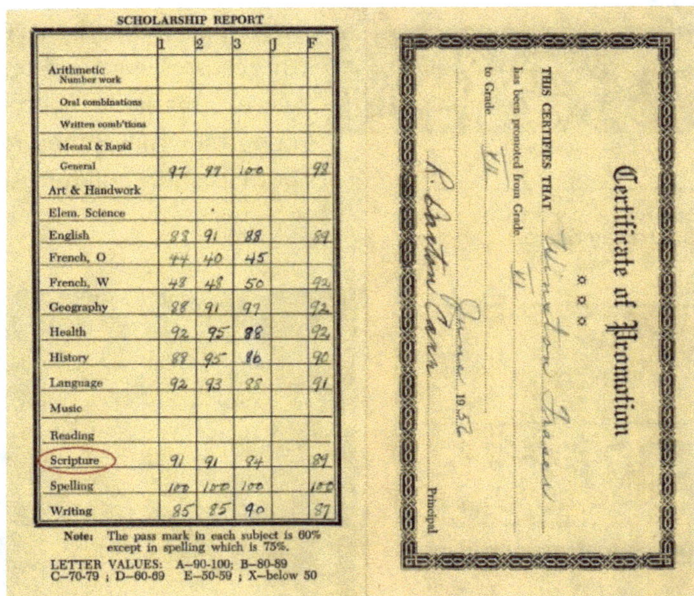

SCHOLARSHIP REPORT

	1	2	3	J	F
Arithmetic Number work					
Oral combinations					
Written comb'tions					
Mental & Rapid					
General	97	97	100		92
Art & Handwork					
Elem. Science					
English	88	91	88		89
French, O	44	40	45		
French, W	48	48	50		92
Geography	88	91	97		92
Health	92	95	88		92
History	88	95	86		90
Language	92	93	88		91
Music					
Reading					
Scripture	91	91	84		89
Spelling	100	100	100		100
Writing	85	85	90		87

Note: The pass mark in each subject is 60% except in spelling which is 75%.

LETTER VALUES: A—90-100; B—80-89
C—70-79 ; D—60-69   E—50-59 ; X—below 50

Certificate of Promotion

* * *

THIS CERTIFIES THAT _Winston Powell_

has been promoted from Grade _VI_

to Grade _VII_

December 19.56

R. Burton Carr .... Principal

1956 Grade 6 report card showing Scripture subject

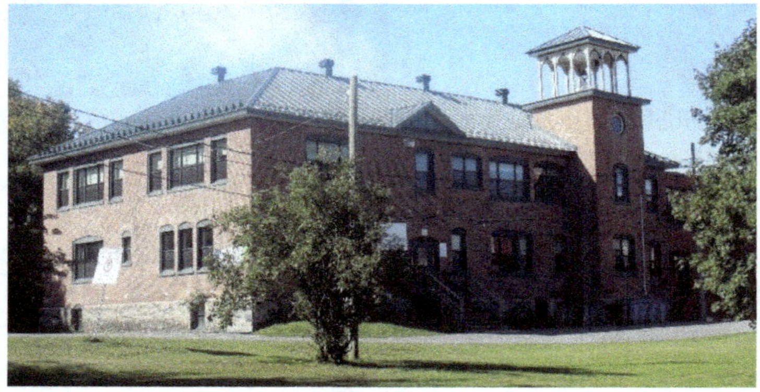

Cookshire High School (author)

Preface

In my schooling days (1950s), exposure to the Scriptures was not limited to Sunday School. Scripture was taught in the elementary grades at Cookshire High School, having equal billing with other subjects such as English, French, Geography, Health, Science and the 3 R's (Reading, 'Riting and 'Rithmetic). In later grades, the Bible was also studied as literature.

Bishop's University

SUBJECT & No.		MID YEAR	FINAL	SUPP.	SUPP.
FIRST YEAR B.Sc. 1961-62					
DIVINITY 101		79	73		
ENGLISH ac 101		64	68		
MATHEMATICS 101		70	71		
CHEMISTRY 101		70	75		
PHYSICS 101		59	74		
FRENCH 101		75	77		
SECOND YEAR 1962-63					
Chemistry 202		72	75		
Divinity 314		78	78		
English 203		67	67		
French 202		80	77		
Physics 202		94	97		
Maths 202		96	76		
Russian 101		90	87		

Bishop's University 1961-62 BSc Program — Divinity courses

In 1961, I entered the Bachelor of Science program at Bishop's University in Lennoxville (Quebec). Among the compulsory courses in first and second years were a pair of Scripture-based courses: Divinity 101 and Divinity 314. According to the university's Academic Calendar for that year, the object of these courses was to provide (i) some basic knowledge of the nature and unity of Holy Scriptures; (ii) a general knowledge of the nature of religion in its various manifestations; and (iii) a study of the Biblical basis of Christian ethics and its application to contemporary moral problems. I clearly recall that an entire term of the Divinity 101 course was dedicated to a phrase-by-phrase analysis of The Lord's Prayer.

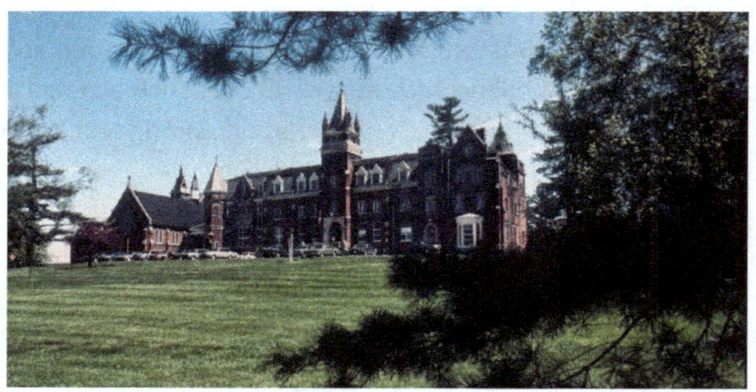

Bishop's University, Lennoxville (Sherbrooke) Que. (author)

Courtship and Marriage

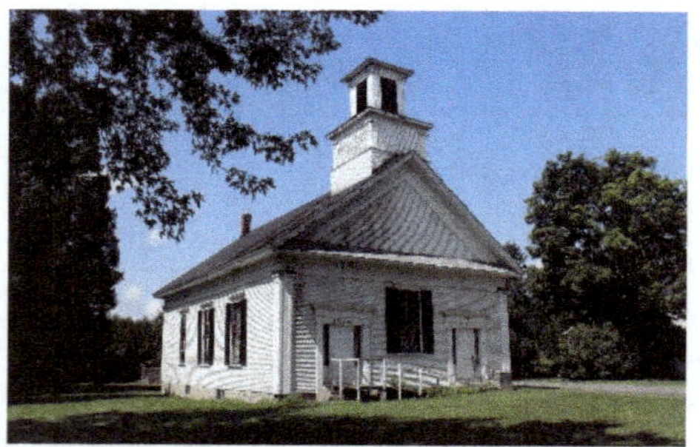

Advent Christian Church, Beebe, Que. (author)

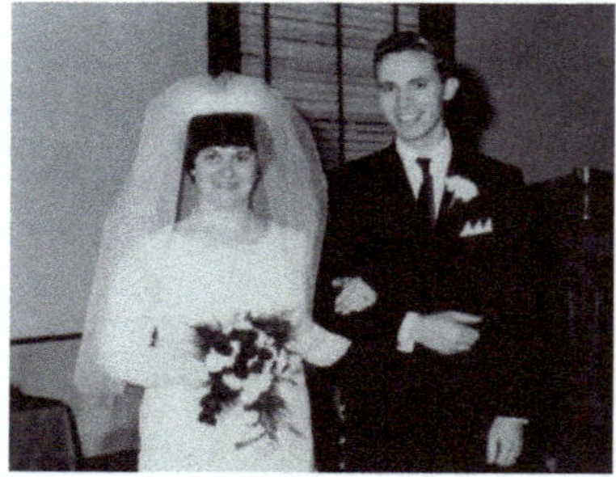

Our wedding portrait, Epiphany 1968 (Fraser family archive)

 A surprising but significant milestone in my association with the Scriptures occurred soon after I met my future wife in 1966. Becky was a member of the Advent Christian Church, some of whose adherents considered members of other denominations to be less Christian or even non Christian. It was natural, then, that Becky would look upon Anglicans with a certain degree of scepticism. So, early on in our relationship, she queried me very directly about the Anglican Church and about my own personal faith. This process caused me to explore more deeply the elements of my faith that I had taken for granted and to show her that the Anglican denomination was indeed a Bible-based Christian denomination. Thankfully, I passed the test and the proof was in the wedding! A few years later, Becky herself would join the

Anglican Church, where she devoted her life to sharing the Gospel by caring for others until her untimely passing in 2015.

St. James Church

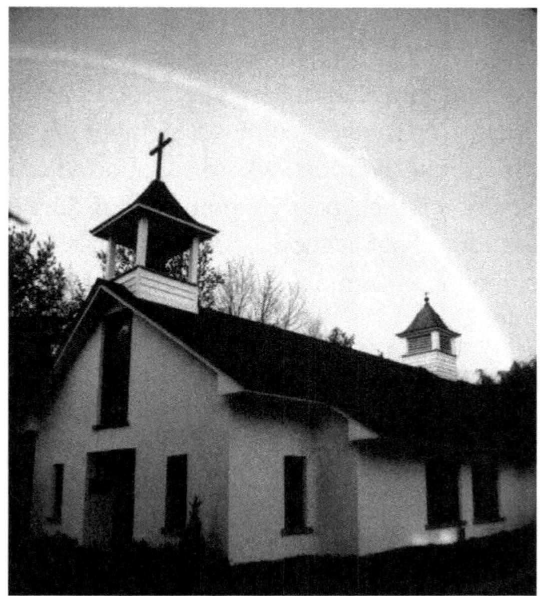

St. James Church, Rosemere, Que. (author)

Upon our marriage on the Feast of the Epiphany in 1968, we joined St. James Anglican Church in Rosemere (Quebec). This represented a real epiphany in my relationship with the Scriptures under the pastoral leadership of a succession of parish priests including the reverends Ed Vokey, Ed Kettleborough, Maurice Bate, Michael Rowe, Murray Tipping, Greg Bailey, Jennifer Davis and David Hart. In addition to learning from their Bible-based sermons, I benefited from participation in Bible studies, prayer groups, healing services and church conferences/workshops. When occasionally called upon to lead a service, I took advantage of the opportunity to delve deeper into the Scriptures for inspiration.

Canadian Bible Society

Involved with the Scriptures though I was throughout my time at St. James, it was in 1995 that my involvement really gained momentum with the launch of a unique Bible-reading project called "Proclamation."

Inspired by a dream that I had experienced, Proclamation was a multi-denominational multilingual gathering together of Christians over a period of ten days to read the Bible aloud, in public, from beginning to end. Following the initial Proclamation event in Rosemere, the Canadian Bible Society adopted the project and expanded it nation-wide under the leadership of

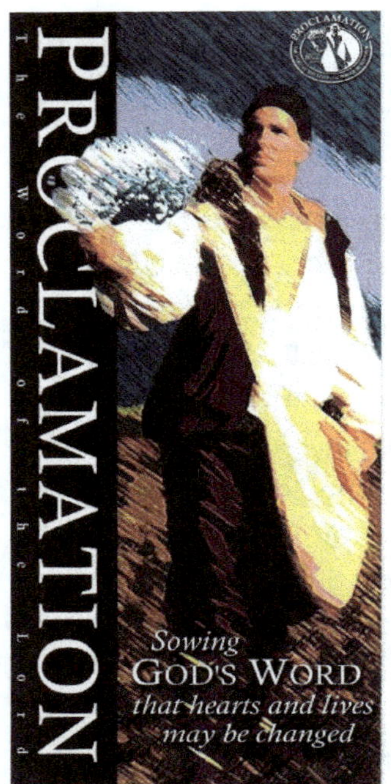

Proclamation poster
(Canadian Bible Society)

Father Greg Bailey and Rev. Georges Legault. In the ensuing years, hundreds of similar Proclamation events were held across Canada and beyond. Becky and I participated in many of them either by sharing in the readings or simply by listening, as together we rediscovered the richness of the Scriptures. The Proclamation experience led to my becoming a member of the CBS Board of Governors, where I supported the fulfillment of the Society's mandate of "Bible translation, publication, distribution and engagement, without doctrinal note or comment."

Photography and Writing

When my lifelong interest in photography eventually turned into a small business, I realized that it was thanks to a God-given ability to see the wonders of creation in a special way. As a result, over the years I have held benefit photo exhibitions in support of several Christian organizations. Following Becky's passing, I embarked on a writing career, self-publishing biographies of Eastern Townships personalities, photographic anthologies and a book on COVID-19. Most recently, I have compiled an illustrated bilingual dictionary of the differences between French and English expressions. Each book featured photographs from my collection.

All of the foregoing experiences have now culminated in the creation of **Illustrated Holy Scriptures** – a project that has been on the back burner for several years. During that time, I built up a personalized list of Bible verses from the New International Version (NIV) and selected photos from my personal collection with which to illustrate them. This book contains an arbitrary selection of approximately 200 Bible verses, starting with the opening text from Genesis and ending with the final words from Revelation. Each of the 66 books of the Bible is represented by at least one passage and most by more than one, with many having several.

May the fruit of my endeavour bring the reader hope, encouragement and a sense of reassurance in these troubled times. And may these biblical appetizers provide motivation for the further exploration of God's life-changing Word.

In shameful recognition of Canadian churches' complicity in the Indian Residential Schools tragedy and as a token gesture toward reconciliation, the proceeds from the sale of this book will be donated to the National Centre for Truth and Reconciliation.

Section 1: The Books of the Law

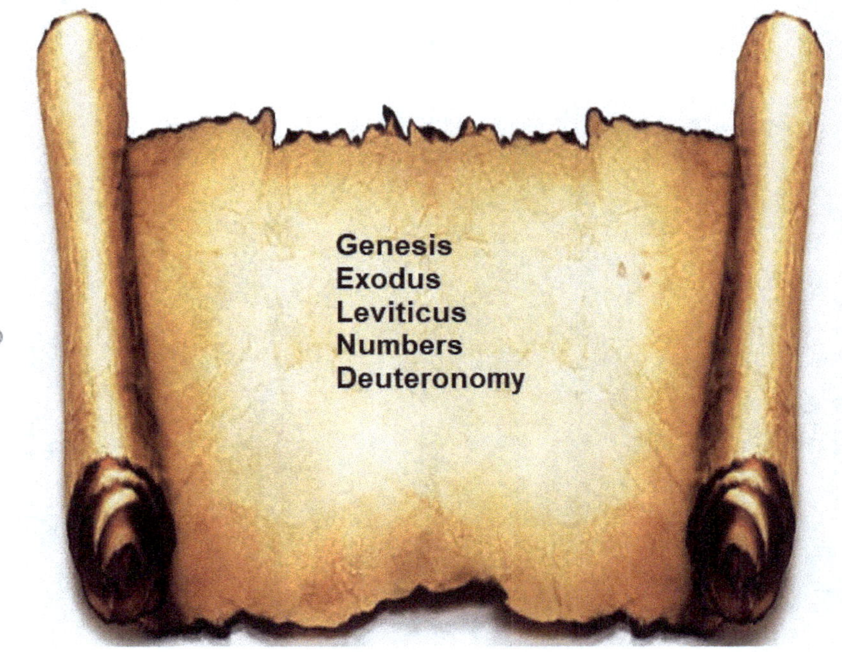

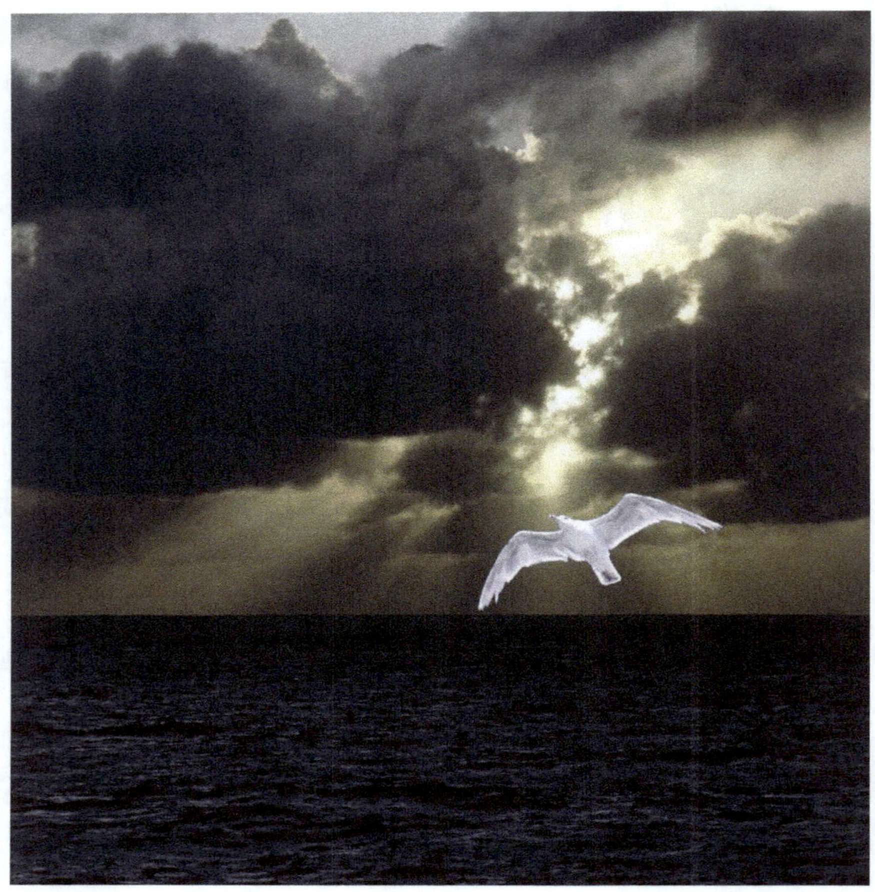

In the beginning God created the heaven and the earth. And the earth was without form, and void; and darkness was upon the face of the deep. And the Spirit of God moved upon the face of the waters.

Bible reference: Genesis 1:2-3

Context: The Beginning

Illustration ID (credit): 01-1140 (author, enhanced by Jim Fraser)

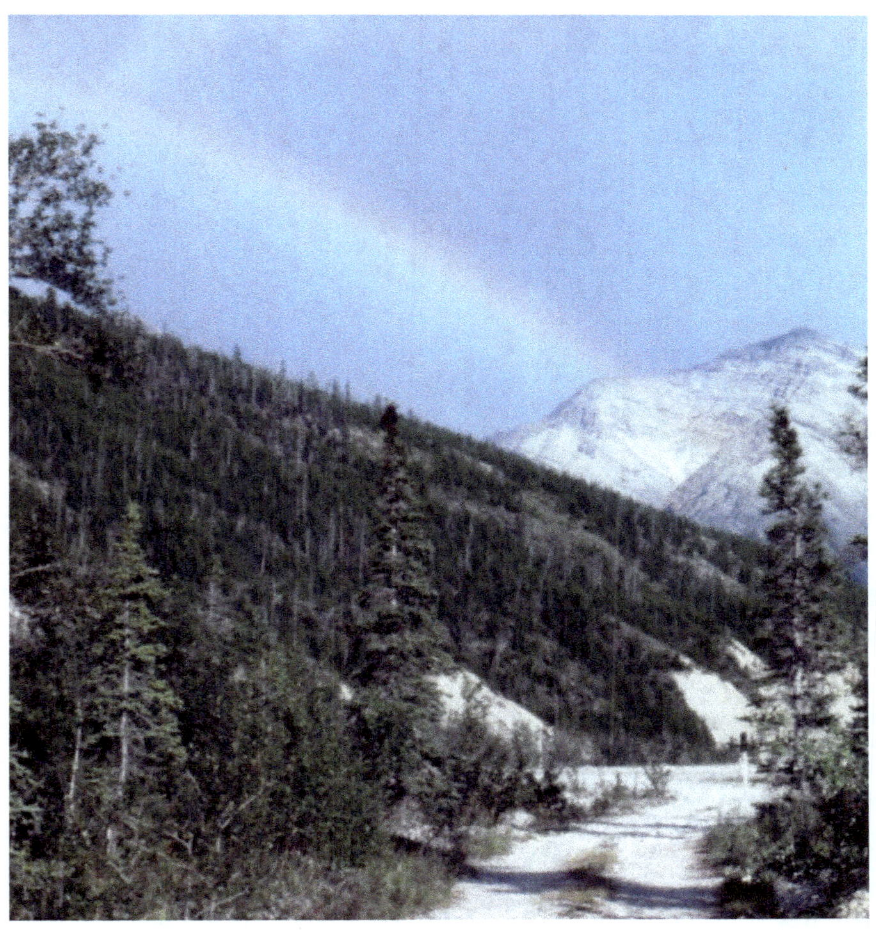

I have set my rainbow in the clouds, and it will be the sign of the covenant between me and the earth.

Bible reference: Genesis 9:13

Context: God's Covenant with Noah

Illustration ID (credit): 02-1140 (author)

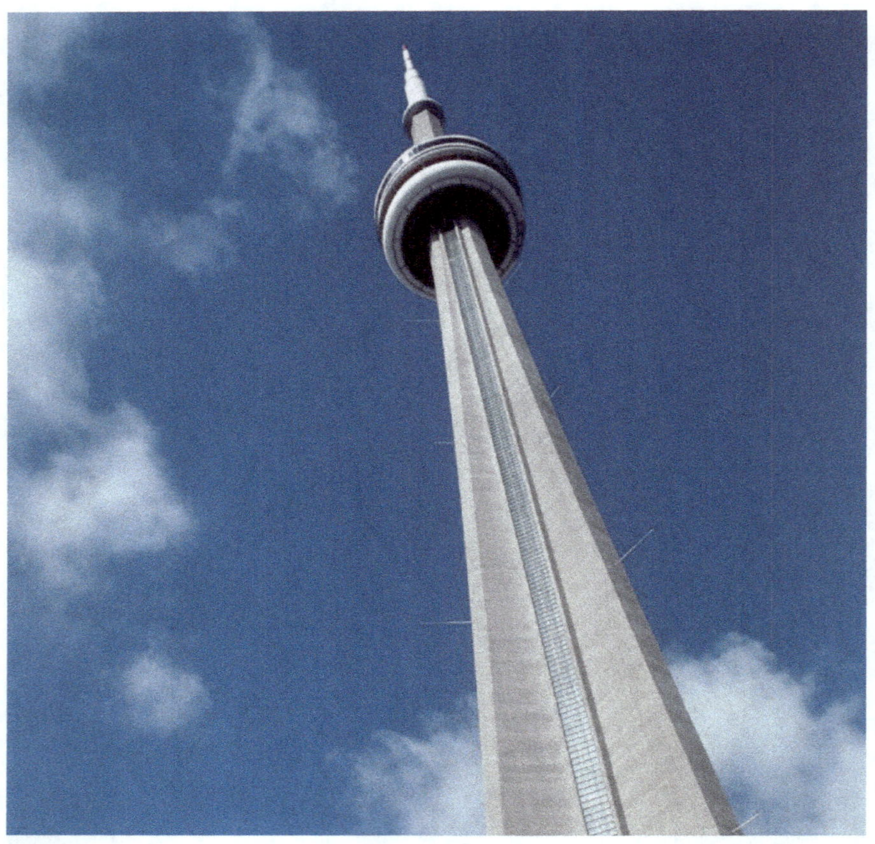

Then they said, "Come, let us build ourselves a city, with a tower that reaches to the heavens, so that we may make a name for ourselves; otherwise we will be scattered over the face of the whole earth."

Bible reference: Genesis 11:4

Context: The Tower of Babel

Illustration ID (credit): fy_99 (author)

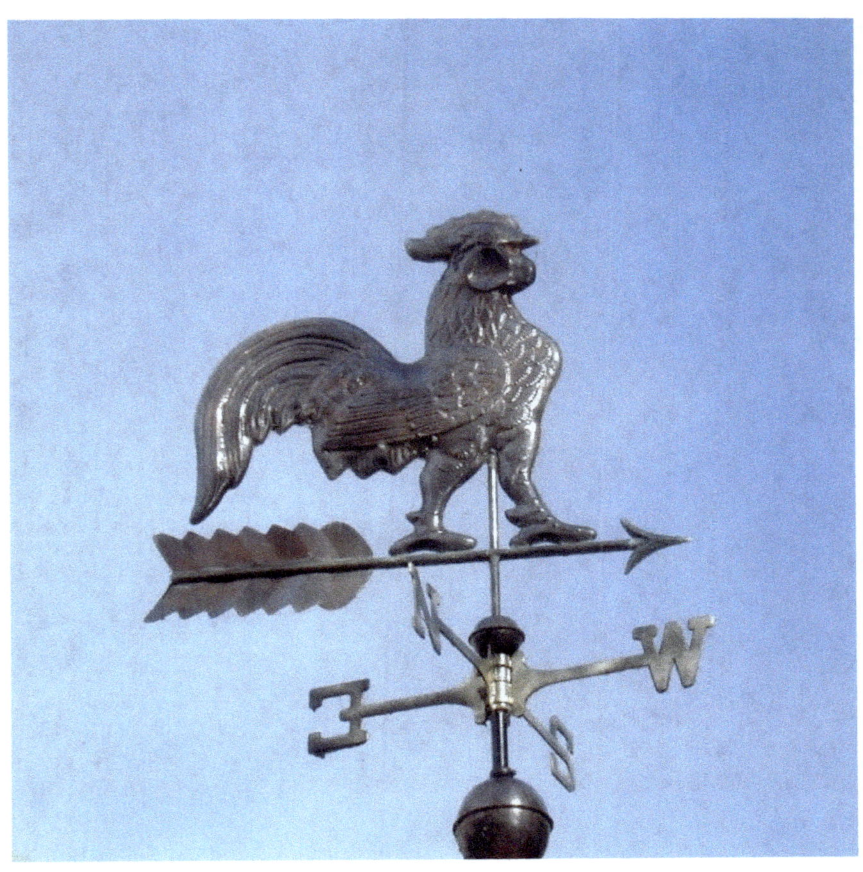

Your descendants will be like the dust of the earth, and you will spread out to the west and to the east, to the north and to the south. All peoples on earth will be blessed through you and your offspring.

Bible reference: Genesis 28:14

Context: Jacob's Dream at Bethel

Illustration ID (credit): fx_4064 (author)

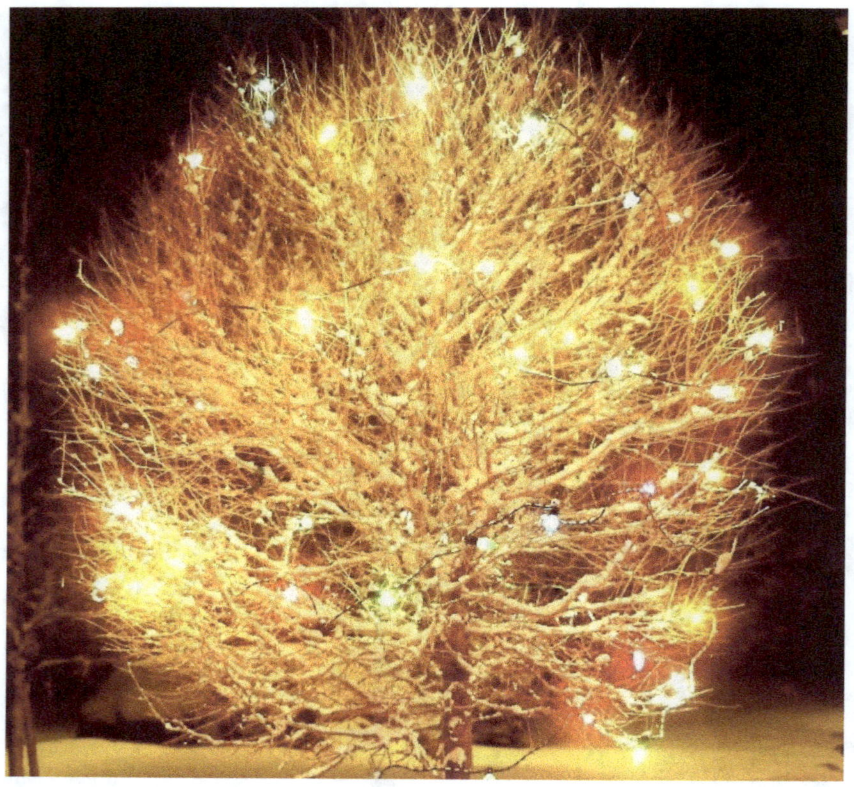

There the angel of the Lord appeared to him in flames of fire from within a bush. Moses saw that though the bush was on fire it did not burn up.

Bible reference: Exodus 3:2

Context: Moses and the Burning Bush

Illustration ID (credit): fs_344 (author)

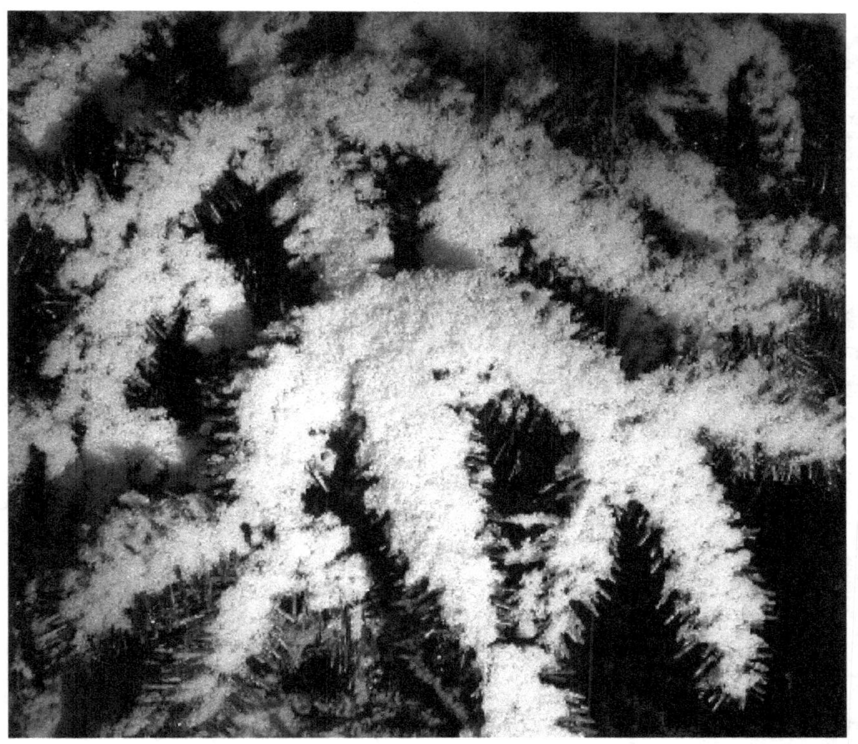

When the dew was gone, thin flakes like frost on the ground appeared on the desert floor. When the Israelites saw it, they said to each other, "What is it?" For they did not know what it was. Moses said to them, "It is the bread the Lord has given you to eat. . . "

Bible reference: Exodus 16:14-15

Context: Manna and Quail

Illustration ID (credit): fy_94 (author)

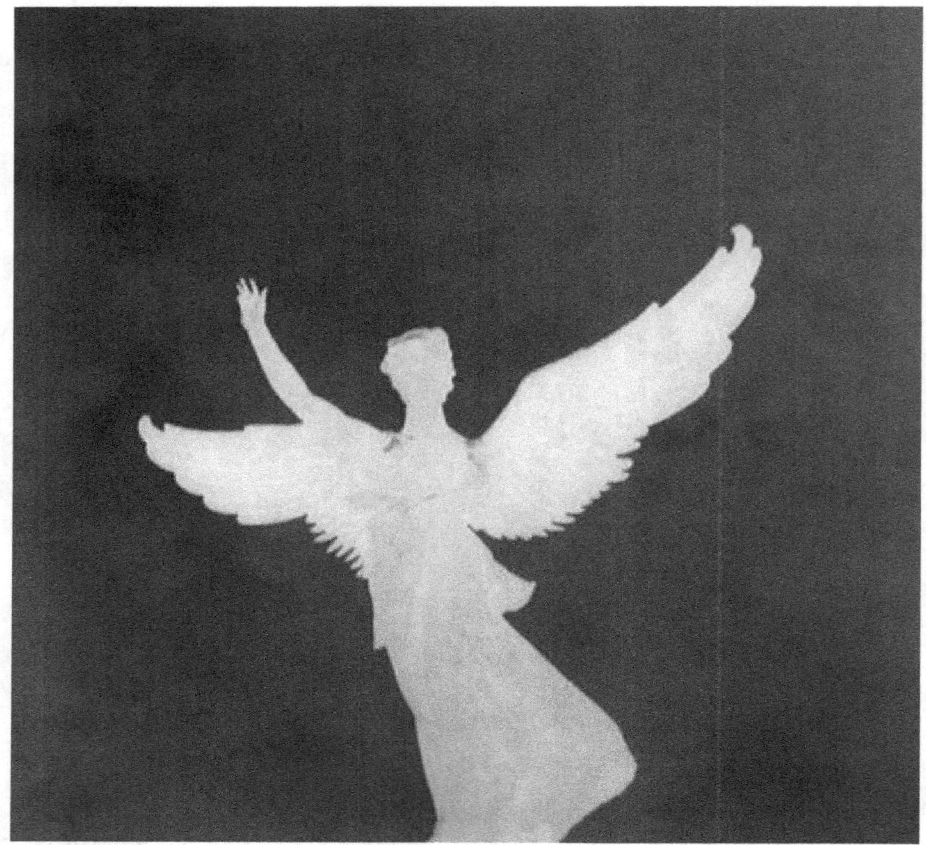

See, I am sending an angel ahead of you to guard you along the way and to bring you to the place I have prepared.

Bible reference: Exodus 23:20

Context: God's Angel to Prepare the Way

Illustration ID (credit): fa_06 (author)

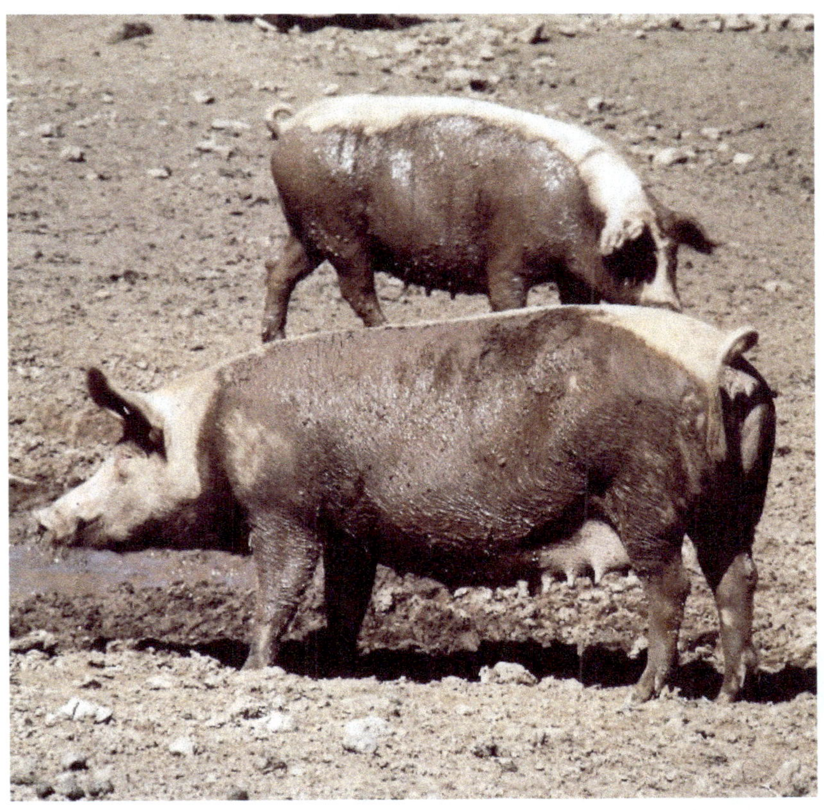

And the pig, though it has a divided hoof, does not chew the cud; it is unclean for you.

Bible reference: Leviticus 11:7

Context: Clean and Unclean Food

Illustration ID (credit): fs_341 (author)

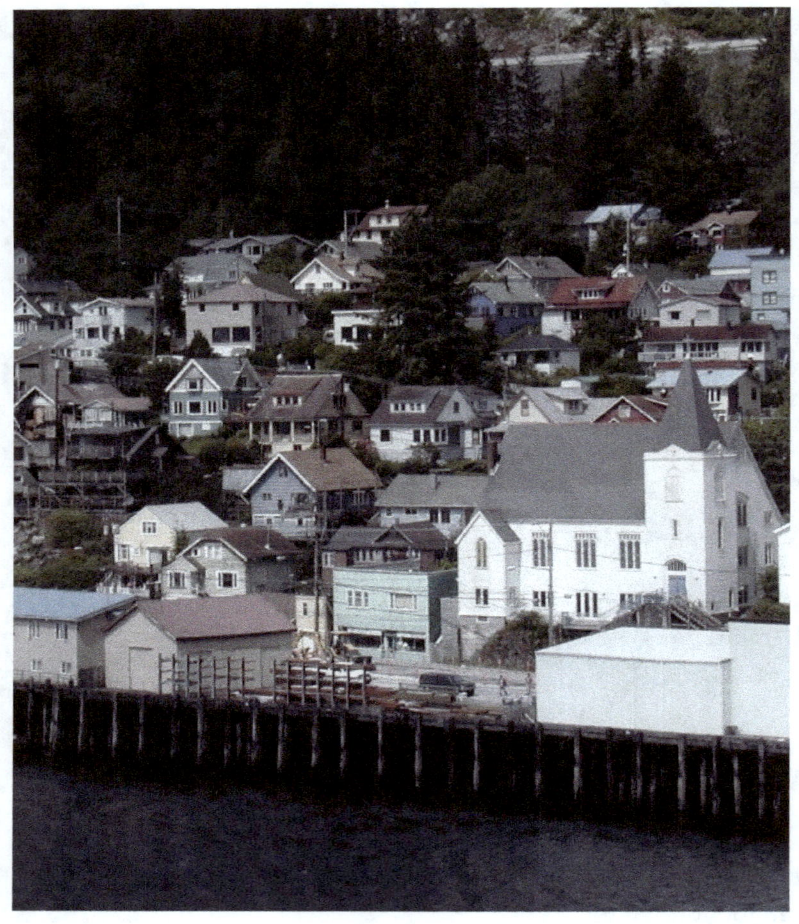

Do not seek revenge or bear a grudge against one of your people, but love your neighbor as yourself. I am the LORD.

Bible reference: Leviticus 19:18

Context: Various Laws

Illustration ID (credit): fx_4640 (author)

The LORD bless you and keep you; the LORD make his face shine upon you and be gracious to you.

Bible reference: Numbers 6:24-25

Context: The Priestly Blessing

Illustration ID (credit): fy_48 (author)

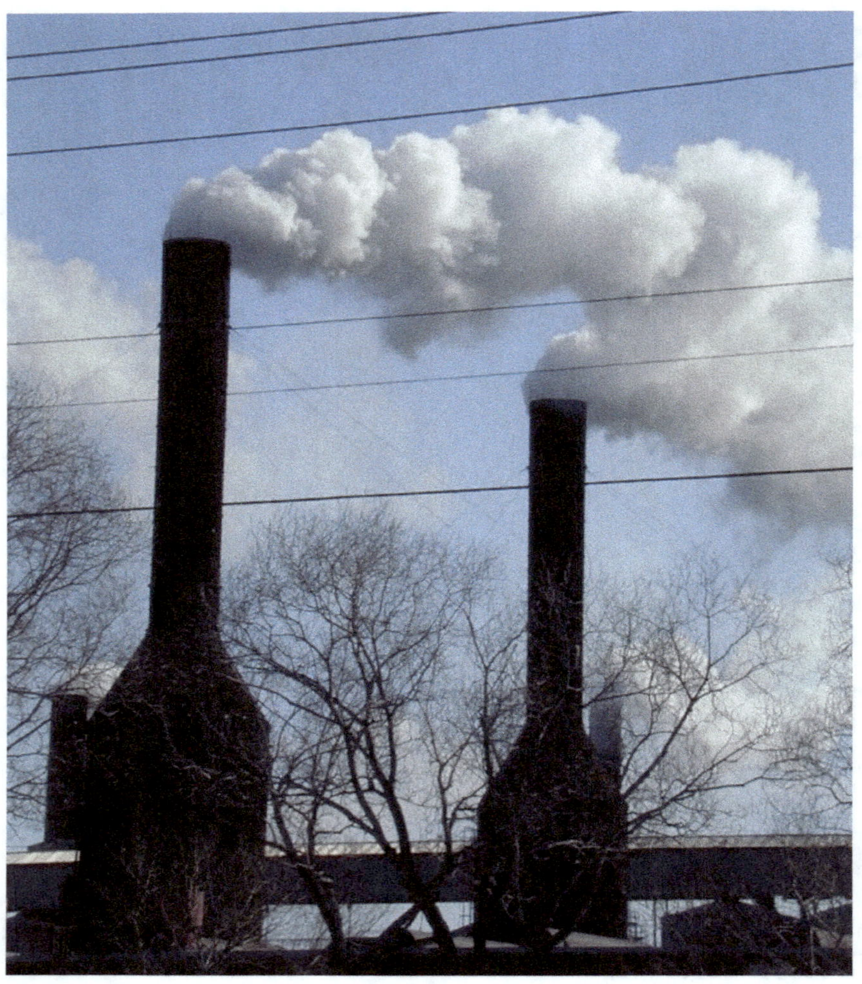

Do not pollute the land where you are.

Bible reference: Numbers 35:33a

Context: Cities of Refuge

Illustration ID (credit): fx_6976 (author)

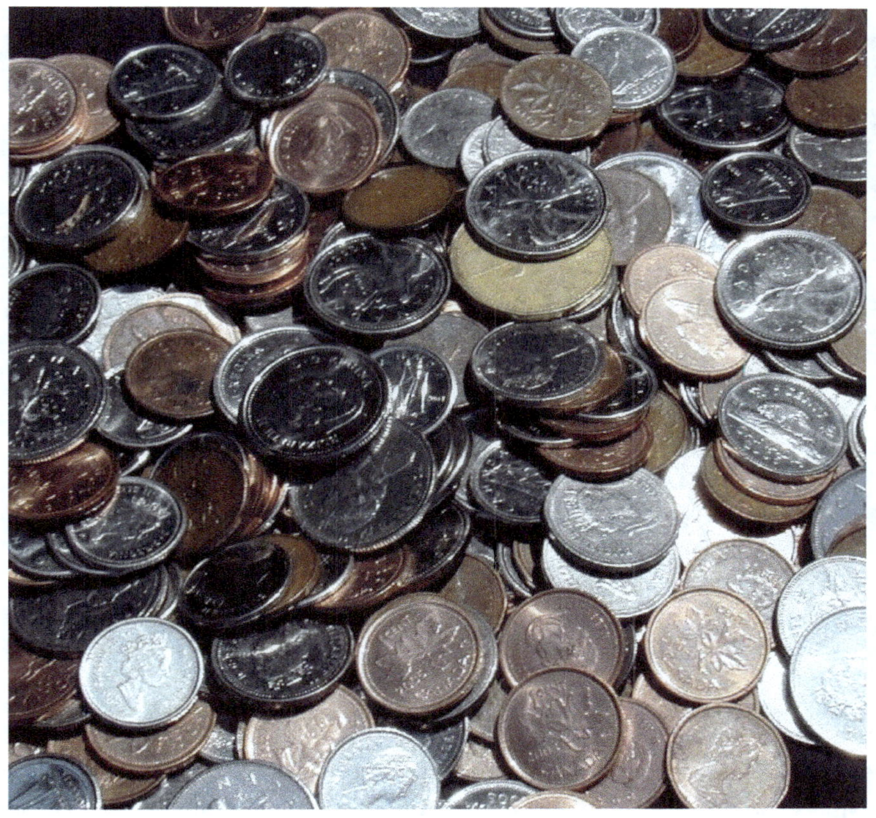

But remember the LORD your God, for it is he who gives you the ability to produce wealth, and so confirms his covenant, which he swore to your forefathers, as it is today.

Bible reference: Deuteronomy 8:18

Context: Do Not Forget the Lord

Illustration ID (credit): fx_4417 (author)

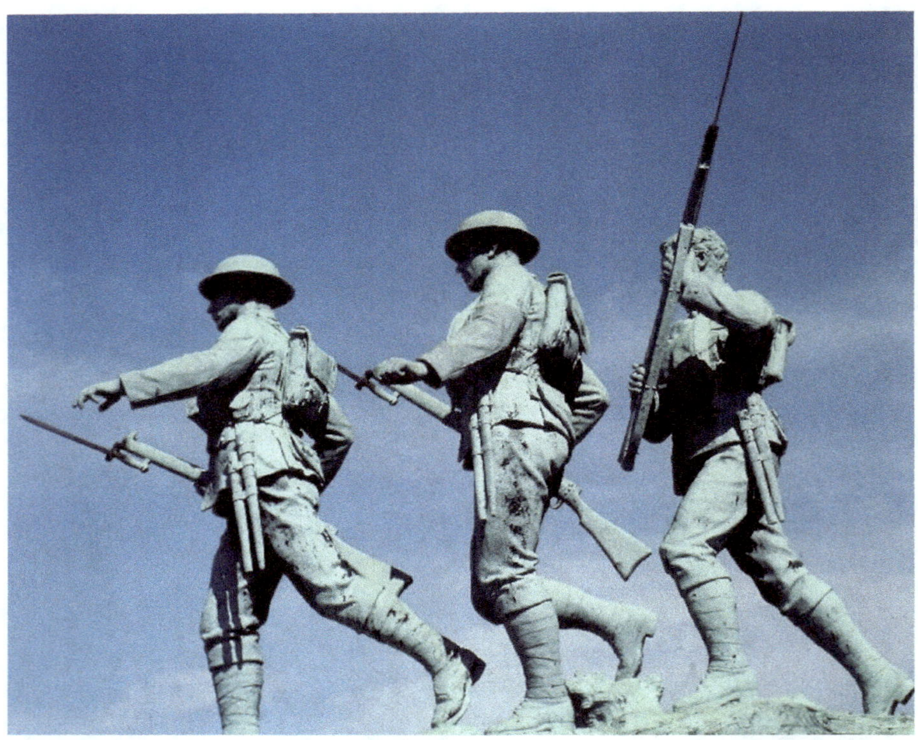

He shall say: "Hear O Israel, today you are going into battle against your enemies. Do not be faint-hearted or afraid; do not be terrified or give way to panic before them. For the LORD your God is the one who goes with you to fight for you against your enemies to give you victory."

Bible reference: Deuteronomy 20:3-4

Context: Going to War

Illustration ID (credit): fy_16 (author)

Section 2: Old Testament Historical Books

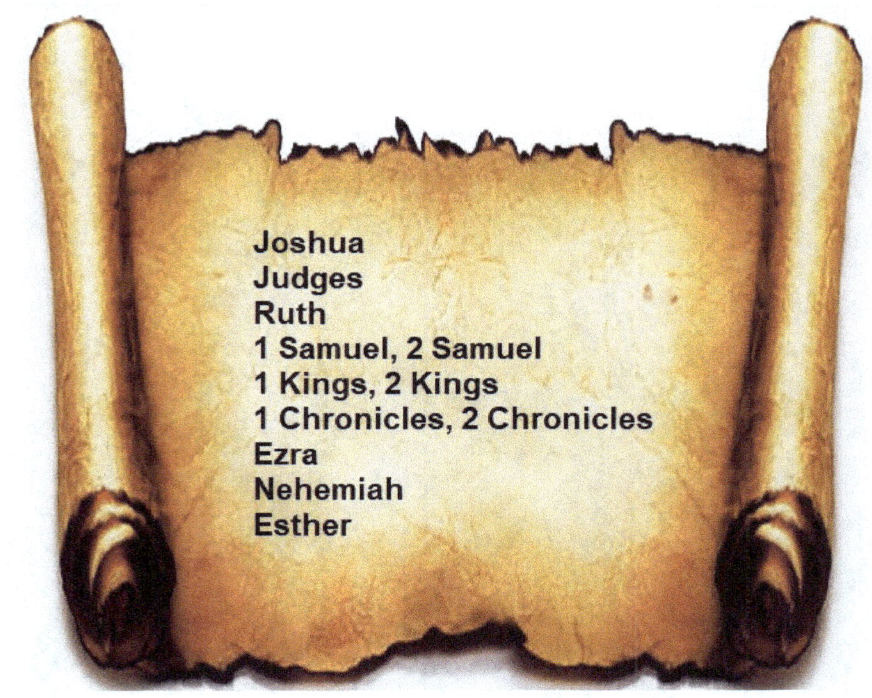

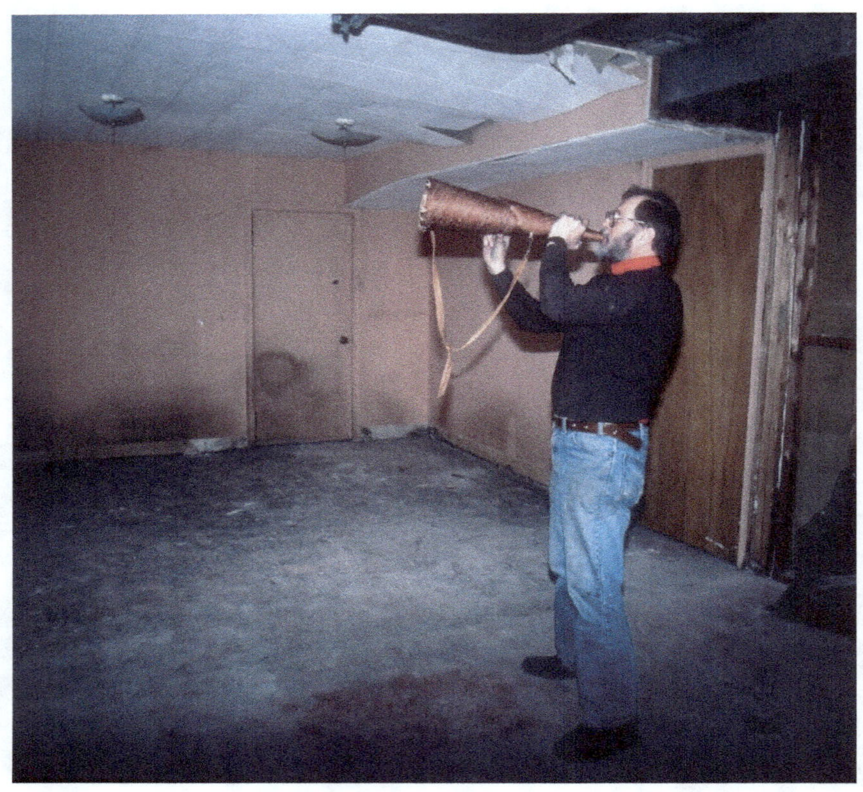

When the trumpets sounded, the army shouted, and at the sound of the trumpet, when the men gave a loud shout, the wall collapsed; so everyone charged straight in, and they took the city.

Bible reference: Joshua 6:20

Context: The Fall of Jericho

Illustration ID (credit): fs_358 (author)

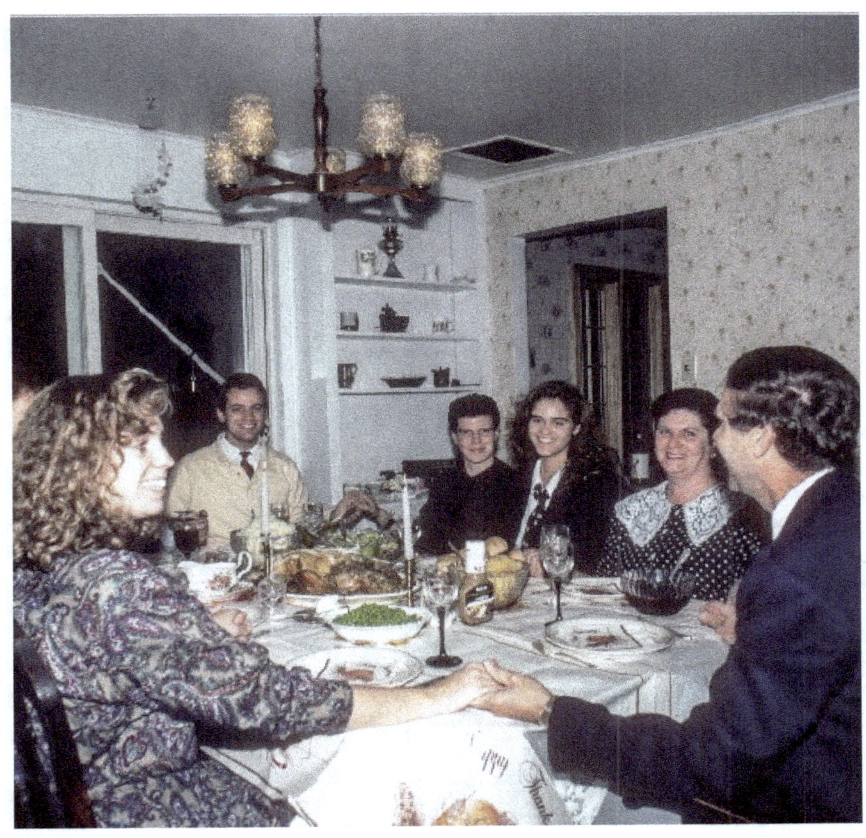

But as for me and my household, we will serve the LORD.

Bible reference: Joshua 24:15b

Context: The Covenant Renewed at Shechem

Illustration ID (credit): fs_3542 (Fraser family archive)

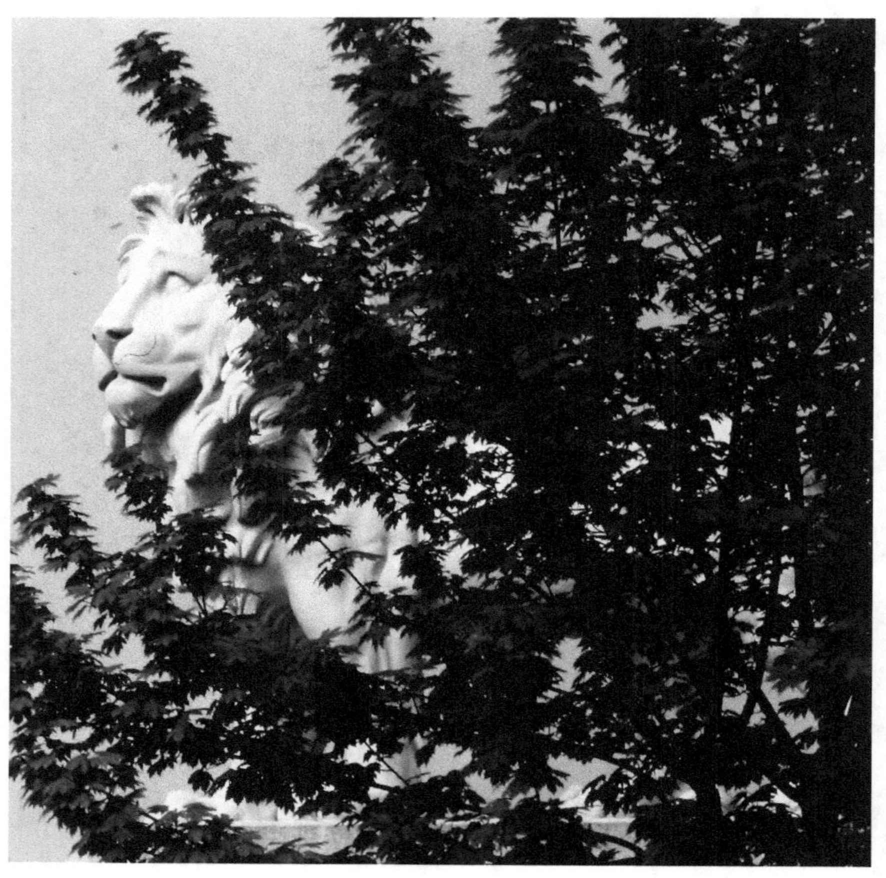

"What is sweeter than honey? What is stronger than a lion?"

Bible reference: Judges 14:18

Context: Samson's Marriage

Illustration ID (credit): fs_353 (author)

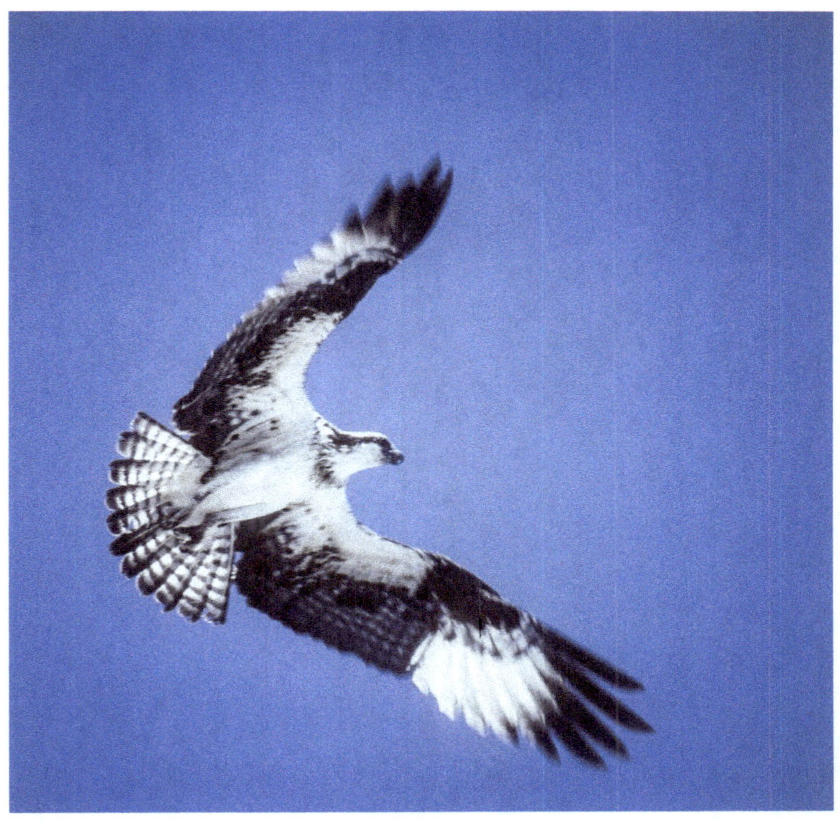

May the LORD repay you for what you have done. May you be richly rewarded by the LORD, the God of Israel, under whose wings you have come to take refuge.

Bible reference: Ruth 2:12

Context: Ruth Meets Boaz

Illustration ID (credit): fx_6250 (Bill Ivy)

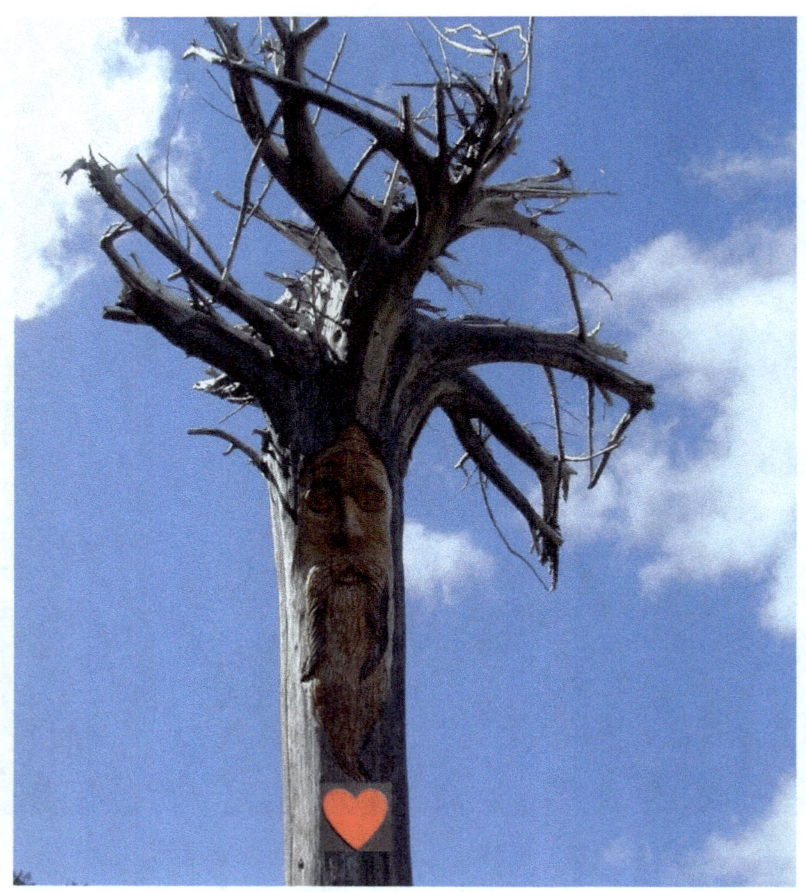

But the LORD said to Samuel, "Do not consider his appearance or his height, for I have rejected him. The LORD does not look at the things man looks at. Man looks at the outward appearance, but the LORD looks at the heart."

Bible reference: 1 Samuel 16:7

Context: Samuel Anoints David

Illustration ID (credit): fx_6141x_tif (author)

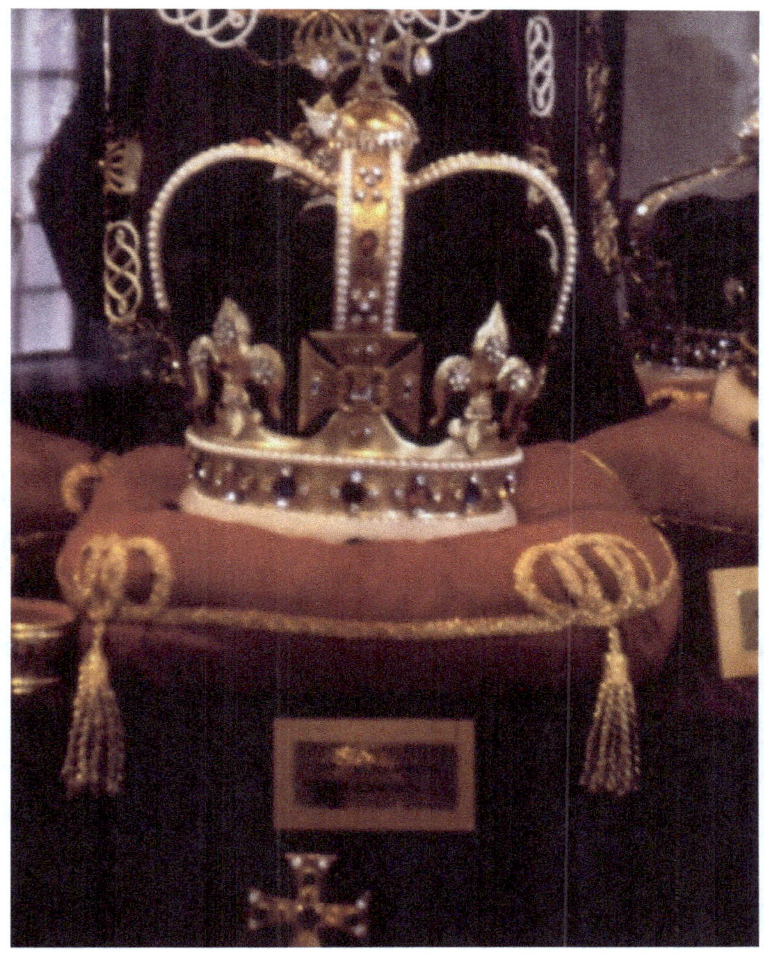

David took the crown from their king's head, and it was placed on his own head. It weighed a talent of gold, and it was set with precious stones.

Bible reference: 2 Samuel 12:30

Context: Nathan Rebukes David

Illustration ID (credit): fa_46 (author)

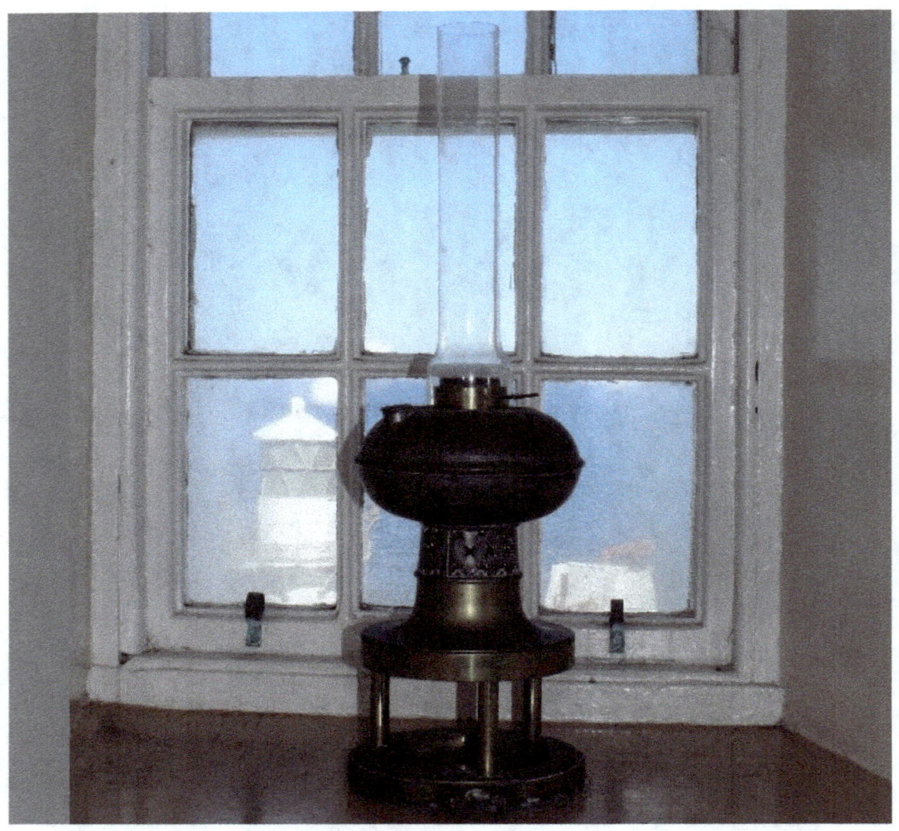

You are my lamp, O LORD; the LORD turns my darkness into light.

Bible reference: 2 Samuel 22:29

Context: David's Song of Praise

Illustration ID (credit): fy_12 (author)

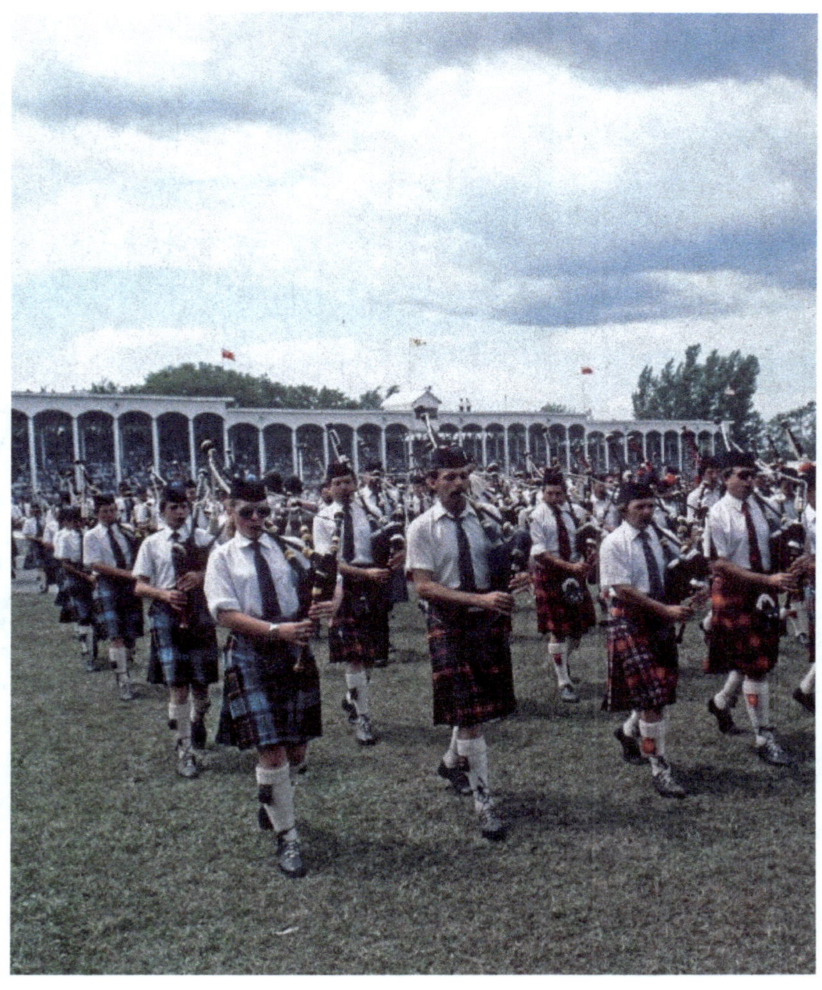

And all the people went up after him, playing pipes and rejoicing greatly, so that the ground shook with the sound.

Bible reference: 1 Kings 1:40

Context: David Makes Solomon King

Illustration ID (credit): fy_86 (author)

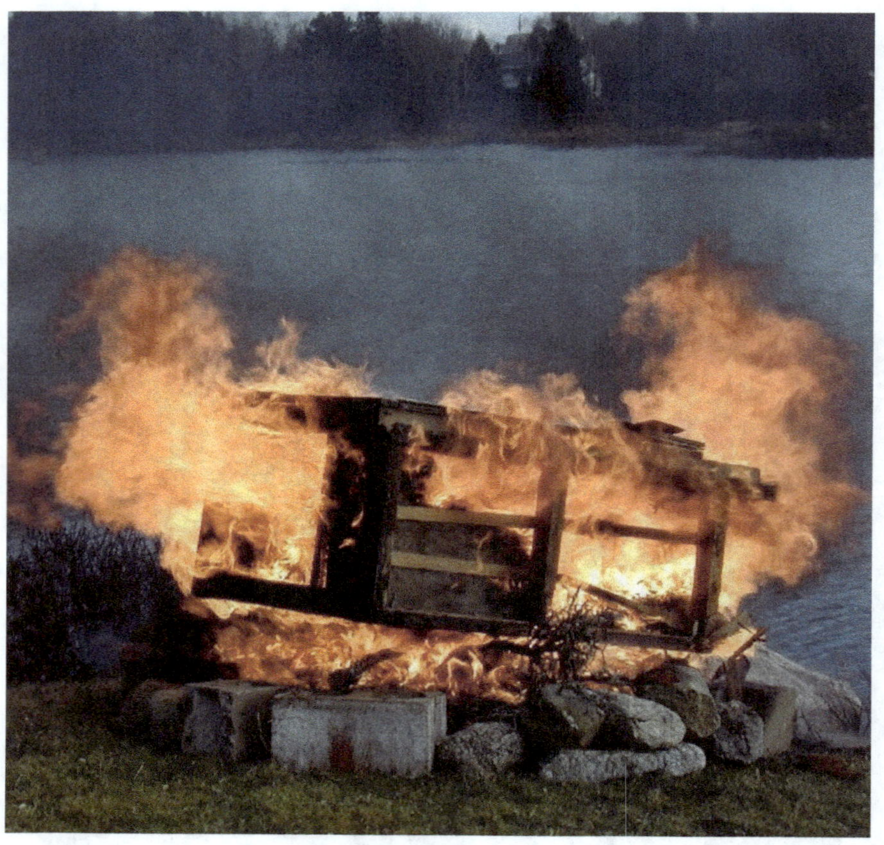

They brought out the sacred pillars of the house of Baal and burned them.

Bible reference: 2 Kings 10:26

Context: Ministers of Baal Killed

Illustration ID (credit): fy_27 (author)

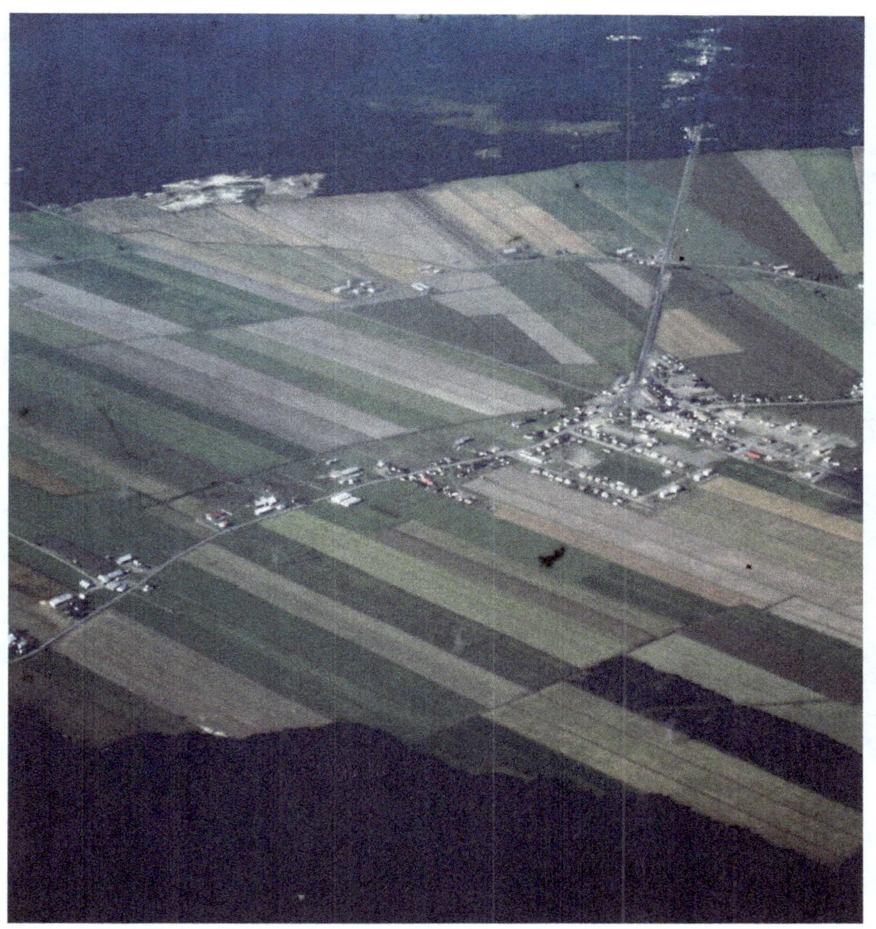

abez cried out to the God of Israel, "Oh, that you would bless me and enlarge my territory! Let your hand be with me, and keep me from harm so that I will be free from pain." And God granted his request.

Bible reference: 1 Chronicles 4:9-10

Context: Other Clans of Judah

Illustration ID (credit): fa_555 (author)

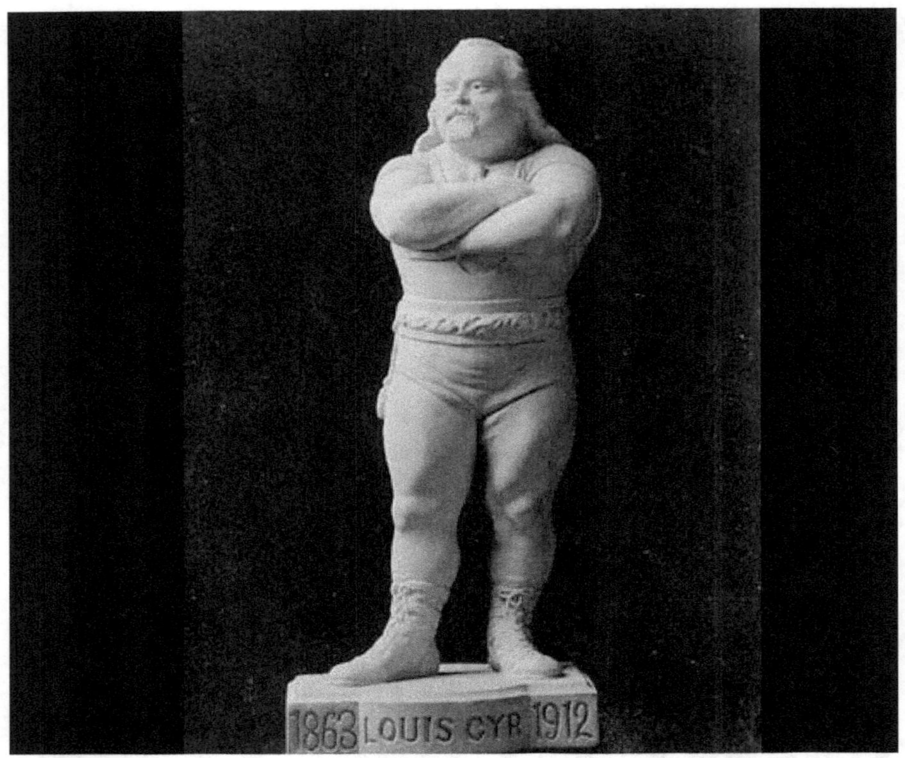

Wealth and honor come from you; you are the ruler of all things. In your hands are strength and power to exalt and give strength to all.

Bible reference: 1 Chronicles 29:12

Context: David's Prayer

Illustration ID (credit): fy_15 (author)

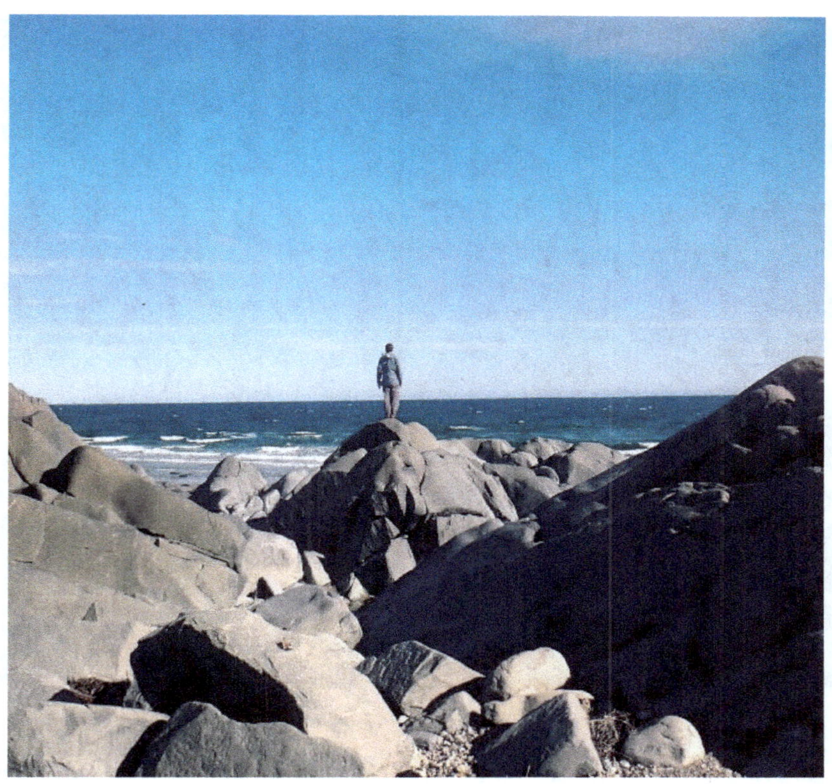

For the eyes of the LORD range throughout the earth to strengthen those whose hearts are fully committed to him.

Bible reference: 2 Chronicles 16:9

Context: Asa's Last Years

Illustration ID (credit): fz_03 (author)

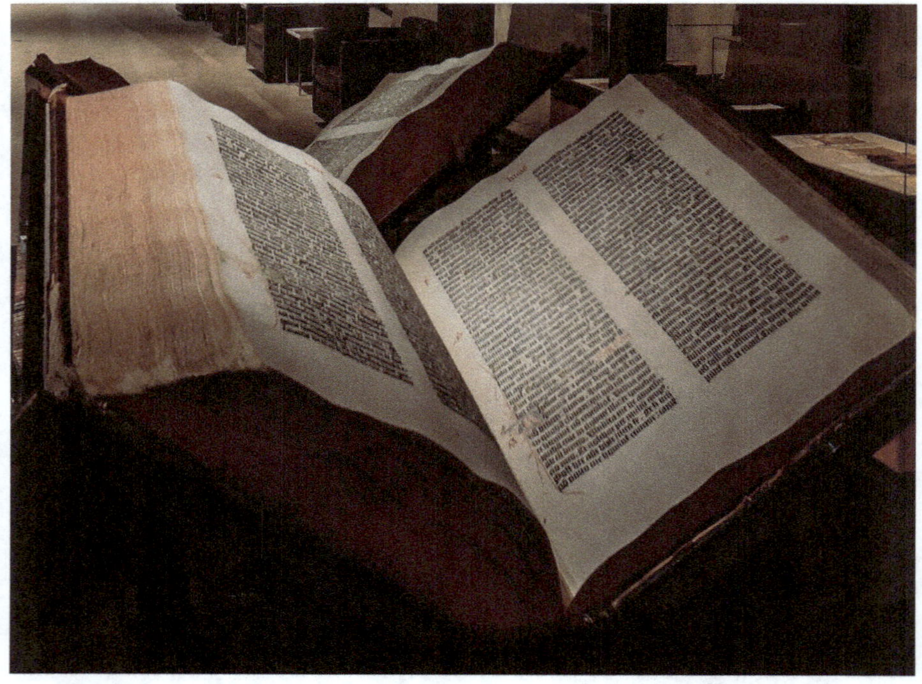

For Ezra had devoted himself to the study and observance of the Law of the LORD , and to teaching its decrees and laws in Israel.

Bible reference: Ezra 7:10

Context: Ezra Comes to Jerusalem

Illustration ID (credit): fa_987 (Ron Planche)

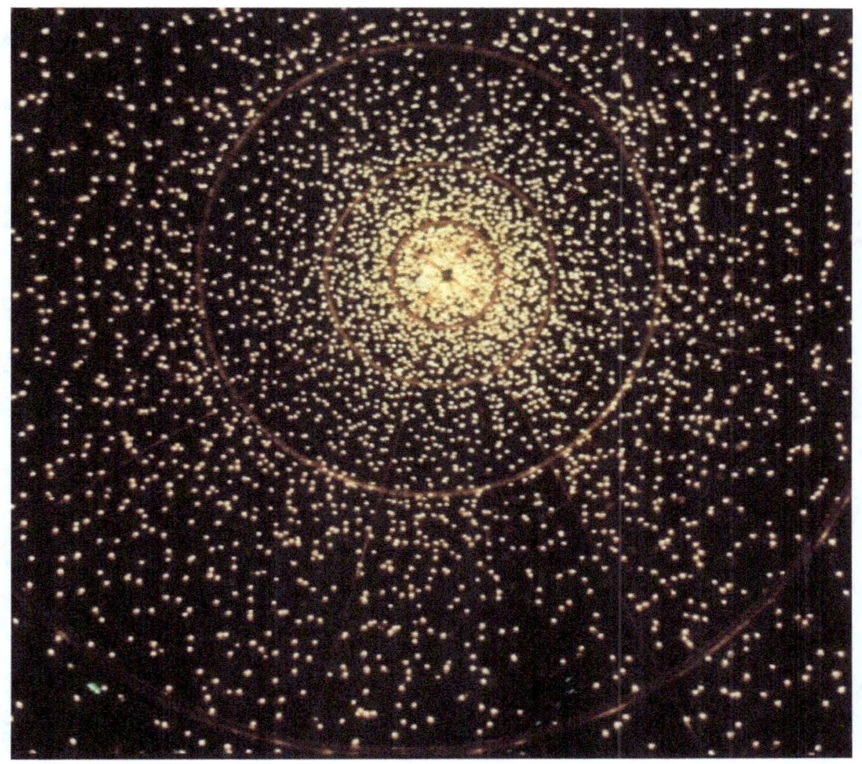

You alone are the LORD. You made the heavens, even the highest heavens, and all their starry host, the earth and all that is on it, the seas and all that is in them. You give life to everything, and the multitudes of heaven worship you.

Bible reference: Nehemiah 9:6

Context: The Israelites Confess Their Sins

Illustration ID (credit): fy_82 (author)

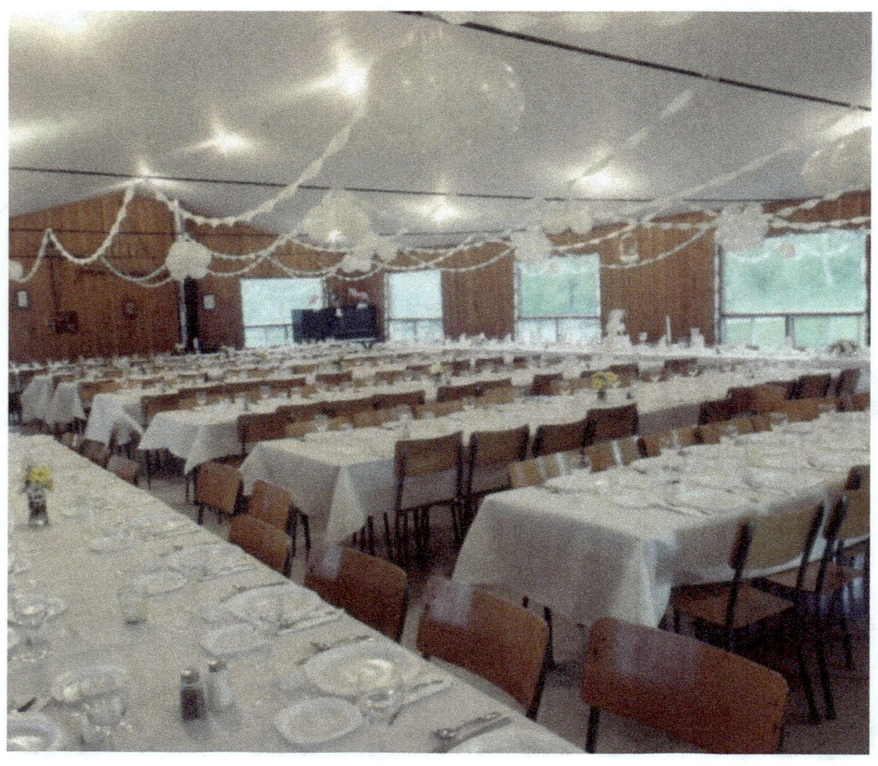

 And in the third year of his reign he gave a banquet for all his nobles and officials.

Bible reference: Esther 1:3

Context: Queen Vashti Deposed

Illustration ID (credit): fy_39 (author)

Section 3: Wisdom Literature

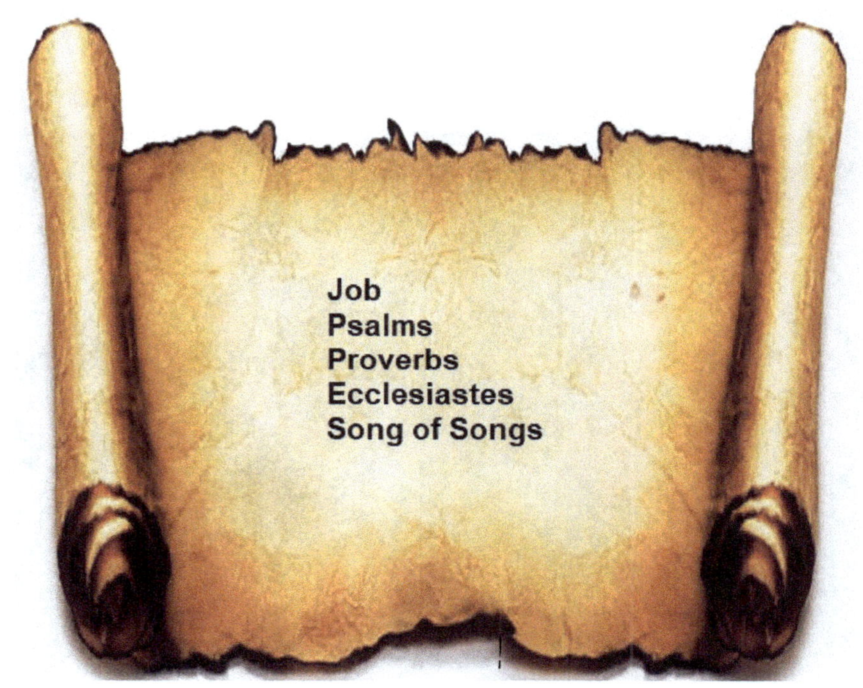

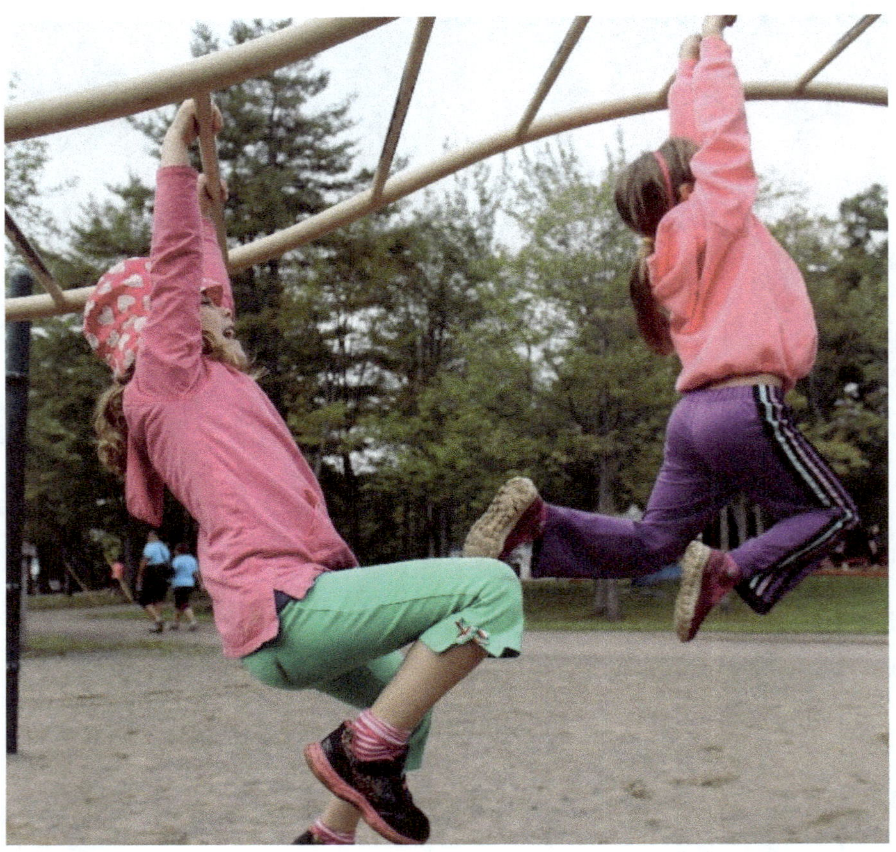

He will yet fill your mouth with laughter and your lips with shouts of joy.

Bible reference: Job 8:21

Context: Bildad

Illustration ID (credit): fc_1918 (author)

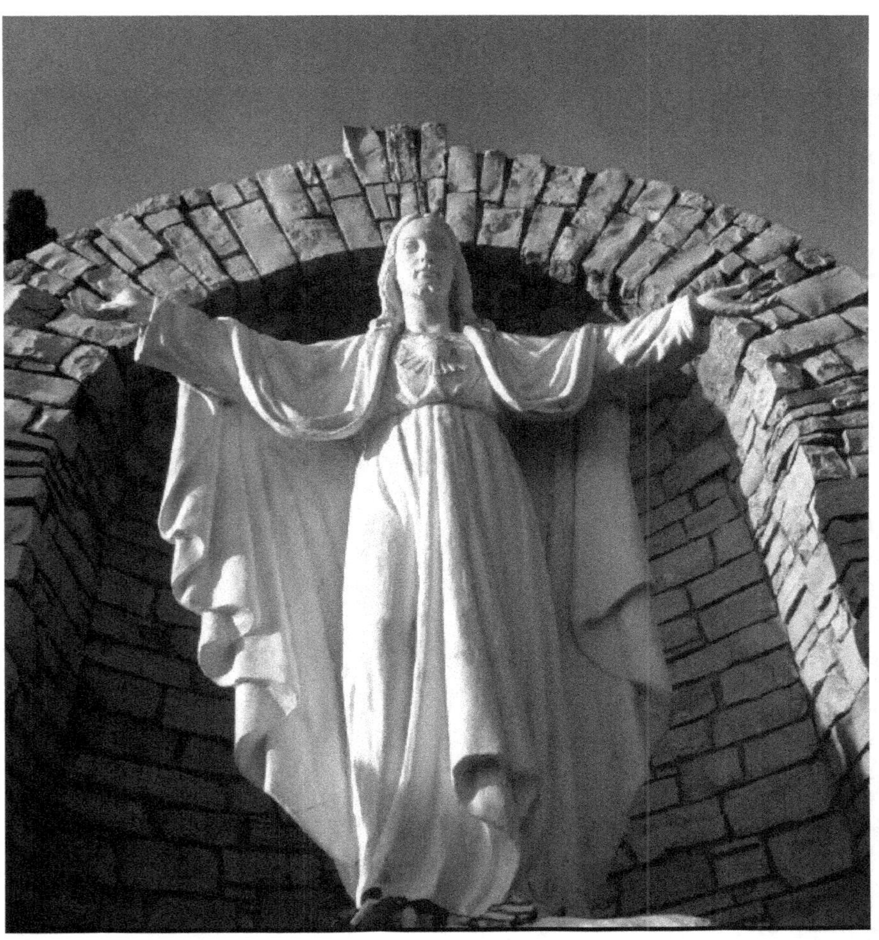

I know that my Redeemer lives, and that in the end he will stand upon the earth.

Bible reference: Job 19:25

Context: Job

Illustration ID (credit): fa_20 (author)

When I consider your heavens, the work of your fingers, the moon and the stars, which you have set in place,

Bible reference: Psalm 8:3

Context: A psalm of David

Illustration ID (credit): fx_2222 (author)

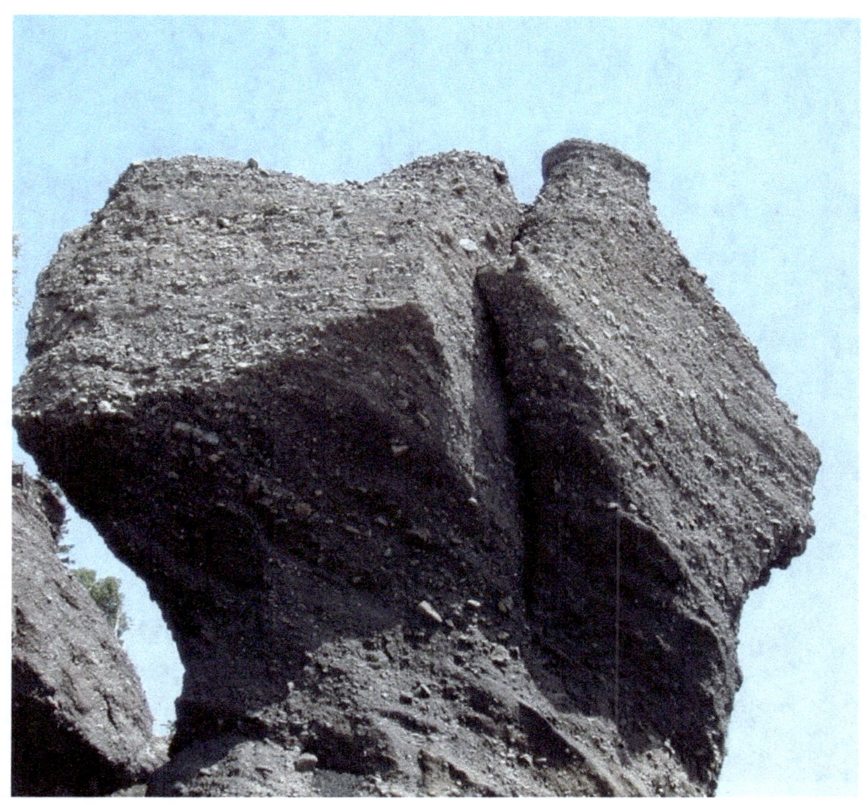

May the words of my mouth and the meditation of my heart be pleasing in your sight, O Lord, my Rock and my Redeemer.

Bible reference: Psalm 19:14

Context: A psalm of David

Illustration ID (credit): fy_34 (author)

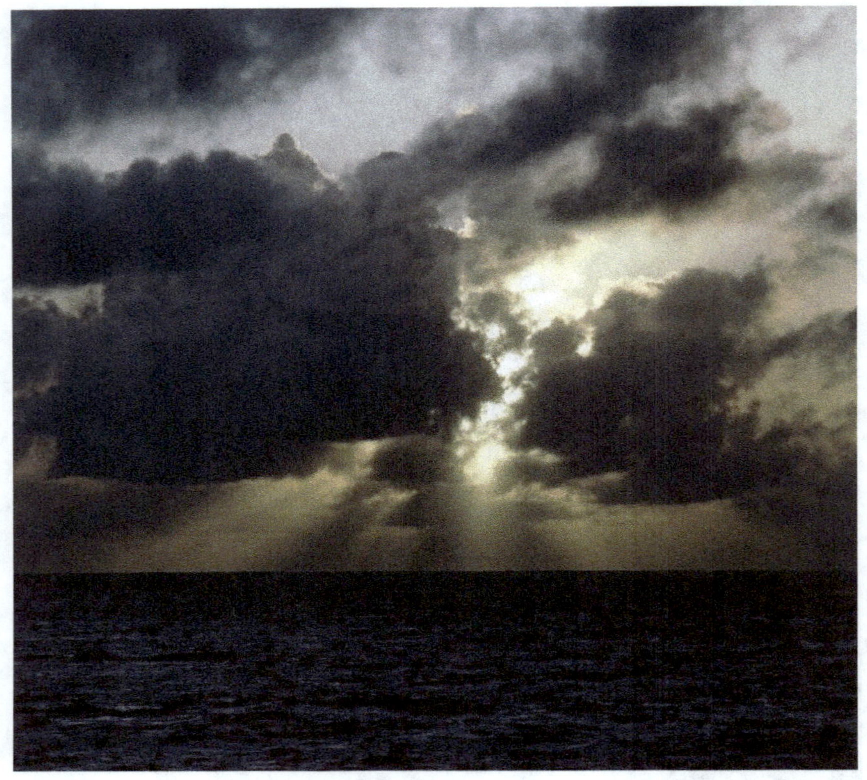

Even though I walk through the valley of the shadow of death, I will fear no evil, for you are with me; your rod and your staff, they comfort me.

Bible reference: Psalm 23:4

Context: A psalm of David

Illustration ID (credit): fv_014 (author)

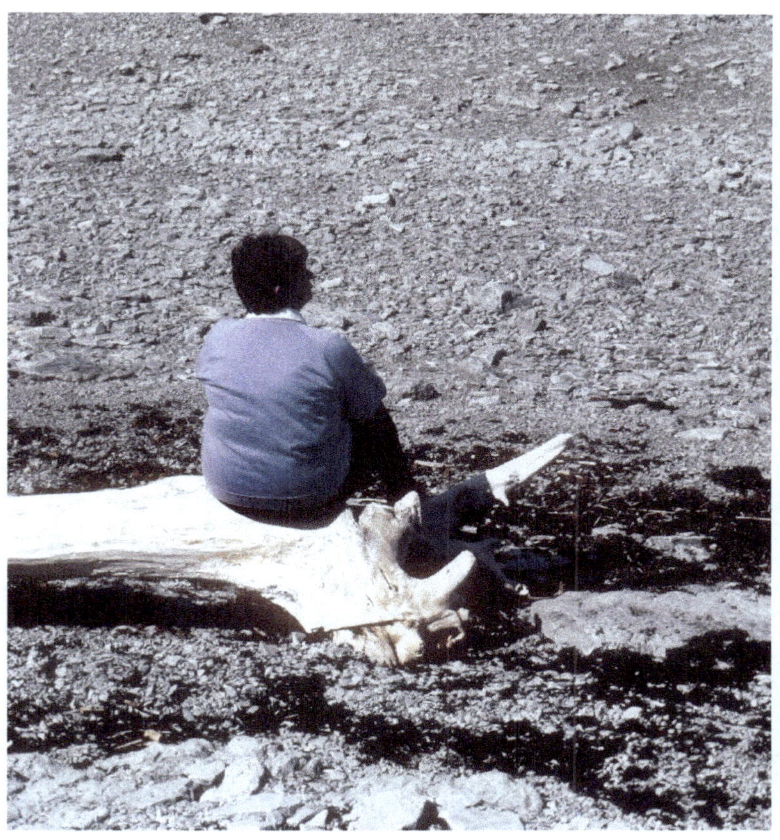

The LORD is close to the broken-hearted and saves those who are crushed in spirit.

Bible reference: Psalm 34:18

Context: Of David

Illustration ID (credit): fv_004 (author)

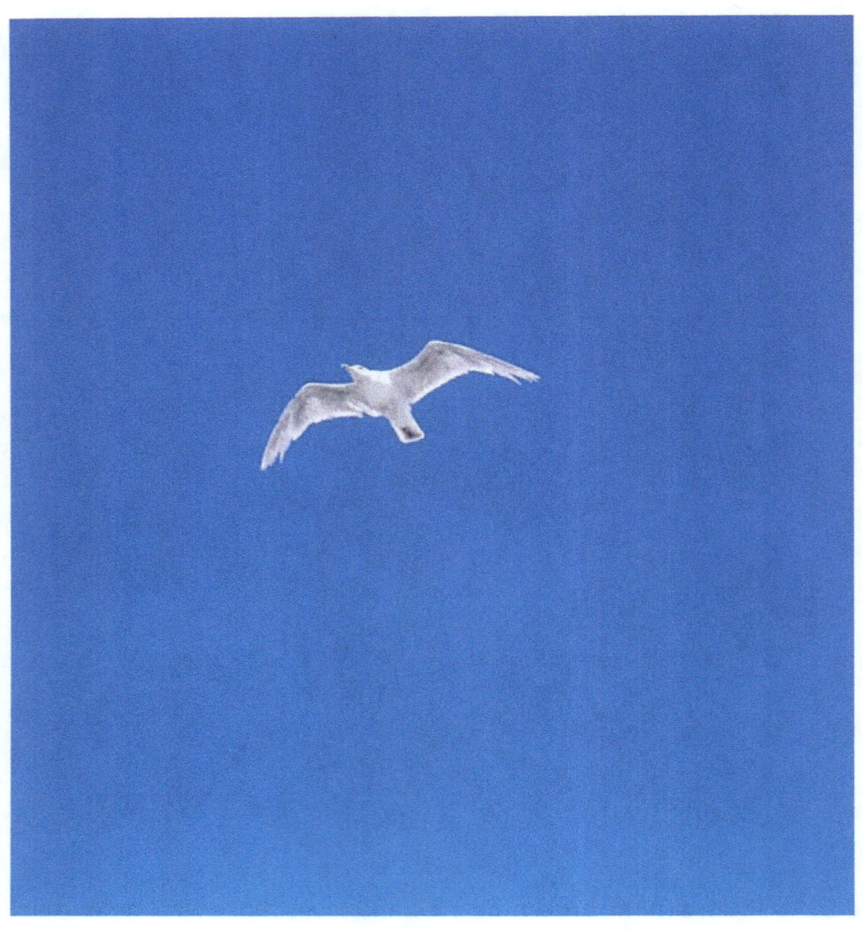

I said, "Oh, that I had the wings of a dove! I would fly away and be at rest."

Bible reference: Psalm 55:6

Context: A maskil of David

Illustration ID (credit): fa_24 (author)

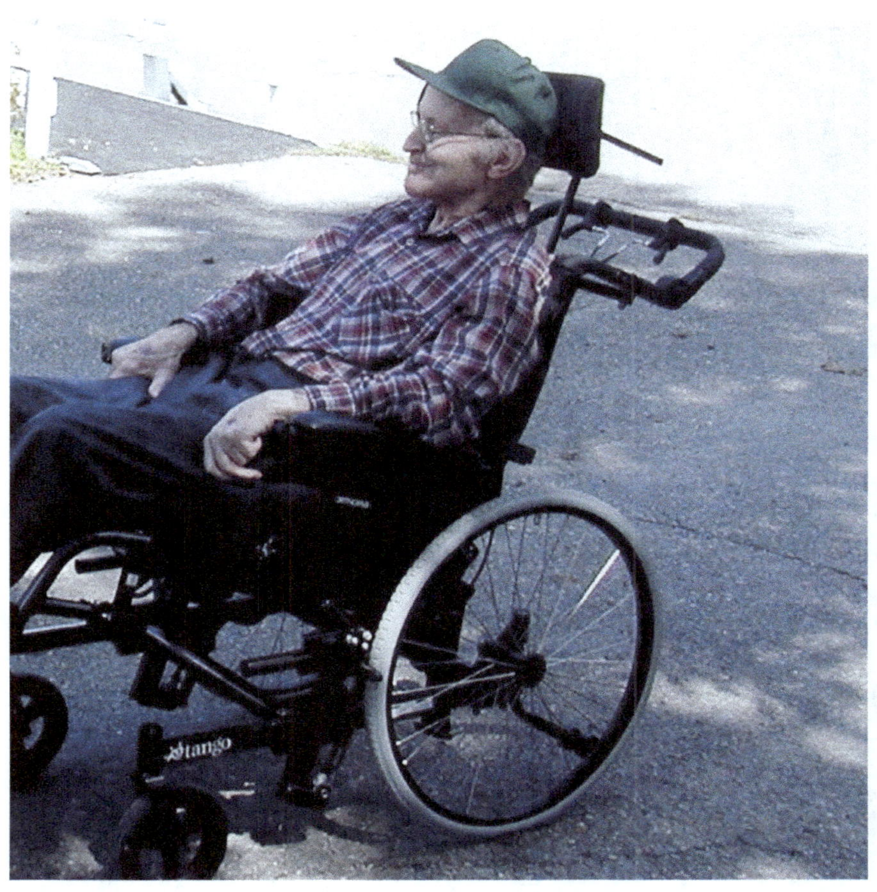

My flesh and my heart may fail, but God is the strength of my heart and my portion forever.

Bible reference: Psalm 73:26

Context: A psalm of Asaph

Illustration ID (credit): fx_0627_1140 (author)

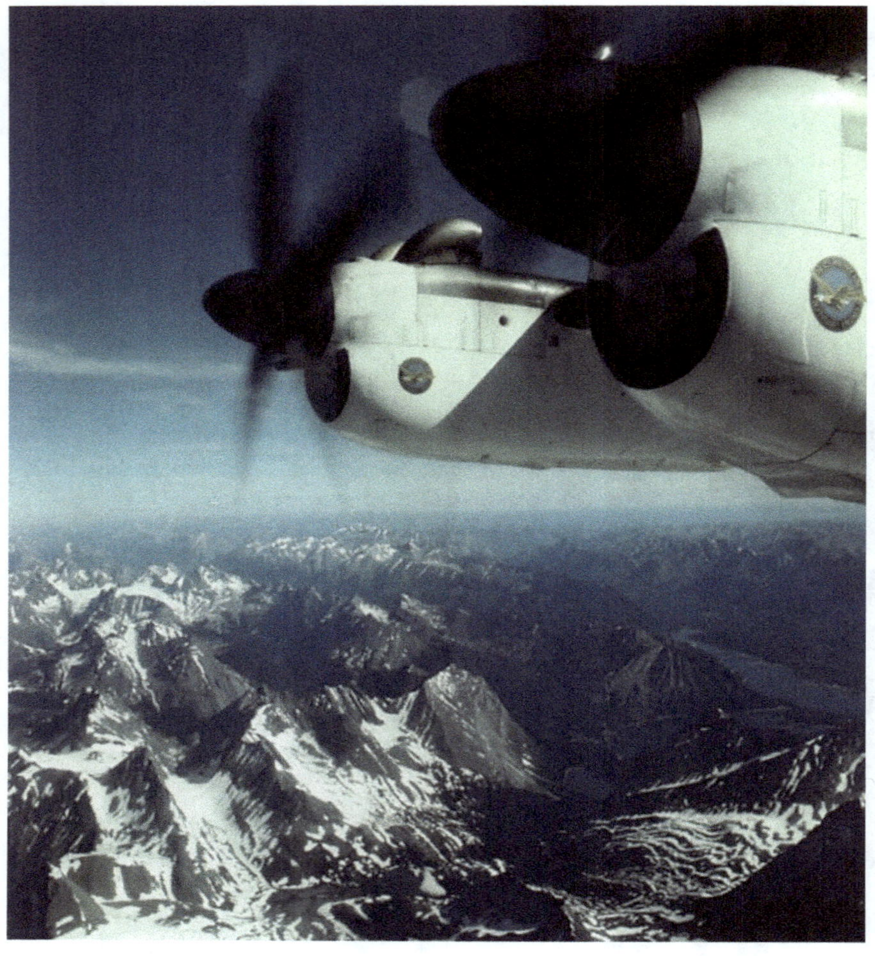

He [the Lord] makes the clouds his chariot and rides on the wings of the wind.

Bible reference: Psalm 104:3b

Context: (unspecified)

Illustration ID (credit): fy_93 (author)

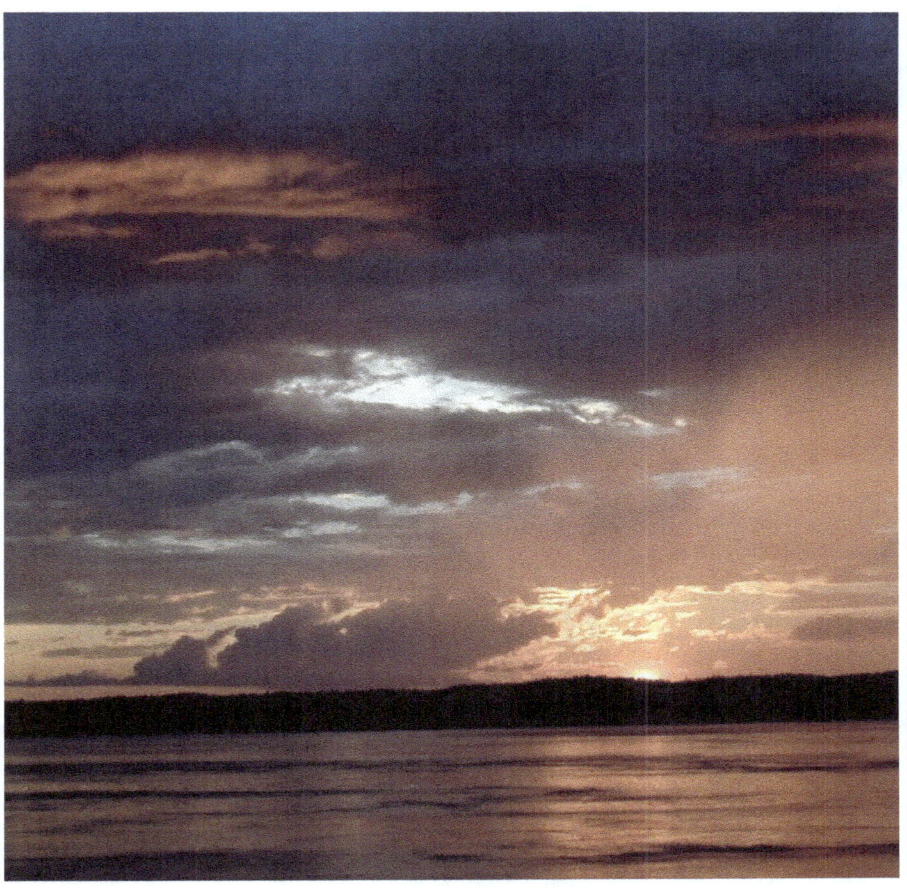

Let the name of the LORD be praised, both now and forevermore. From the rising of the sun to the place where it sets, the name of the LORD is to be praised.

Bible reference: Psalm 113:3

Context: (unspecified)

Illustration ID (credit): fx_8655 (author)

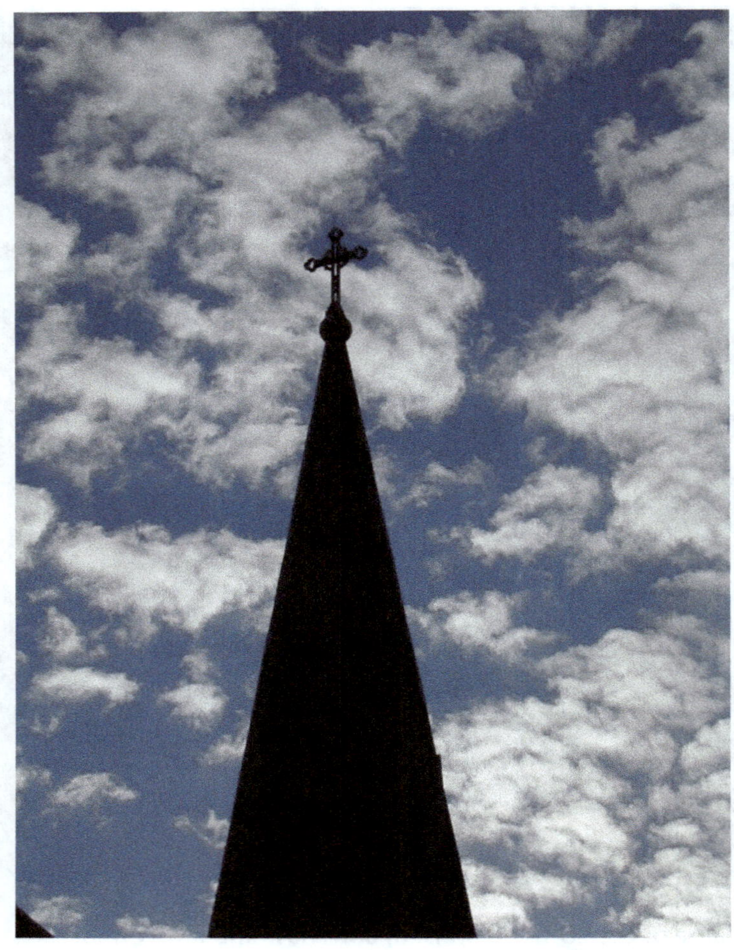

May you be blessed by the LORD, the Maker of heaven and earth. The highest heavens belong to the LORD, but the earth he has given to man.

Bible reference: Psalm 115:15-16

Context: (unspecified)

Illustration ID (credit): fx_6129 (author)

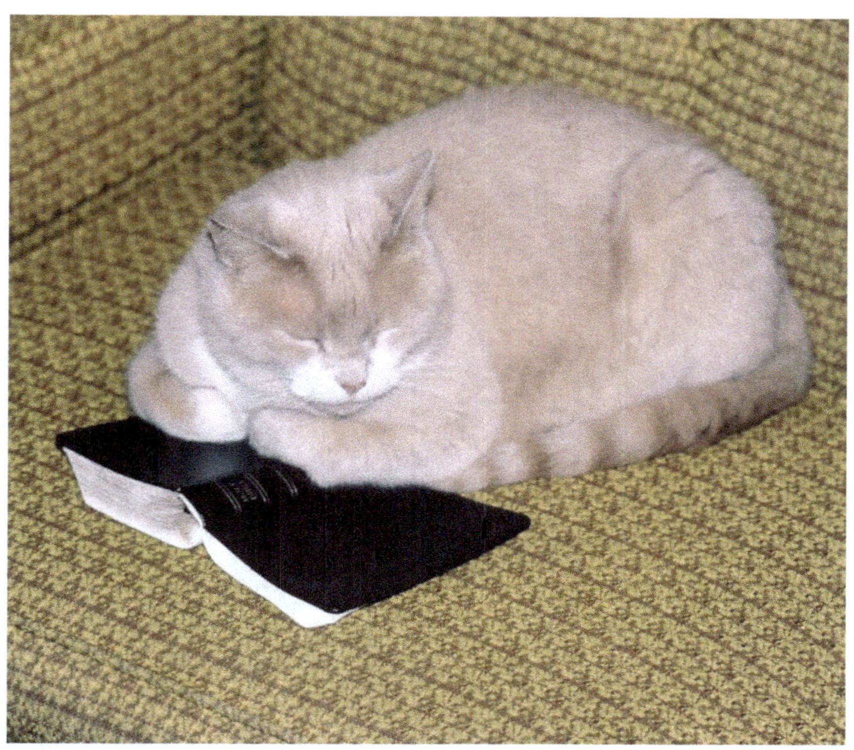

Open my eyes that I may see wonderful things in your law.

Bible reference: Psalm 119:18

Context: Gimel

Illustration ID (credit): fa_34 (author)

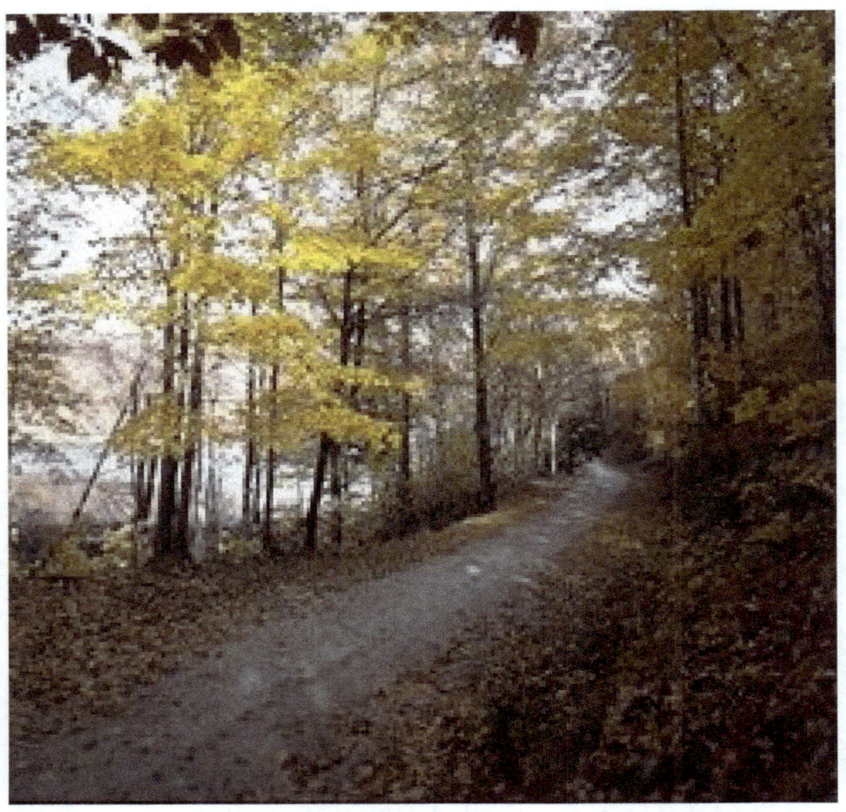

Your word is a lamp to my feet and a light for my path.

Bible reference: Psalm   119:105

Context: Nun

Illustration ID (credit): fx_5900 (author)

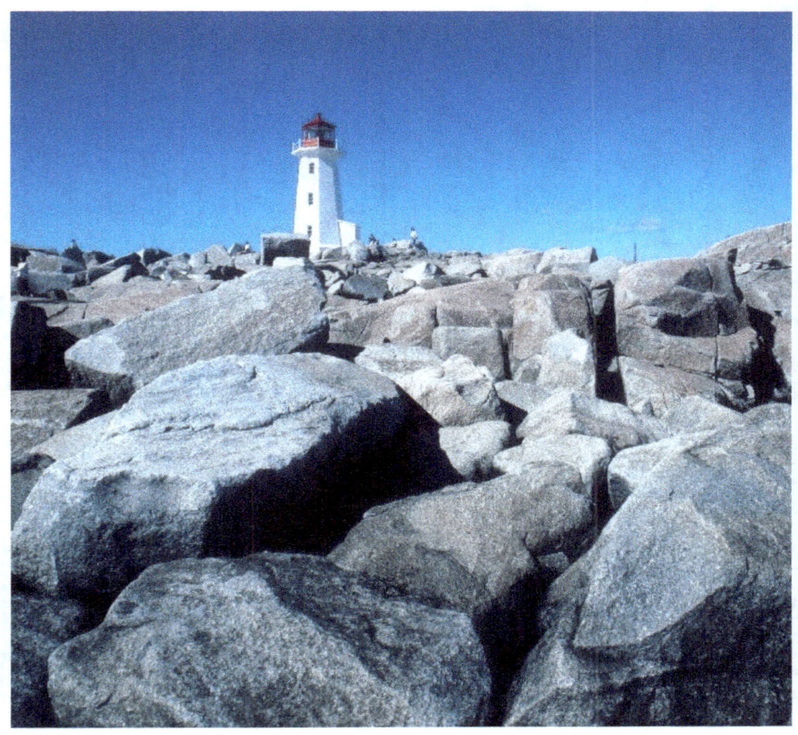

You are my refuge and my shield; I have put my hope in your word.

Bible reference: Psalm 119:114

Context: Samekh

Illustration ID (credit): fa_567 (author)

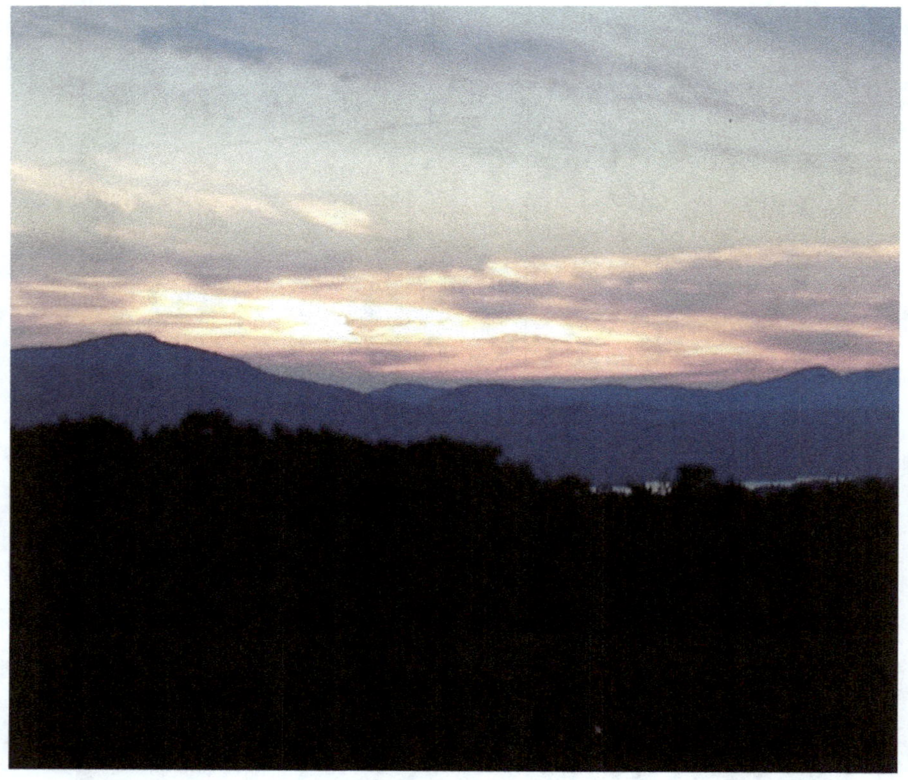

As the mountains surround Jerusalem so the LORD surrounds his people both now and forevermore.

Bible reference: Psalm 125:2

Context: A song of ascents

Illustration ID (credit): fy_21 (author)

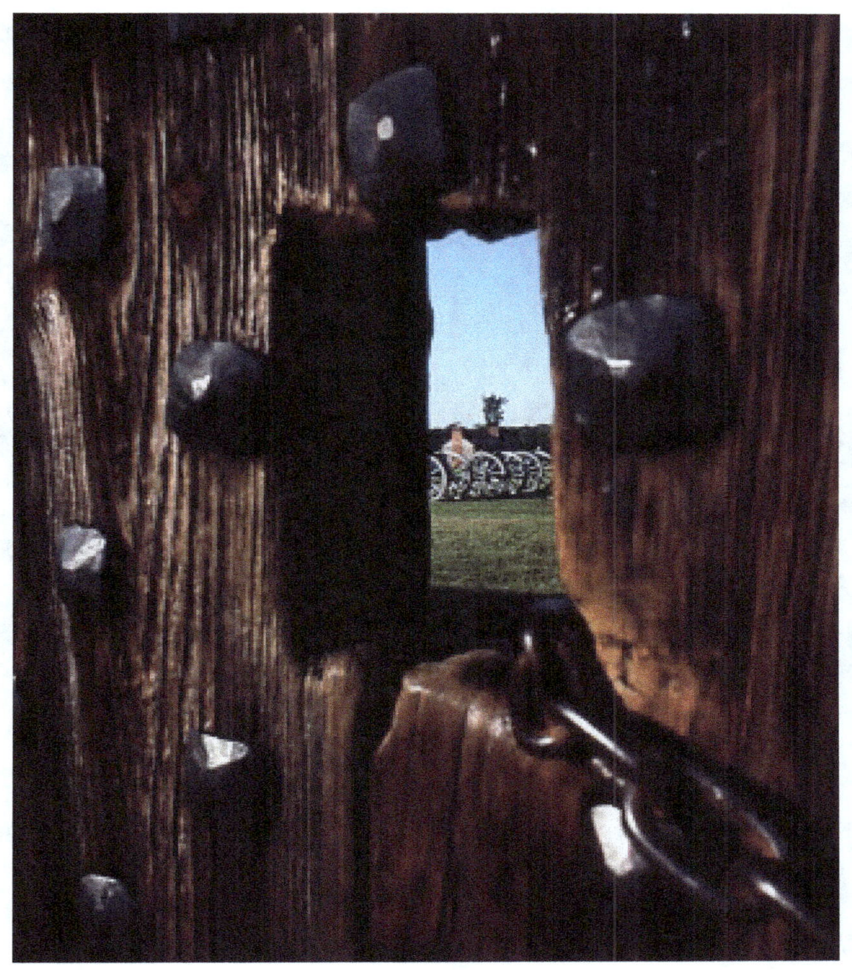

He is my loving God and my fortress, my stronghold and my deliverer,

Bible reference: Psalm 144:2

Context: Of David

Illustration ID (credit): fy_83 (author)

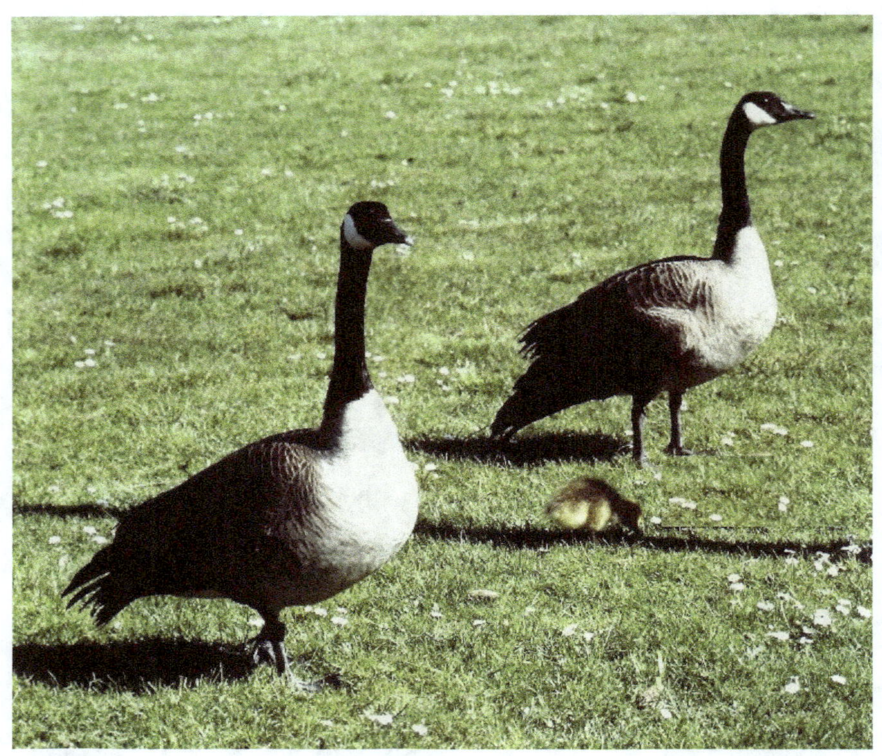

Listen, my son, to your father's instruction and do not forsake your mother's teaching.

Bible reference: Proverbs 1:8

Context: Warning Against Enticement

Illustration ID (credit): fv_009 (author)

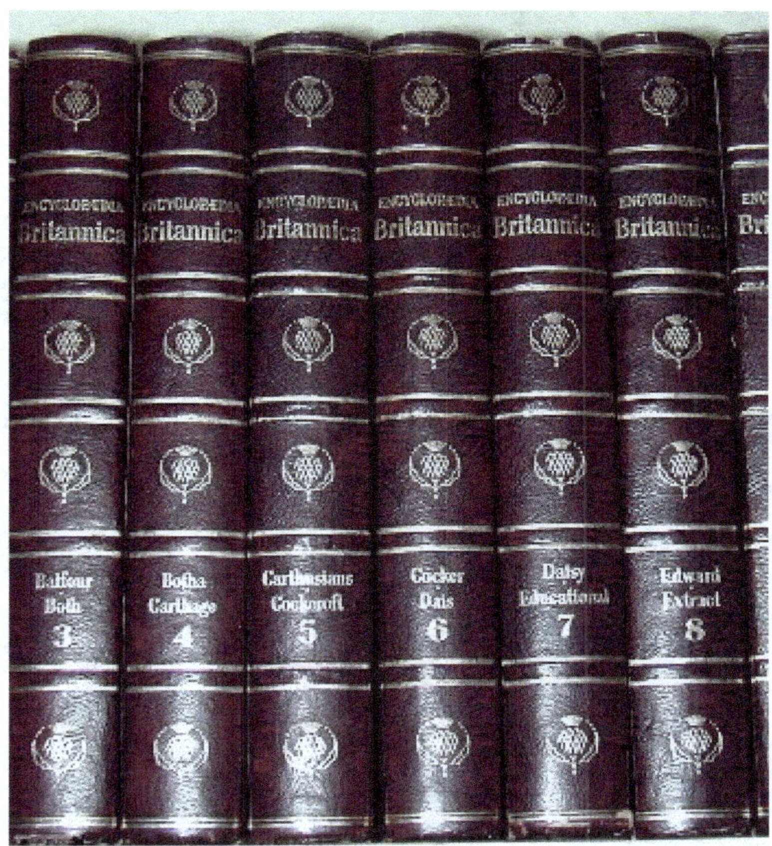

For the Lord gives wisdom; from his mouth come knowledge and understanding.

Bible reference: Proverbs 2:6

Context: Moral Benefits of Wisdom

Illustration ID (credit): fx_1844 (author)

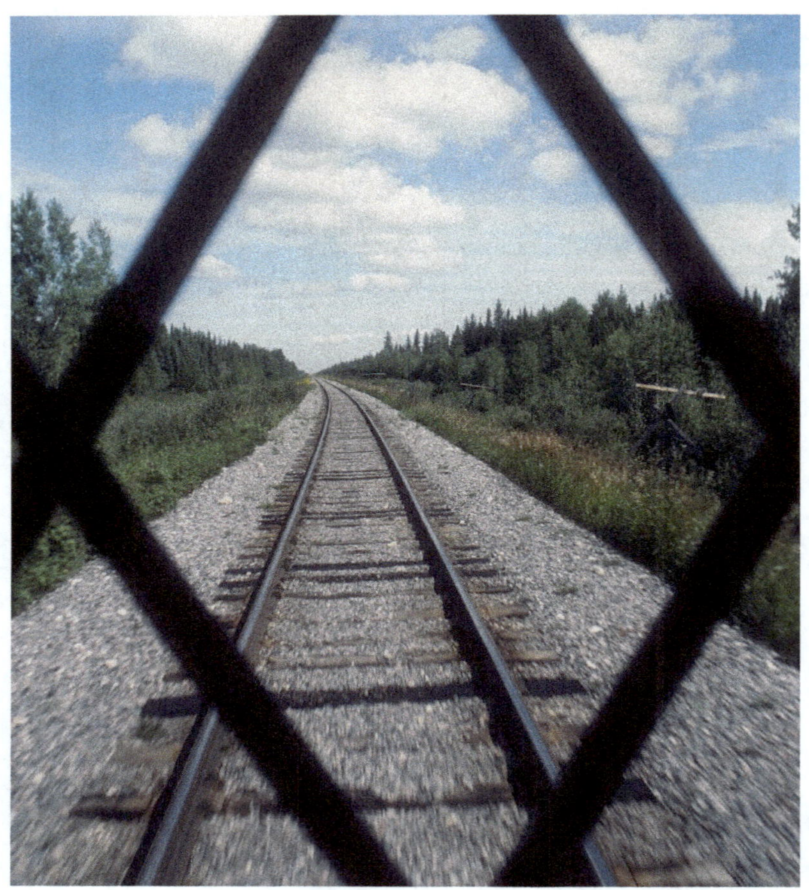

Trust in the LORD with all your heart and lean not on your own understanding; in all your ways acknowledge him, and he will make your paths straight.

Bible reference: Proverbs 3:5-6

Context: Further Benefits of Wisdom

Illustration ID (credit): fy_43 (author)

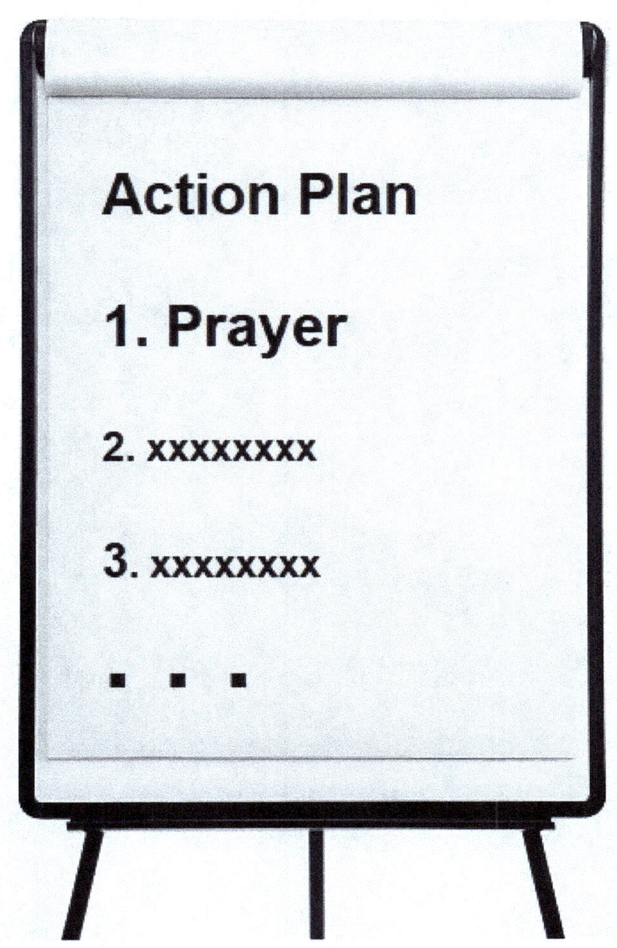

Commit to the LORD whatever you do, and your plans will succeed.

Bible reference: Proverbs 16:3

Context: Proverbs of Solomon

Illustration ID (credit): fs_133304651 (istockphoto, enhanced by author)

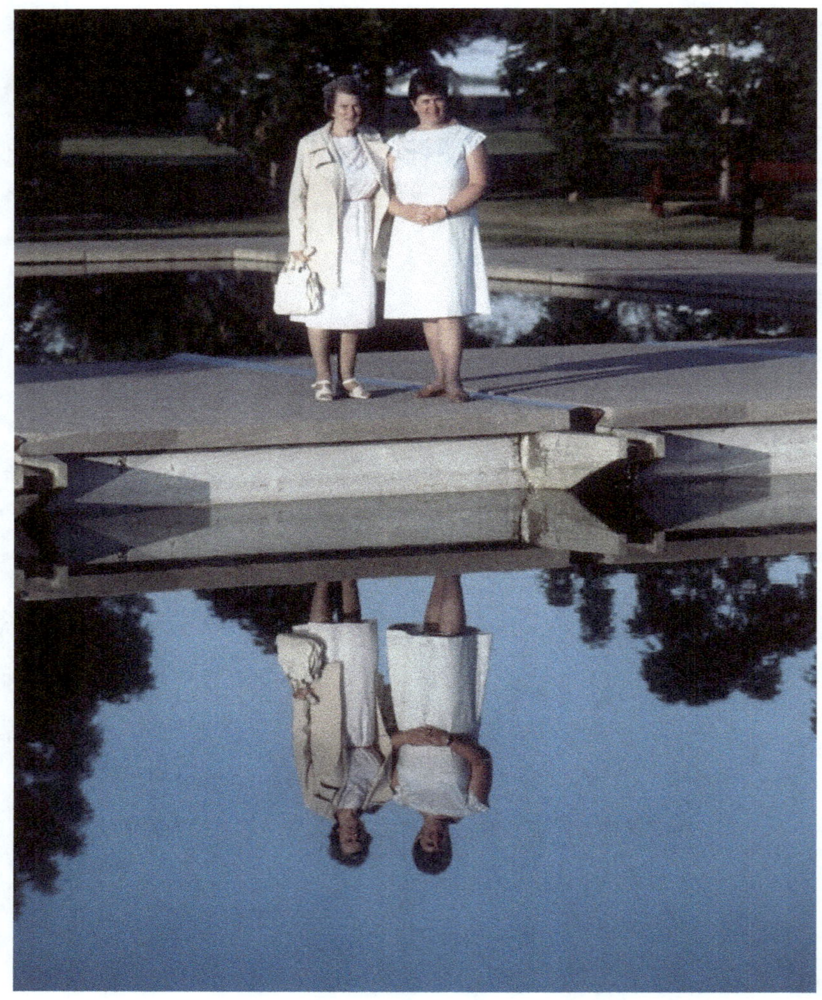

As water reflects a face, so a man's heart reflects the man.

Bible reference: Proverbs 27:19

Context: More Proverbs of Solomon

Illustration ID (credit): fy_74 (author)

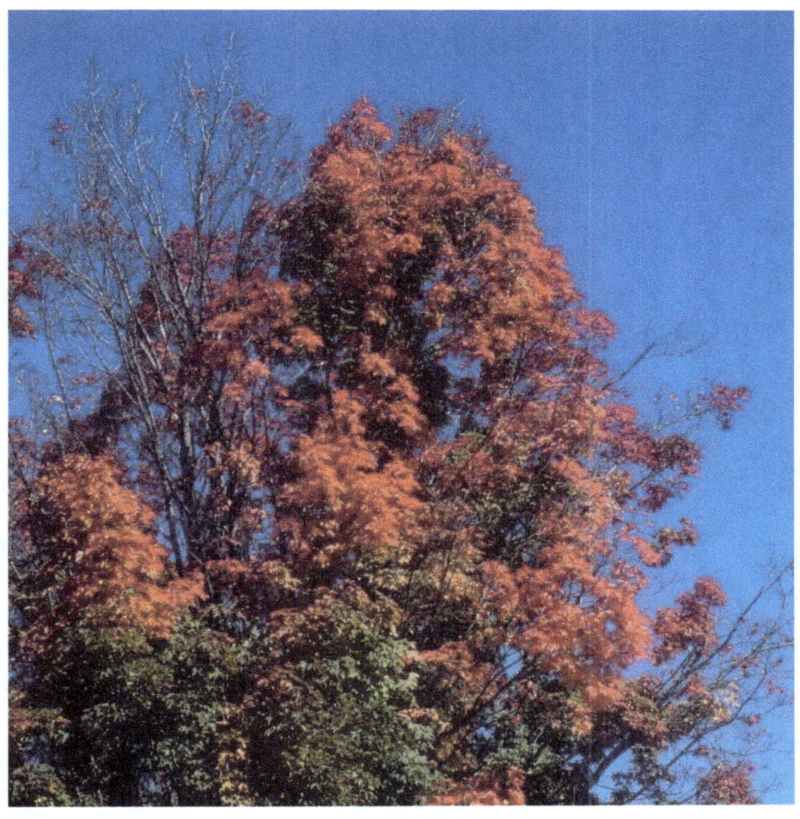

There is a time for everything, and a season for every activity under heaven:

Bible reference: Ecclesiastes 3:1

Context: A Time for Everything

Illustration ID (credit): fy_63 (author)

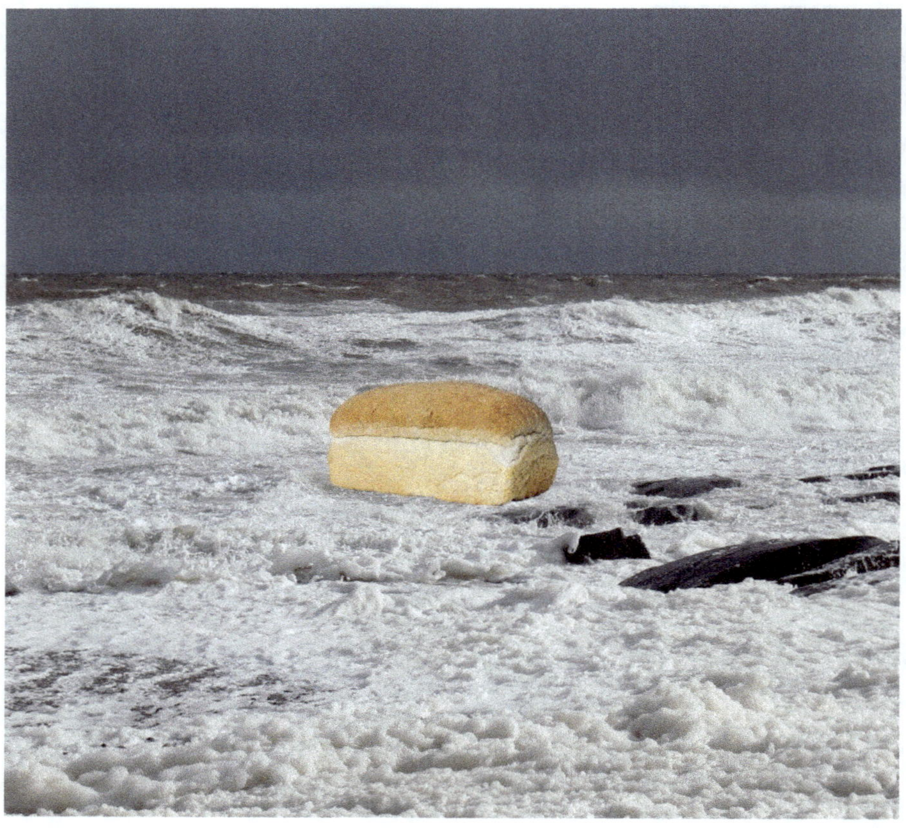

Cast your bread upon the waters, for after many days you will find it again.

Bible reference: Ecclesiastes 11:1

Context: Bread Upon the Waters

Illustration ID (credit): fx_4480e (author, enhanced by Jim Fraser)

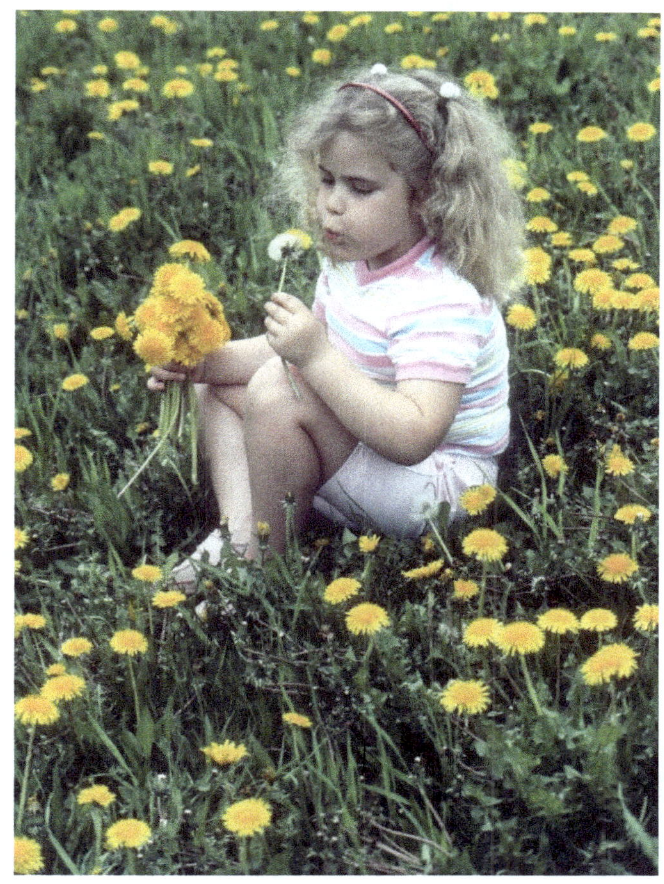

See! The winter is past; the rains are over and gone. Flowers appear on the earth;

Bible reference: Song of Songs 2:11-12

Context: Beloved

Illustration ID (credit): fy_24 (author)

Section 4: The Prophets

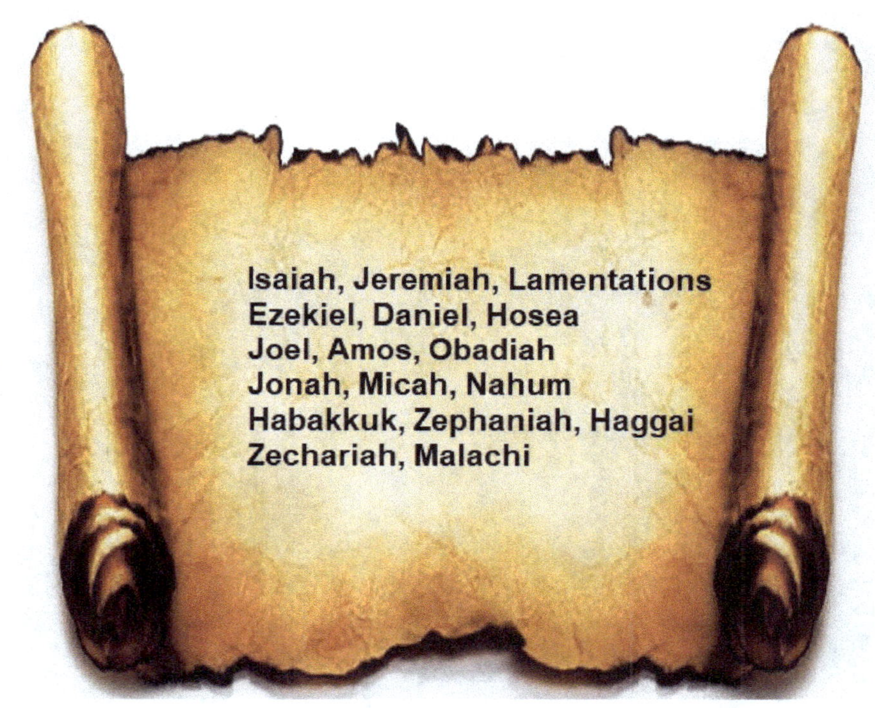

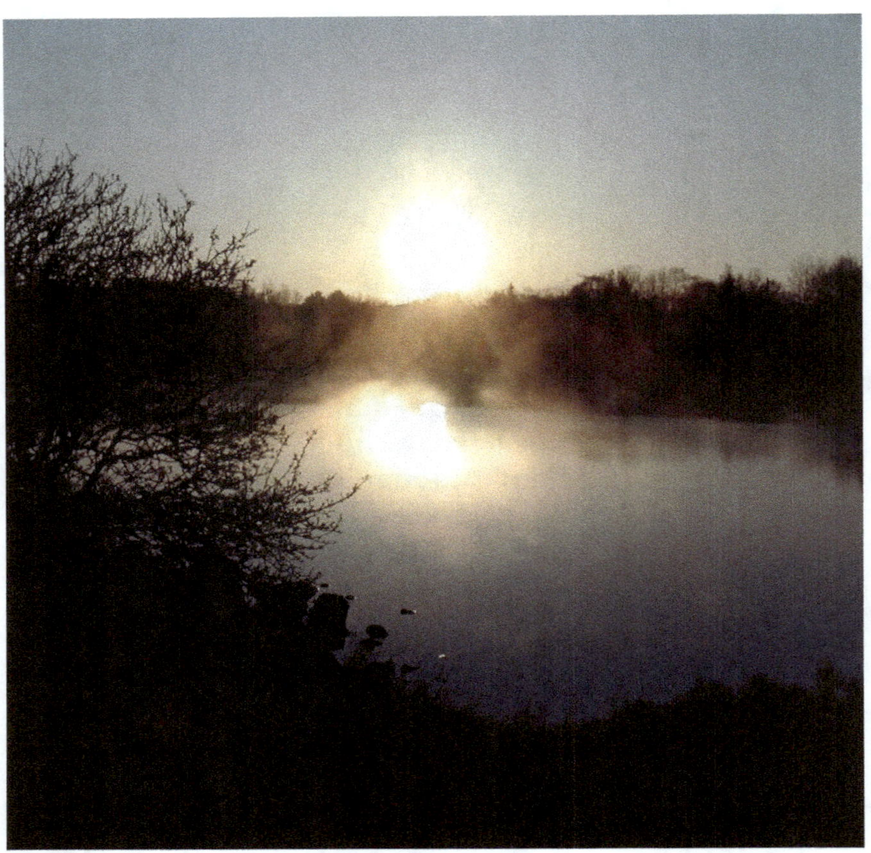

The people walking in darkness have seen a great light; on those living in the land of the shadow of death a light has dawned.

Bible reference: Isaiah 9:2

Context: To Us a Child Is Born

Illustration ID (credit): fx_4277 (author)

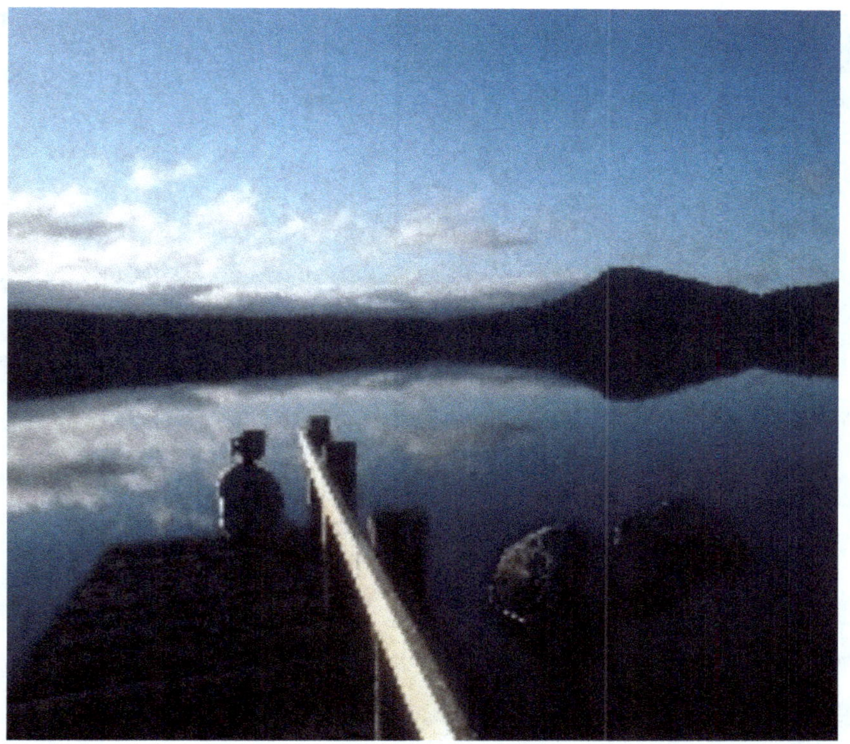

You will keep in perfect peace him whose mind is steadfast, because he trusts in you. Trust in the LORD forever, for the LORD, the LORD, is the Rock eternal.

Bible reference: Isaiah 26:3-4

Context: A Song of Praise

Illustration ID (credit): fy_14 (author)

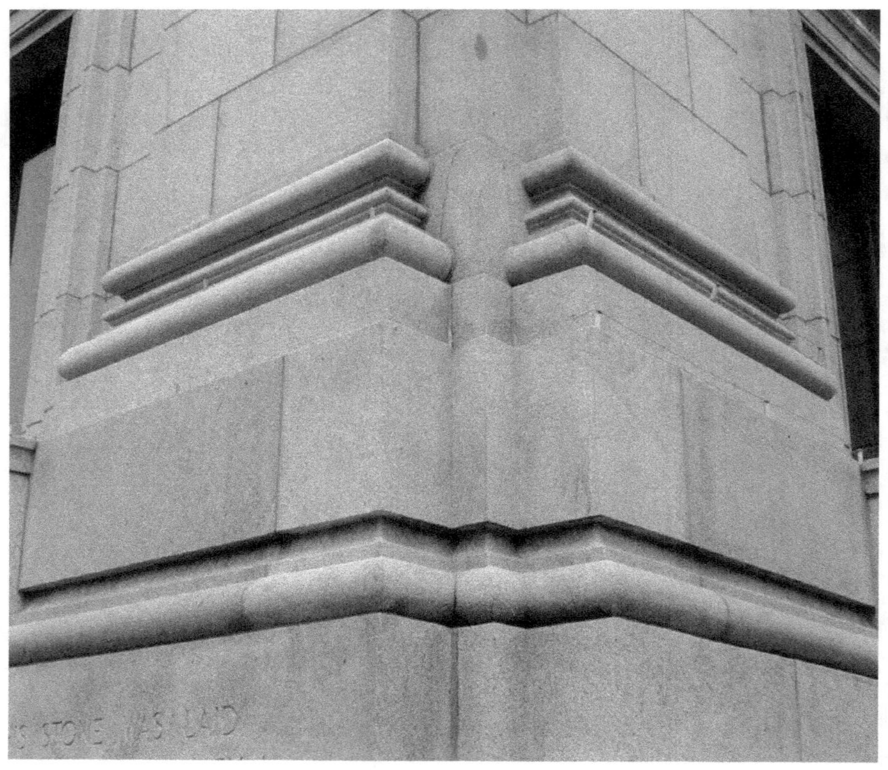

So this is what the Sovereign Lord says: "See, I lay a stone in Zion, a tested stone, a precious cornerstone for a sure foundation; . . ."

Bible reference: Isaiah 28:16a

Context: Woe to Ephraim

Illustration ID (credit): fa_47 (author)

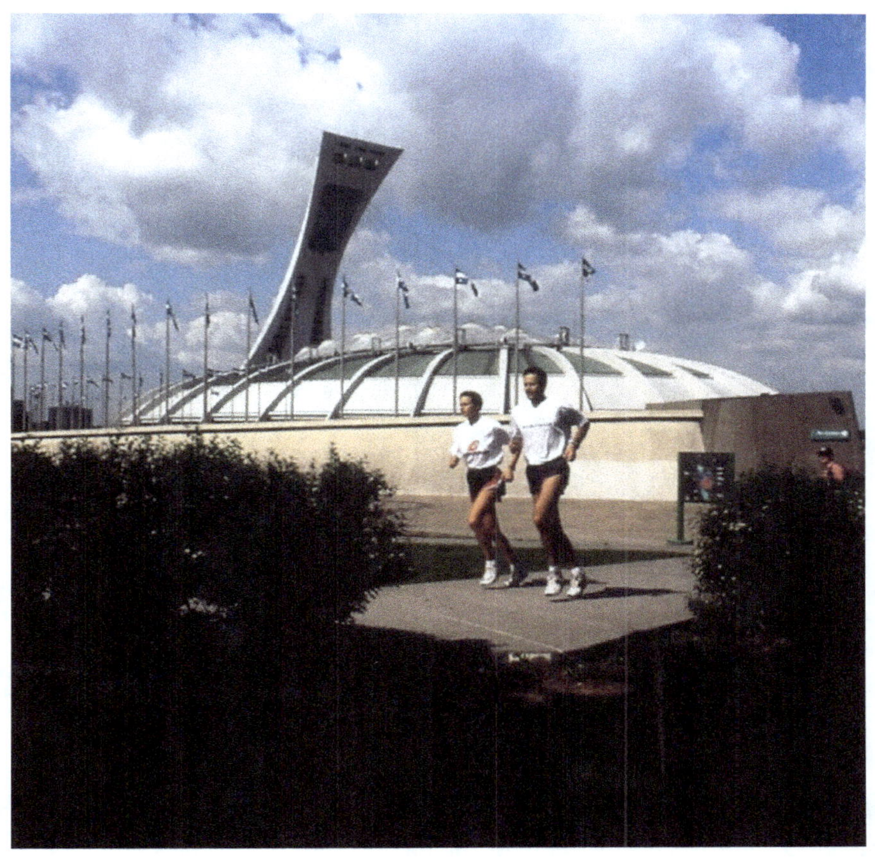

. . . but those who hope in the LORD will renew their strength. They will soar on wings like eagles; they will run and not grow weary, they will walk and not be faint.

Bible reference: Isaiah 40:31

Context: Comfort for God's People

Illustration ID (credit): fy_26b (author)

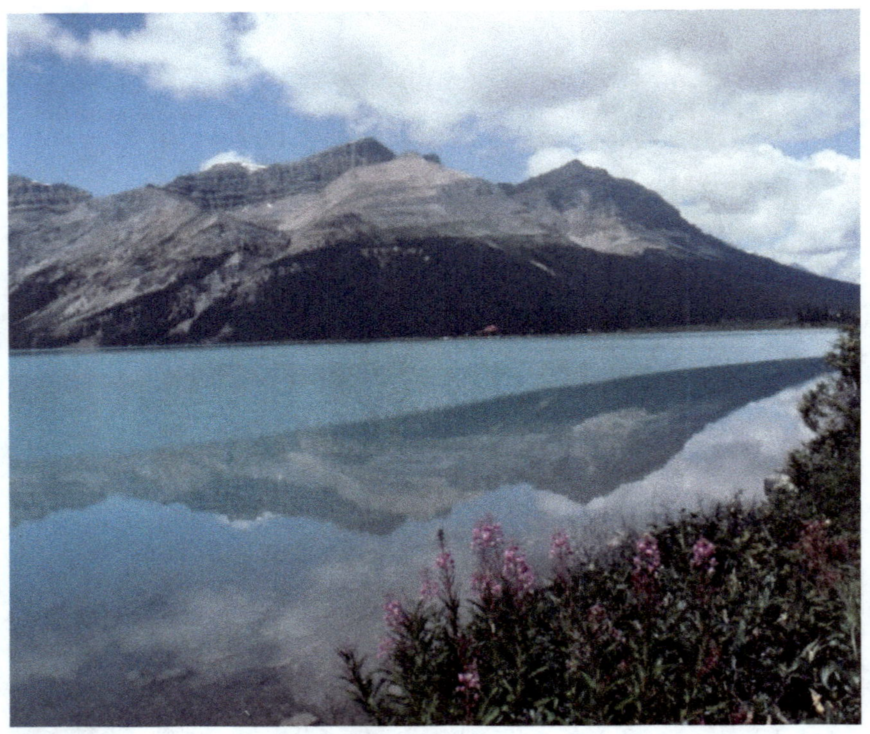

Shout for joy, O heavens; rejoice, O earth; burst into song, O mountains! For the LORD comforts his people and will have compassion on his afflicted ones.

Bible reference: Isaiah 49:13

Context: Restoration of Israel

Illustration ID (credit): fv_010 (author)

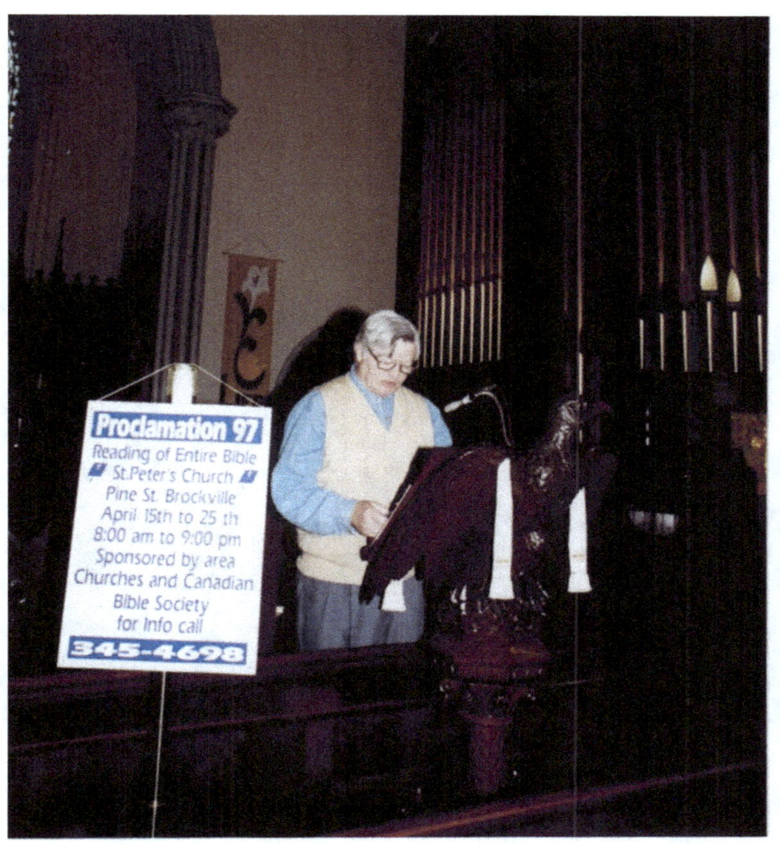

. . . so is my word that goes out from my mouth: It will not return to me empty, but will accomplish what I desire and achieve the purpose for which I sent it.

Bible reference: Isaiah 55:11

Context: Invitation to the Thirsty

Illustration ID (credit): CCI_1101 (author)

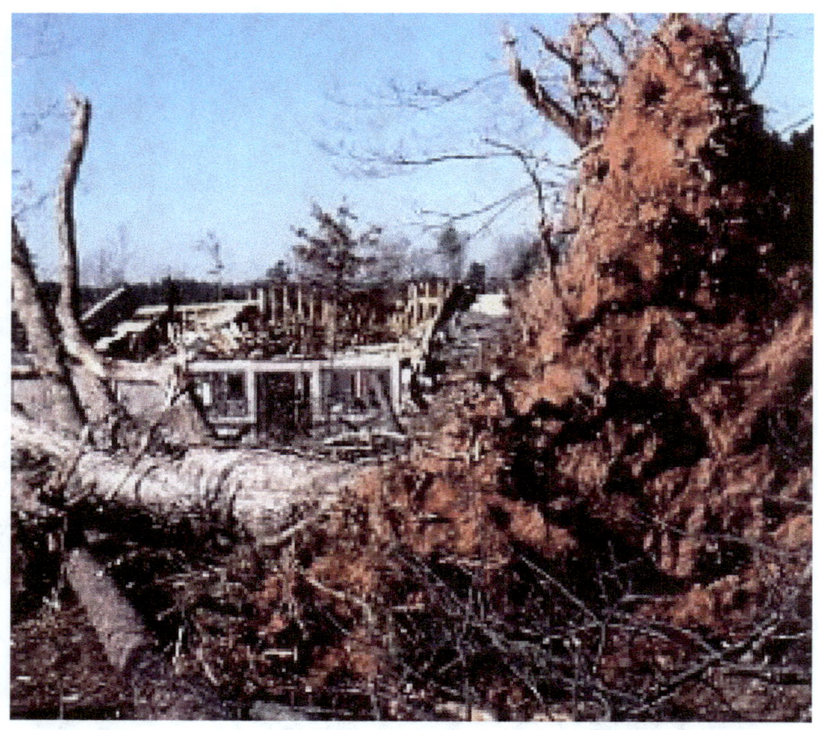

This is what the LORD Almighty says: "Look! Disaster is spreading from nation to nation; a mighty storm is rising from the ends of the earth."

Bible reference: Jeremiah 25:32

Context: The Cup of God's Wrath

Illustration ID (credit): fptorn01 (author)

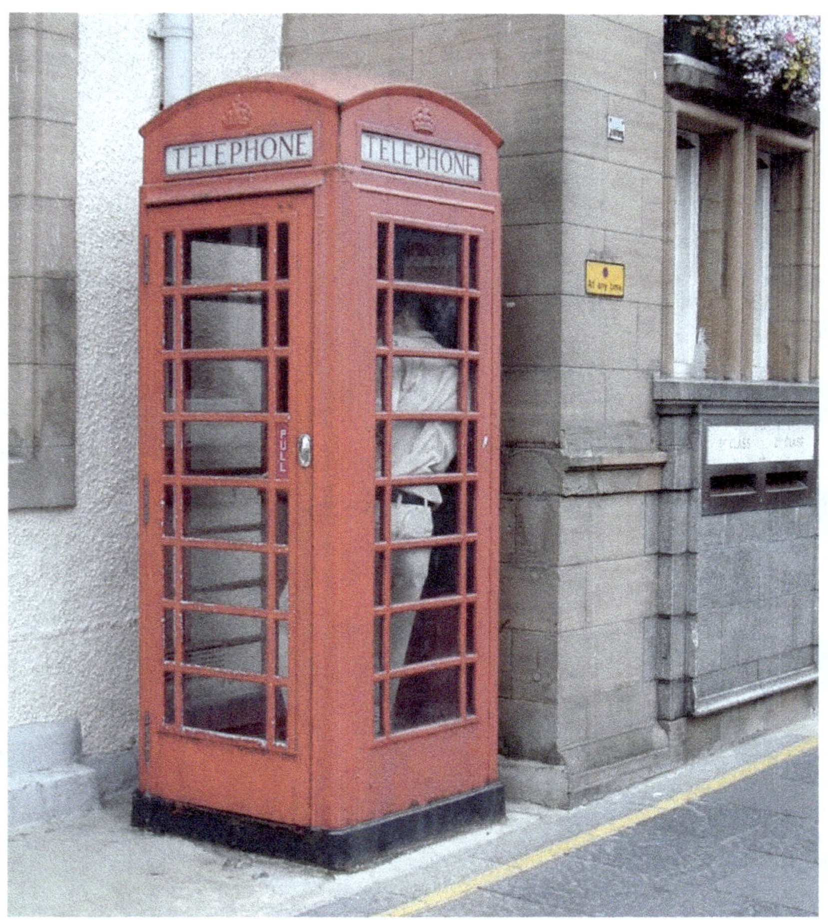

Call to me and I will answer you and tell you great and unsearchable things you do not know.

Bible reference: Jeremiah 33:3

Context: Promise of Restoration

Illustration ID (credit): fx_3186 (author)

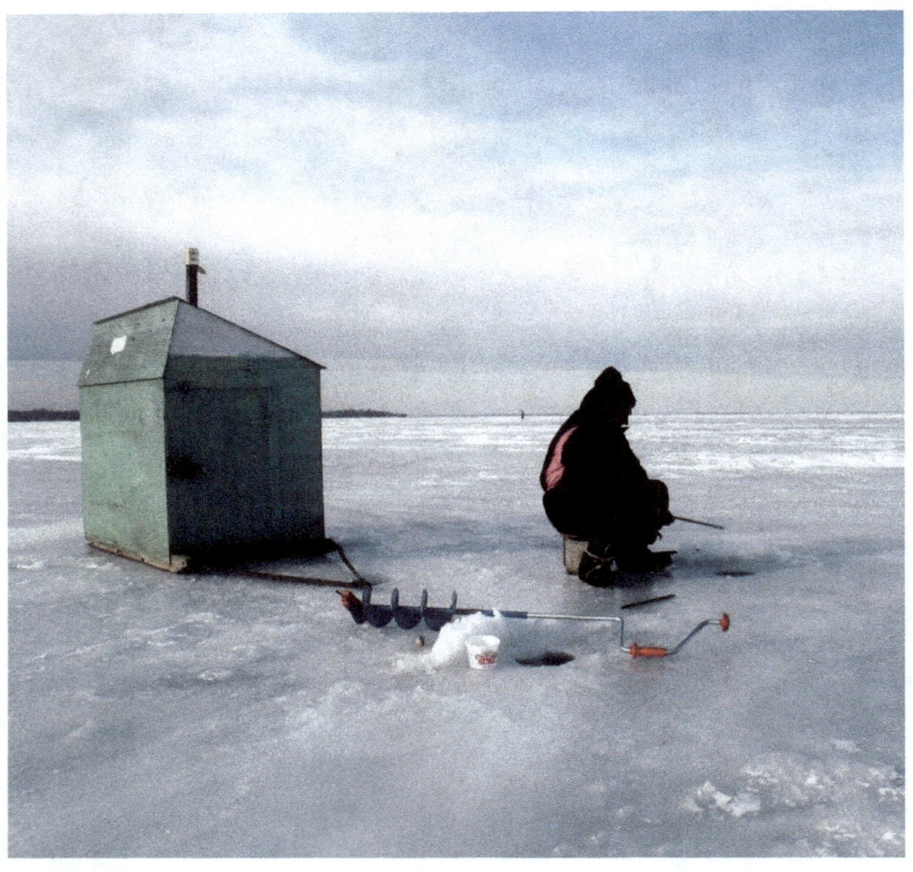

I say to myself, "The LORD is my portion; therefore I will wait for him."

Bible reference: Lamentations 3:24

Context: (unspecified)

Illustration ID (credit): fv_003 (author)

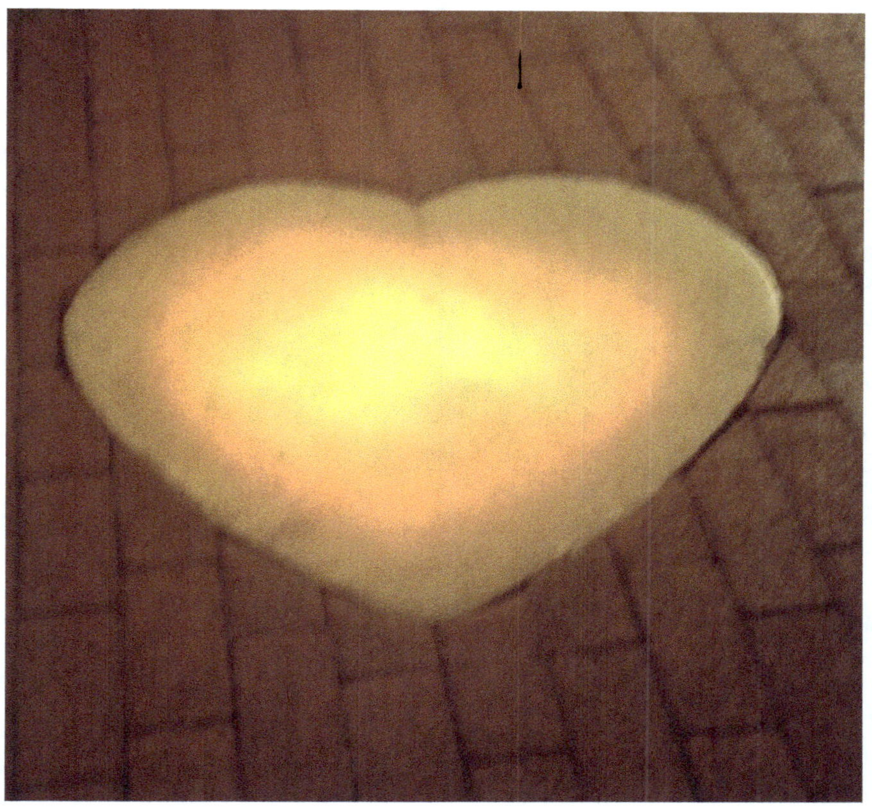

I will give you a new heart and put a new spirit in you; I will remove from you your heart of stone and give you a heart of flesh.

Bible reference: Ezekiel 36:26

Context: A Prophecy of the Mountains of Israel

Illustration ID (credit): fc_3062 (author)

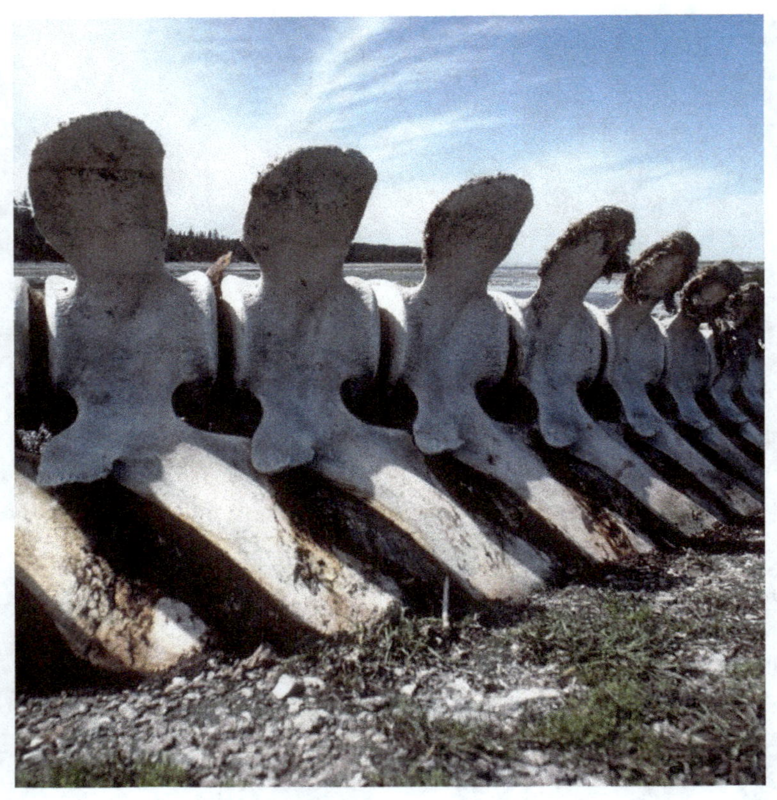

Then he said to me, "Prophesy to these bones and say to them, 'Dry bones, hear the word of the Lord! This is what the Sovereign Lord says to these bones: I will make breath[a] enter you, and you will come to life. I will attach tendons to you and make flesh come upon you and cover you with skin; I will put breath in you, and you will come to life. Then you will know that I am the Lord.'"

Bible reference: Ezekiel 37:4-6

Context: The Valley of Dry Bones

Illustration ID (credit): fa_333 (author)

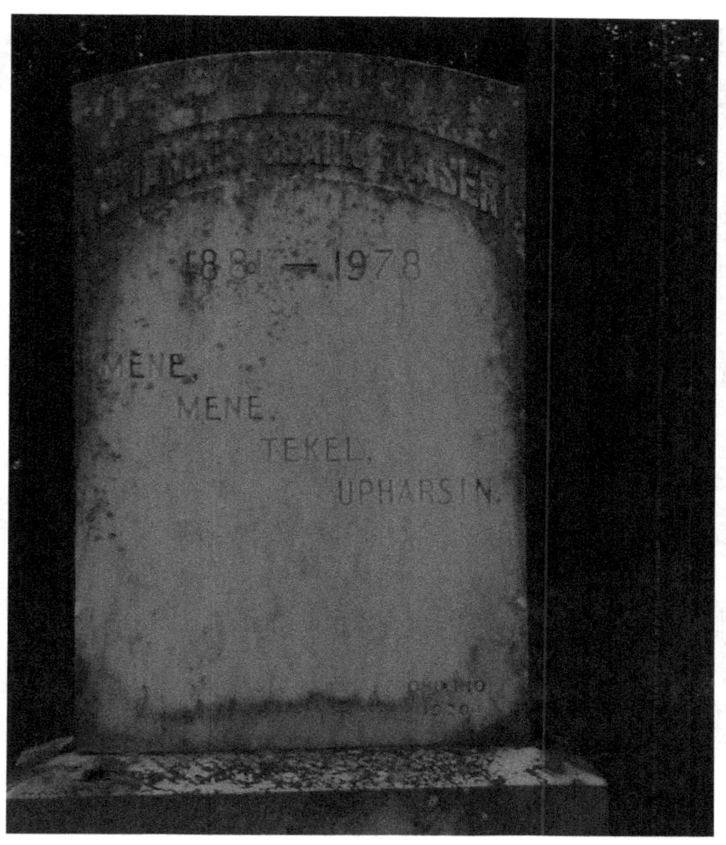

"This is the inscription that was written: mene, mene, tekel, parsin. "Here is what these words mean: Mene: God has numbered the days of your reign and brought it to an end. Tekel: You have been weighed on the scales and found wanting. Peres: Your kingdom is divided and given to the Medes and Persians."

Bible reference: Daniel 5:25-28

Context: The Writing on the Wall

Illustration ID (credit): fy_101 (author)

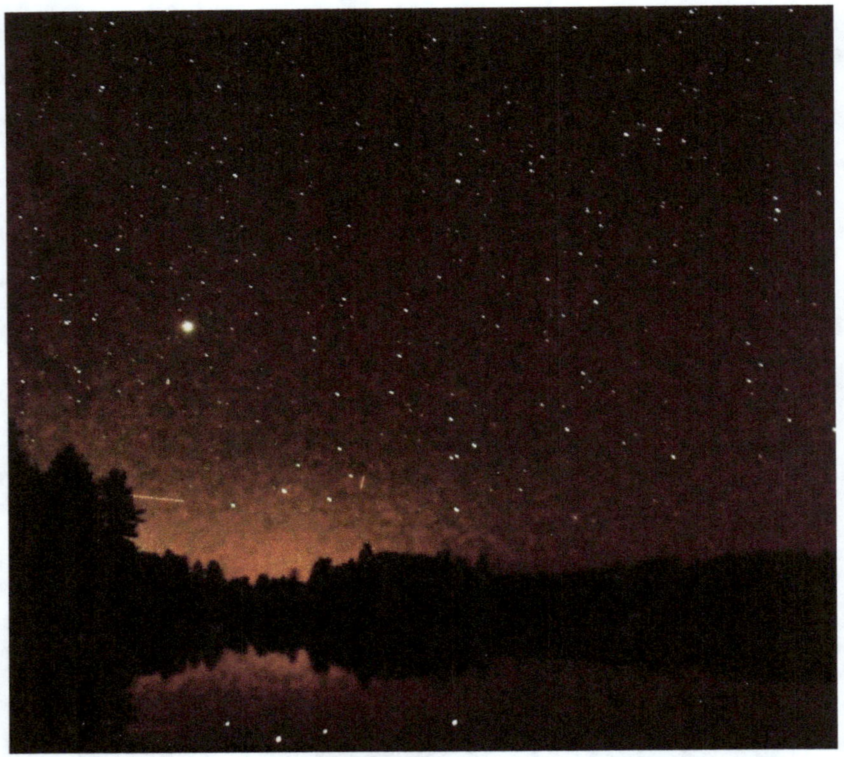

Those who are wise will shine like the brightness of the heavens, and those who lead many to righteousness, like the stars for ever and ever.

Bible reference: Daniel 12:3

Context: The End Times

Illustration ID (credit): fy_45 (Kira-Marie Lazda)

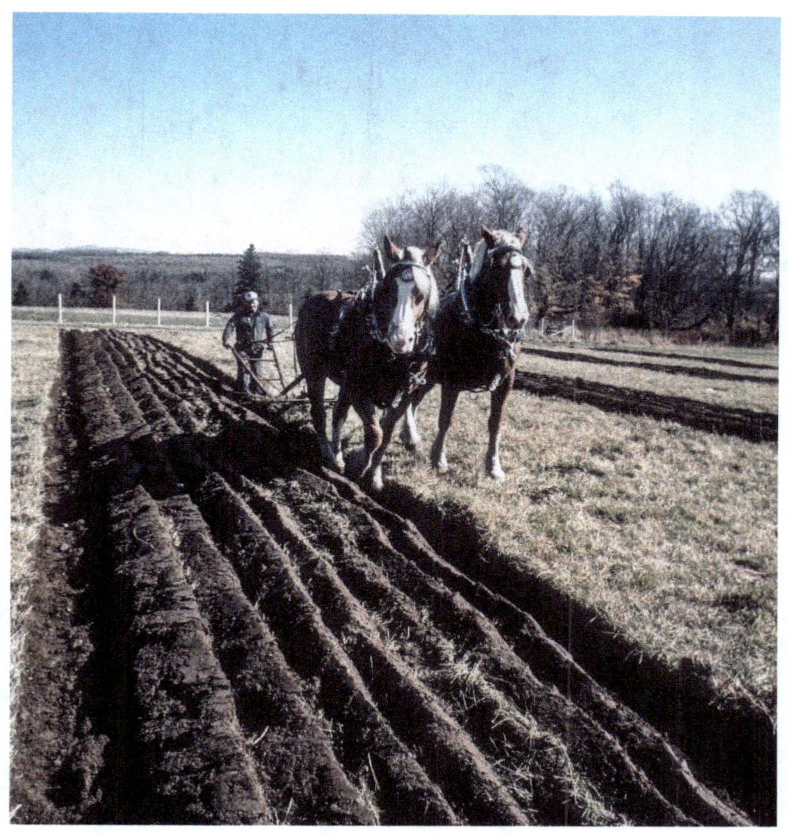

Sow for yourselves righteousness, reap the fruit of unfailing love, and break up your unplowed ground; for it is time to seek the LORD, until he comes and showers righteousness on you.

Bible reference: Hosea 10:12

Context: Punishment for Israel

Illustration ID (credit): fy_75 (author)

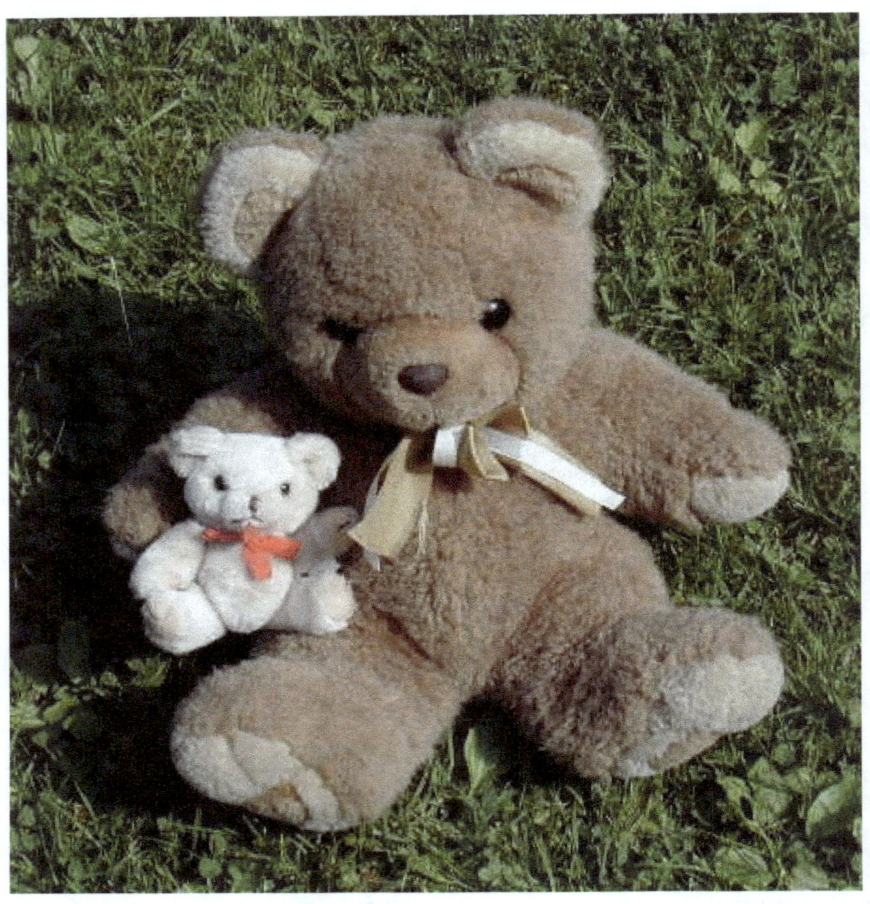

Return to the LORD your God, for he is gracious and compassionate, slow to anger and abounding in love

Bible reference: Joel 2:13

Context: Rend Your Heart

Illustration ID (credit): fy_28 (author)

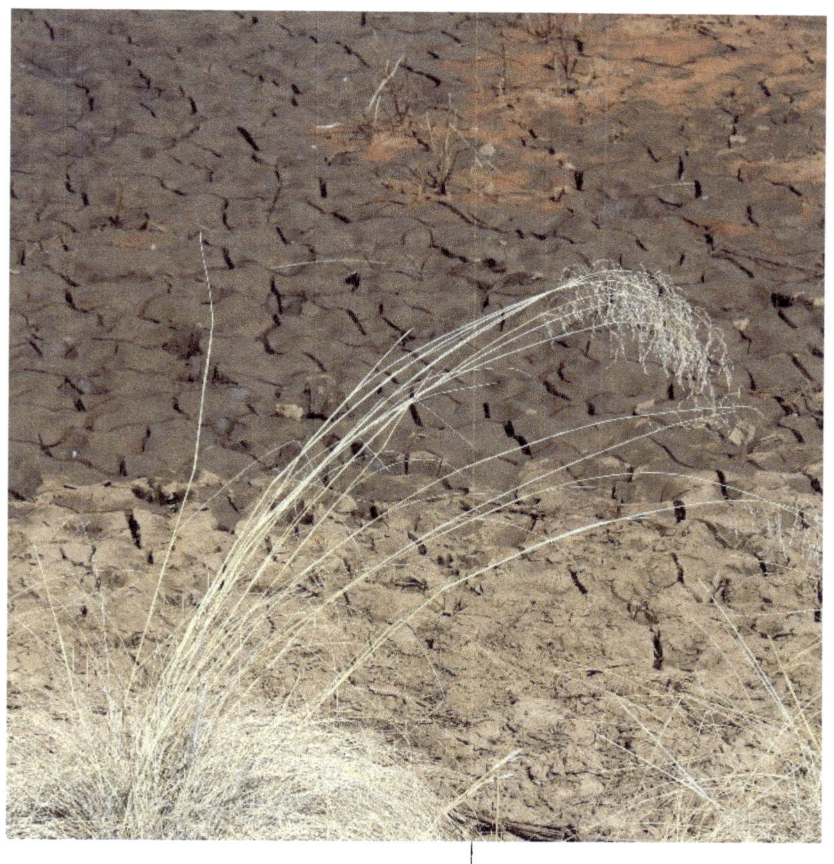

"The days are coming," declares the Sovereign Lord, "when I will send a famine through the land — not a famine of food or a thirst for water, but a famine of hearing the words of the Lord. . ."

Bible reference: Amos 8:11

Context: A Basket of Ripe Fruit

Illustration ID (credit): fc_0982 (author)

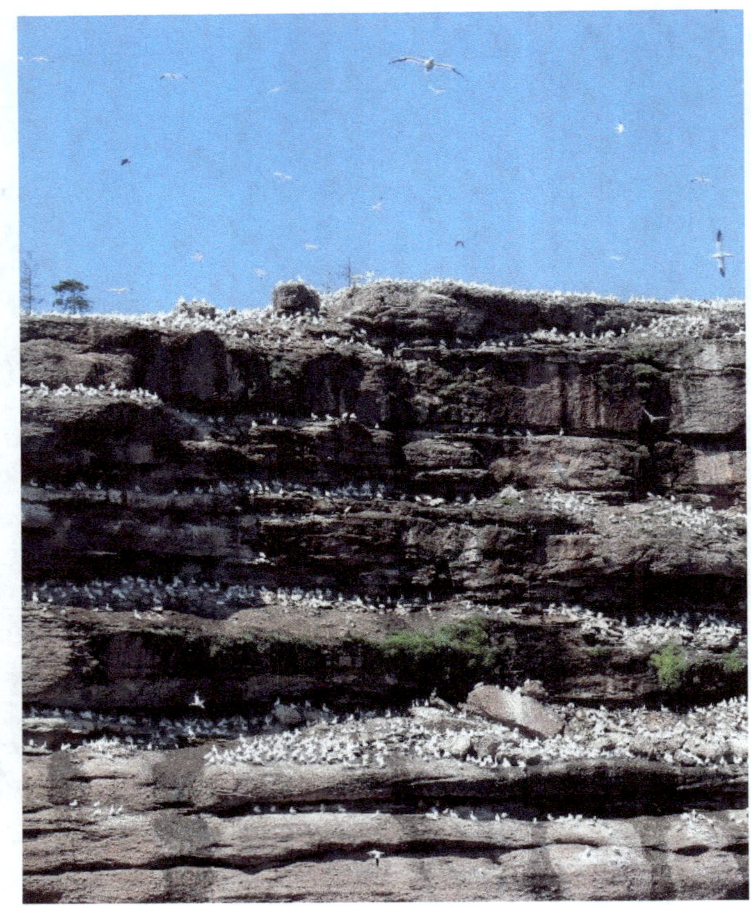

The pride of your heart has deceived you, you who live in the clefts of the rocks and make your home on the heights, you who say to yourself, 'Who can bring me down to the ground?'

Bible reference: Obadiah 1:3

Context: (unspecified)

Illustration ID (credit): fx_1111 (author)

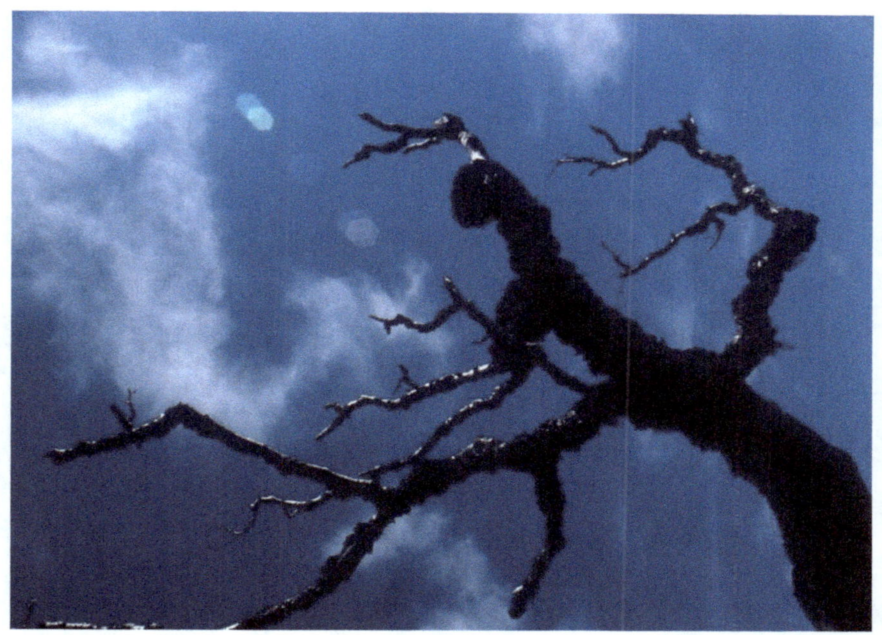

But the Lord said, "You have been concerned about this plant, though you did not tend it or make it grow. It sprang up overnight and died overnight . . . ."

Bible reference: Jonah 4:10

Context: Jonah's Anger at the Lord's Compassion

Illustration ID (credit): fa_02 (author)

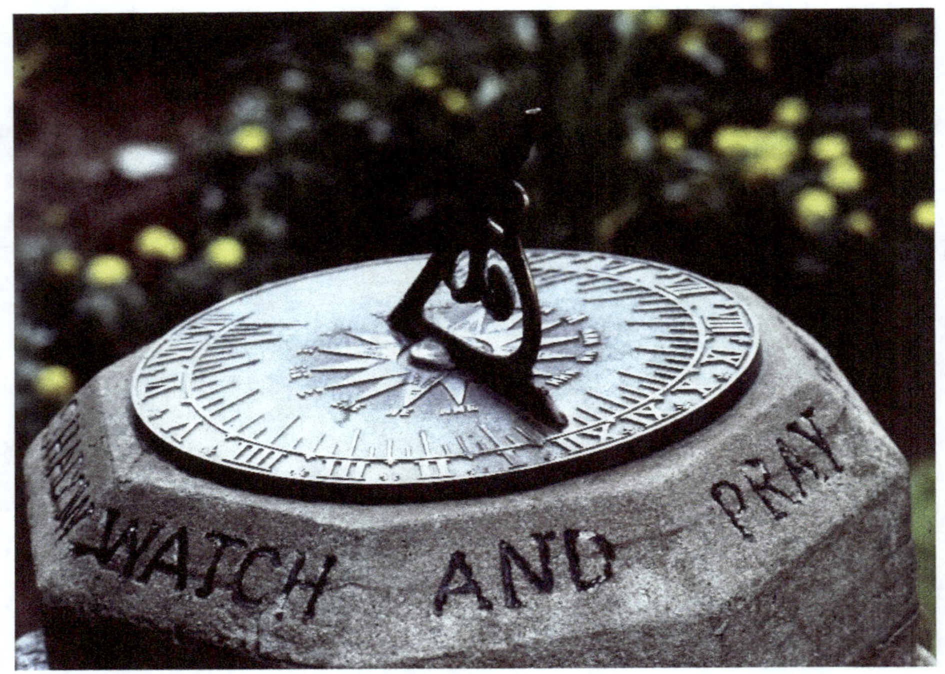

But as for me, I watch in hope for the LORD, I wait for God my Savior; my God will hear me.

Bible reference: Micah 7:7

Context: Israel's Misery

Illustration ID (credit): fs_343 (author)

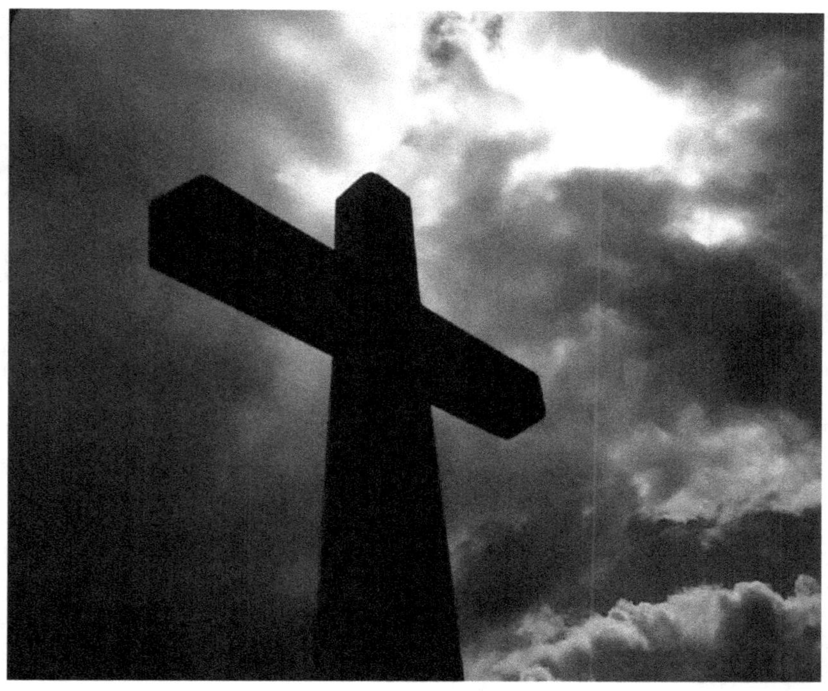

The LORD is good, a refuge in times of trouble. He cares for those who trust in him,

Bible reference: Nahum 1:7

Context: The Lord's Anger Against Nineveh

Illustration ID (credit): fa_42 (author)

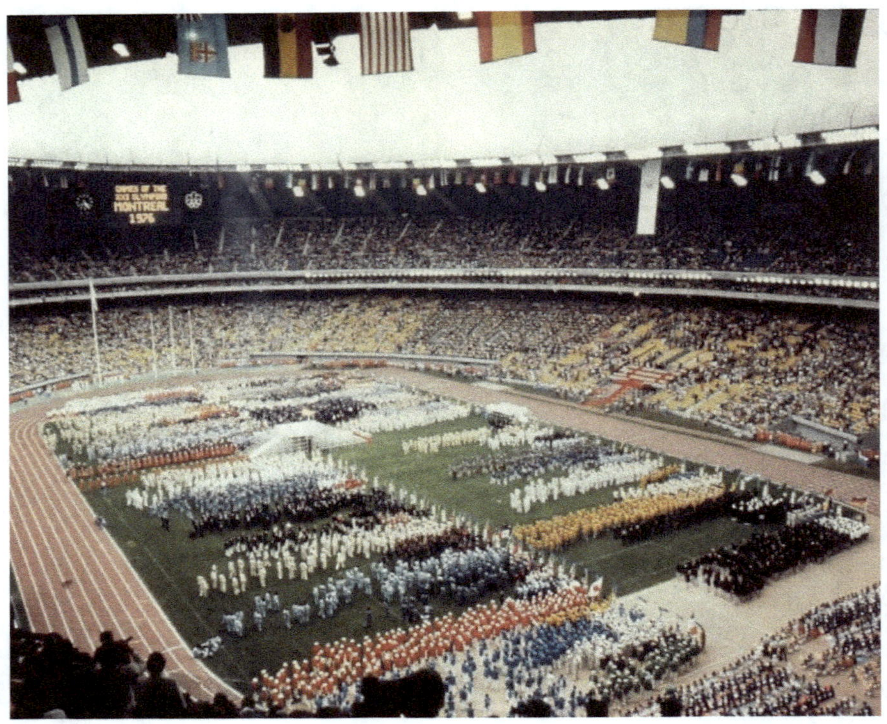

Look at the nations and watch — and be utterly amazed. For I am going to do something in your days that you would not believe, even if you were told.

Bible reference: Habakkuk 1:5

Context: The Lord's Answer

Illustration ID (credit): fy_31 (author)

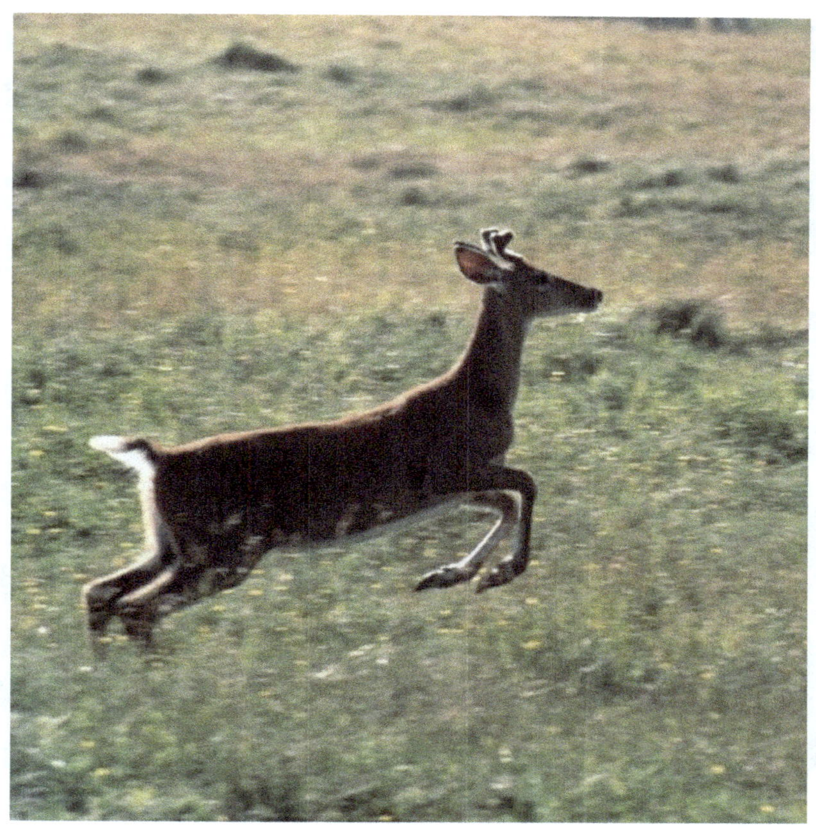

The Sovereign LORD is my strength; he makes my feet like the feet of a deer, he enables me to go on the heights.

Bible reference: Habakkuk 3:19

Context: Habakkuk's Prayer

Illustration ID (credit): fy_42 (author)

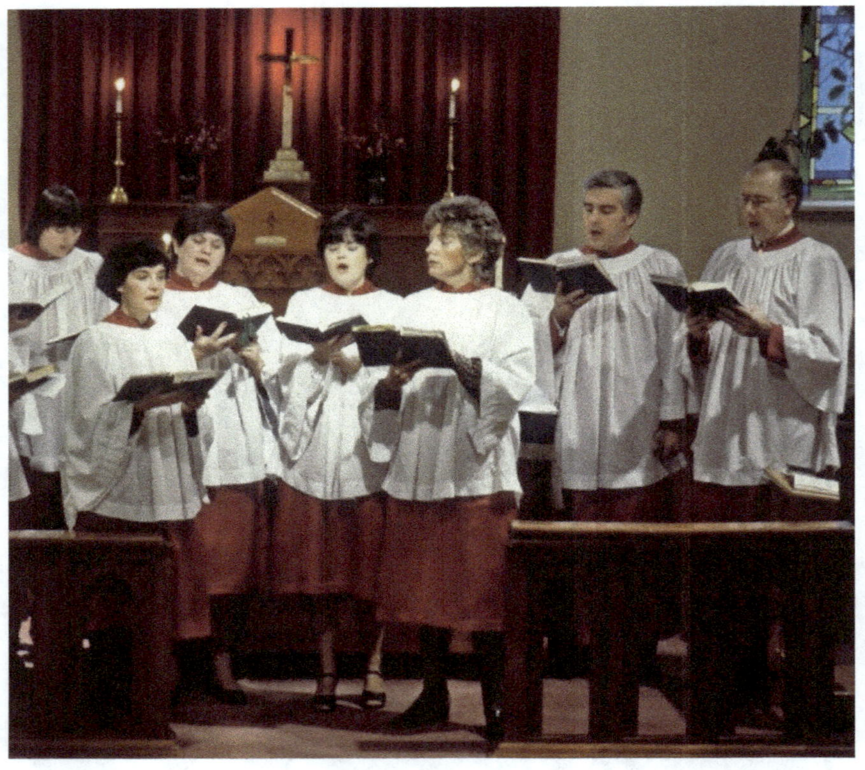

The LORD your God is with you, he is mighty to save. He will take great delight in you, he will quiet you with his love, he will rejoice over you with singing.

Bible reference: Zephaniah 3:17

Context: The Future of Jerusalem

Illustration ID (credit): fy_201 (author)

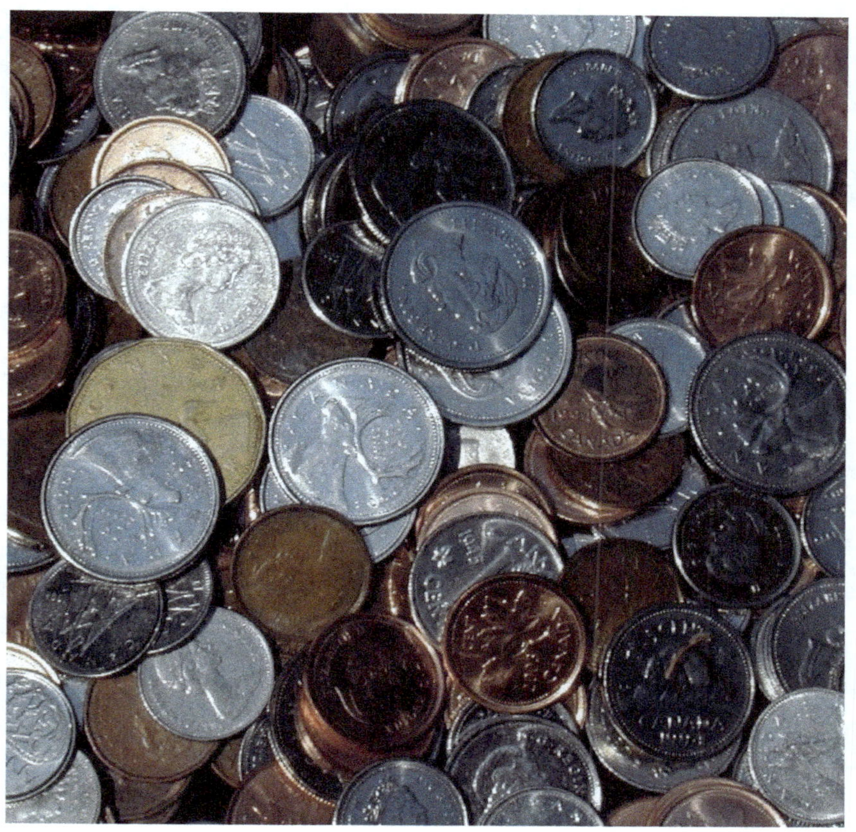

"The silver is mine and the gold is mine," declares the LORD Almighty.

Bible reference: Haggai 2:8

Context: The Promised Glory of the New House

Illustration ID (credit): fz_11 (author)

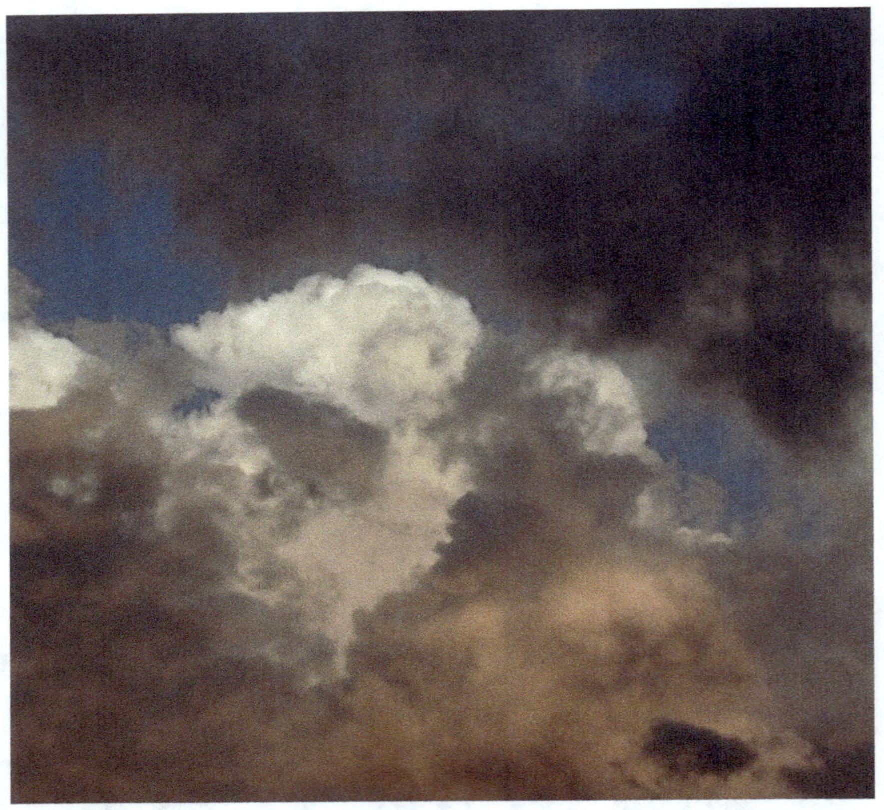

Ask the Lord for rain in the springtime; it is the Lord who sends the thunderstorms. He gives showers of rain to all people, and plants of the field to everyone.

Bible reference: Zechariah 10:1

Context: The Lord Will Care for Judah

Illustration ID (credit): fx_7674 (author)

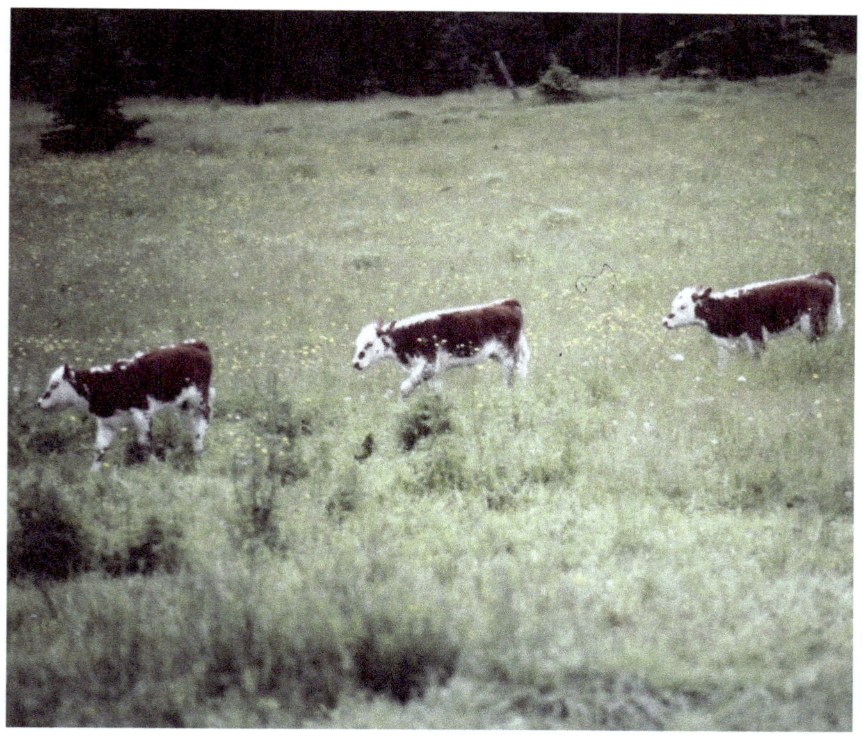

But for you who revere my name, the sun of righteousness will rise with healing in its wings. And you will go out and leap like calves released from the stall.

Bible reference: Malachi 4:2

Context: The Day of the Lord

Illustration ID (credit): fs_342 (author)

Section 5: The Gospels

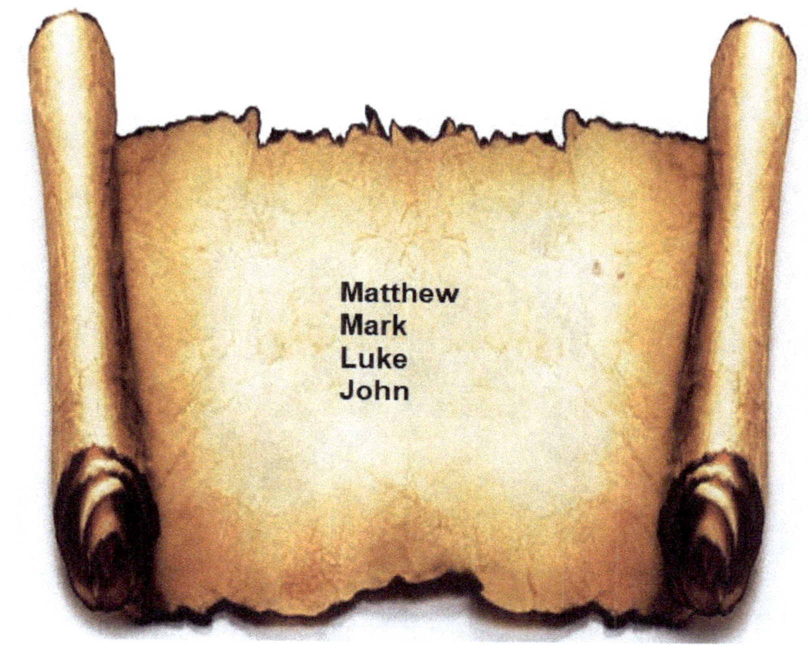

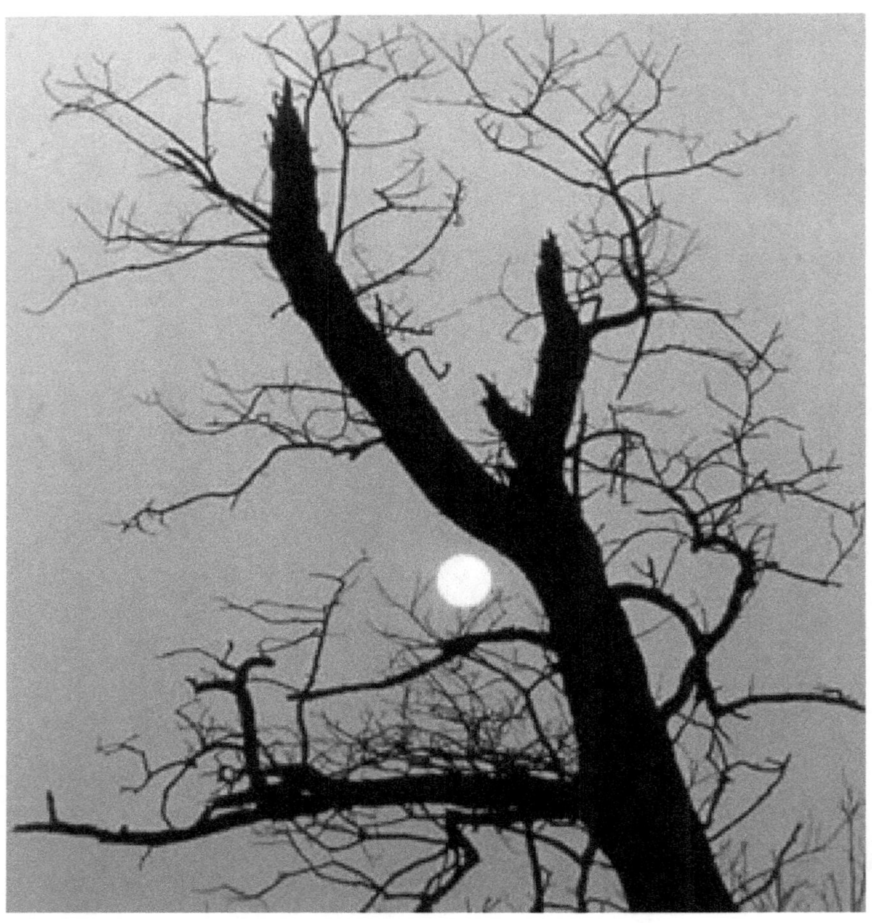

The ax is already at the root of the trees, and every tree that does not produce good fruit will be cut down and thrown into the fire.

Bible reference: Matthew 3:10

Context: John the Baptist Prepares the Way

Illustration ID (credit): fv_015 (author)

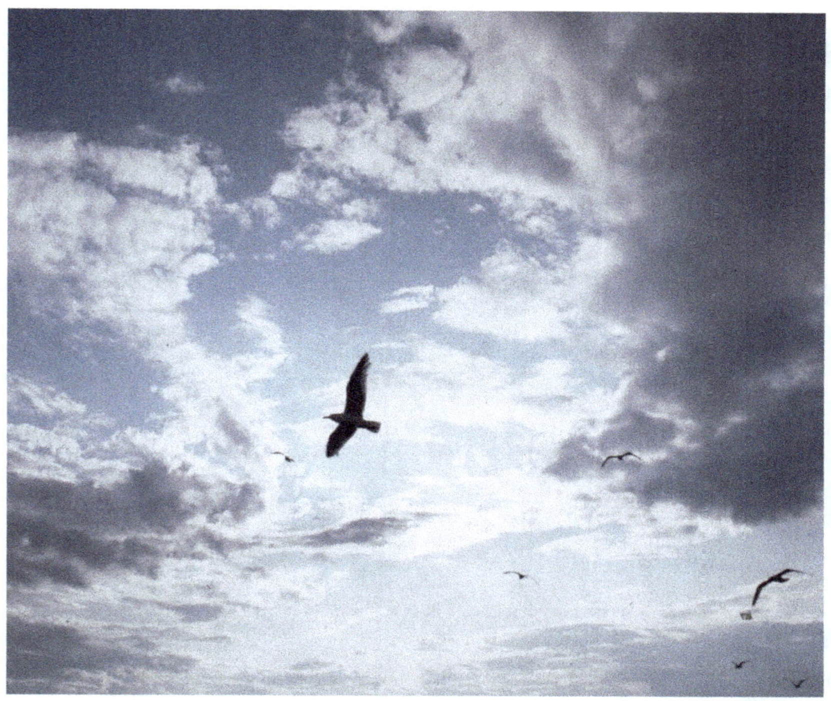

As soon as Jesus was baptized, he went up out of the water. At that moment heaven was opened, and he saw the Spirit of God descending like a dove . . .

Bible reference: Matthew 3:16

Context: The Baptism of Jesus

Illustration ID (credit): fa_08 (author)

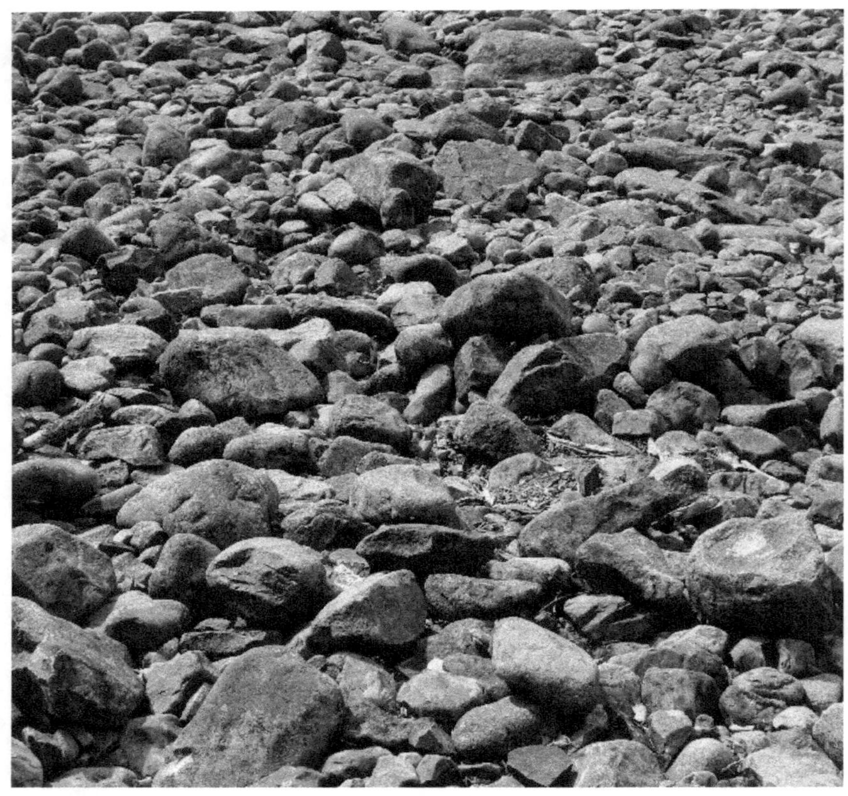

The tempter came to him and said, "If you are the Son of God, tell these stones to become bread."

Bible reference: Matthew 4:3

Context: The Temptation of Jesus

Illustration ID (credit): fc_3859 (author)

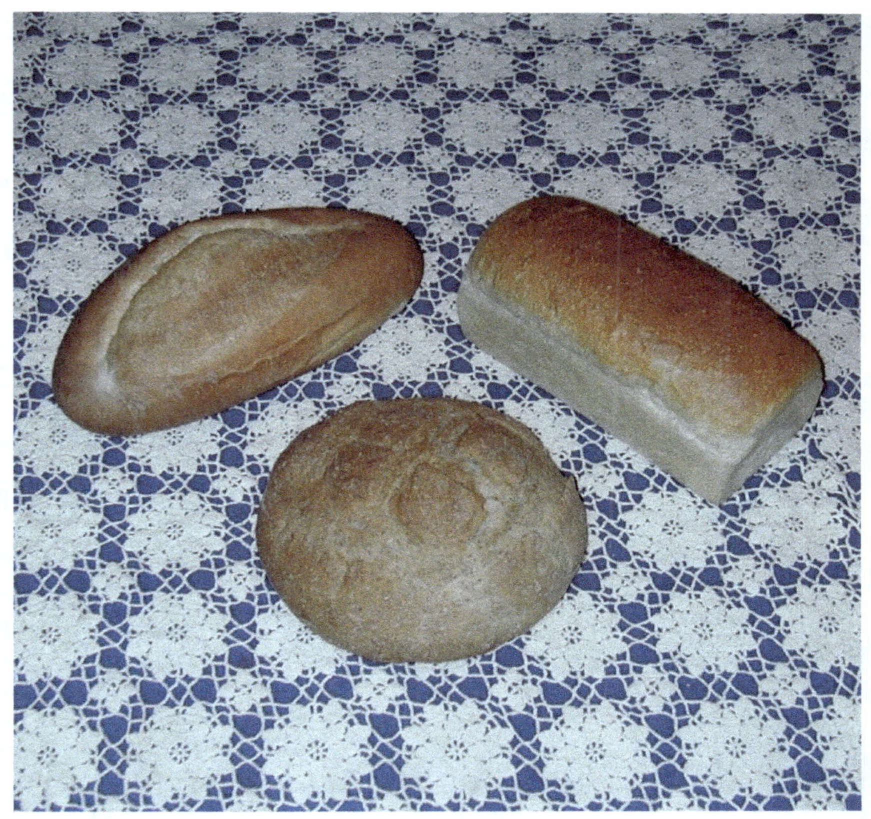

Jesus answered, "It is written: 'Man shall not live on bread alone, but on every word that comes from the mouth of God.' . . ."

Bible reference: Matthew 4:4

Context: The Temptation of Jesus

Illustration ID (credit): fa_21 (author)

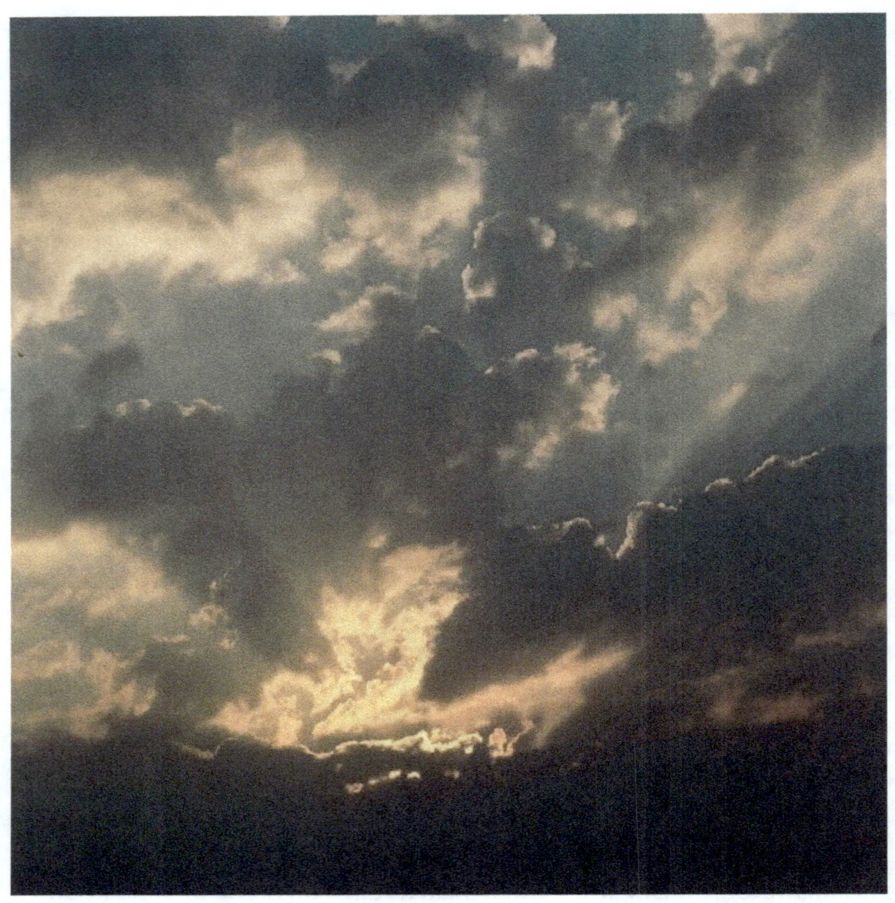

In the same way, let your light shine before men, that they may see your good deeds and praise your Father in heaven.

Bible reference: Matthew 5:16

Context: Salt and Light

Illustration ID (credit): fa_655 (author)

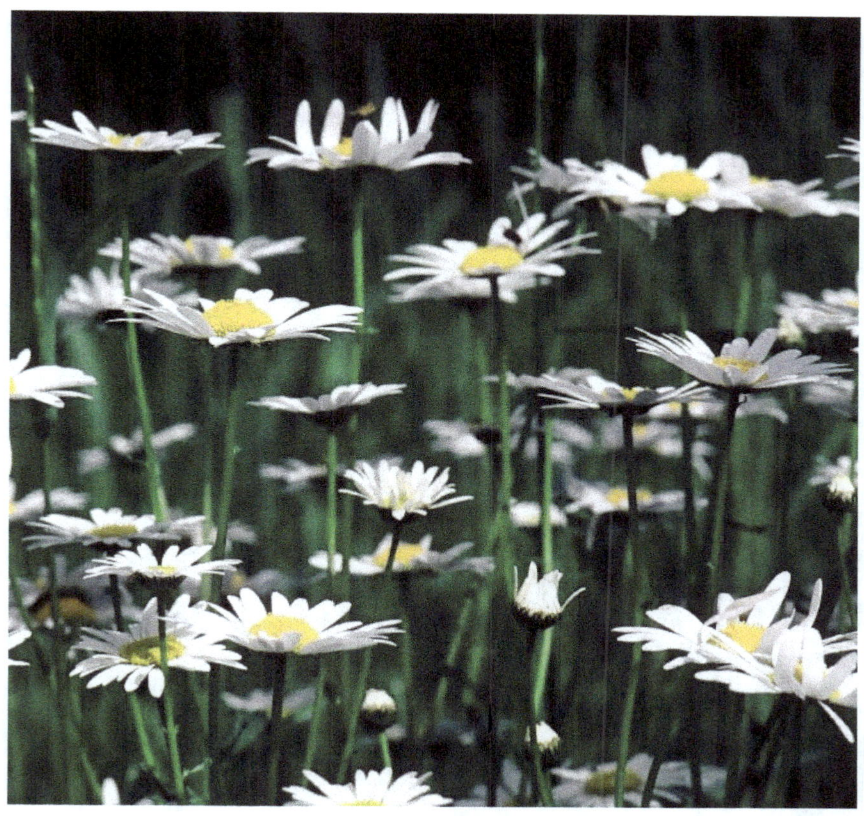

If that is how God clothes the grass of the field, which is here today and tomorrow is thrown into the fire, will he not much more clothe you — you of little faith?

Bible reference: Matthew 6:30

Context: Treasures in Heaven

Illustration ID (credit): fa_28 (author)

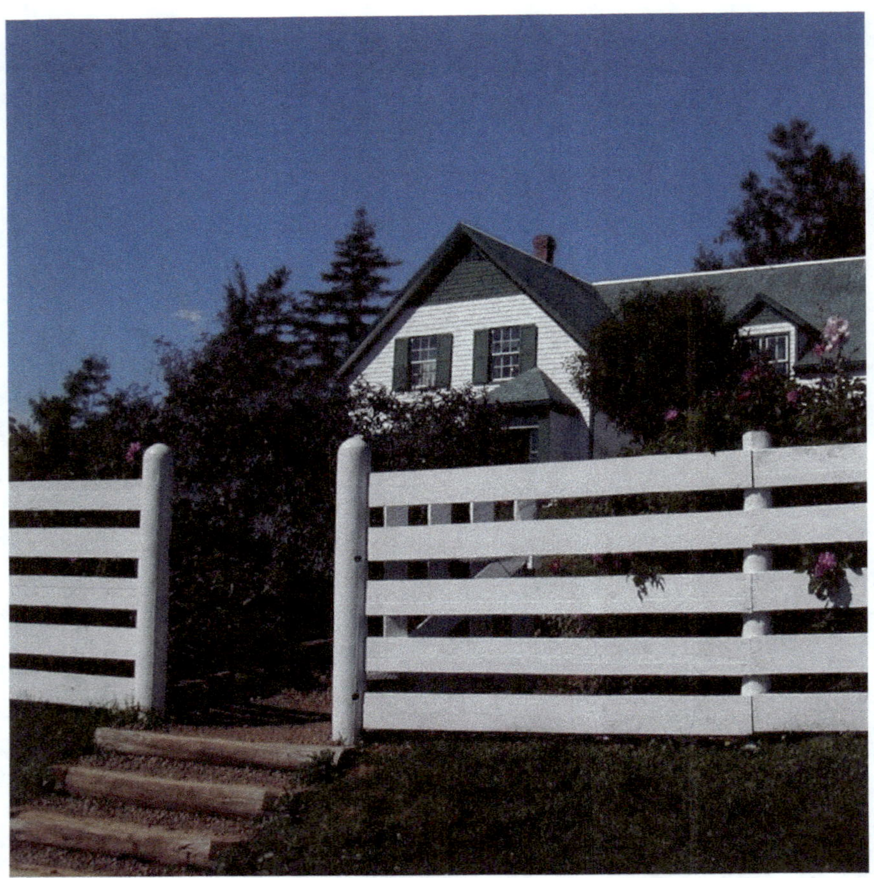

But small is the gate and narrow the road that leads to life, and only a few find it.

Bible reference: Matthew 7:14

Context: The Narrow and Wide Gates

Illustration ID (credit): fx_3823 (author)

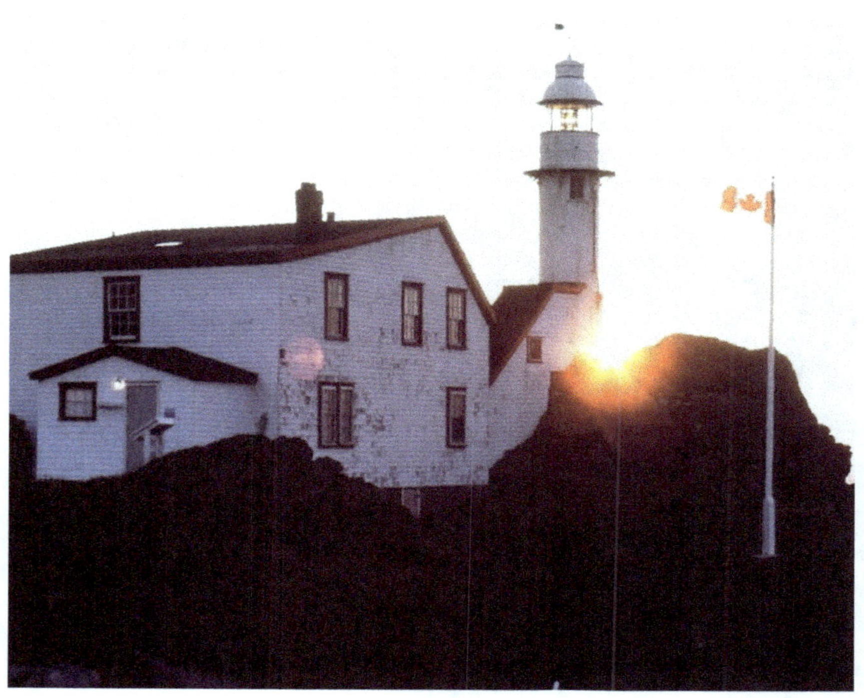

Therefore everyone who hears these words of mine and puts them into practice is like a wise man who built his house on the rock.

Bible reference: Matthew 7:24

Context: The Wise and Foolish Builders

Illustration ID (credit): fs_350 (author)

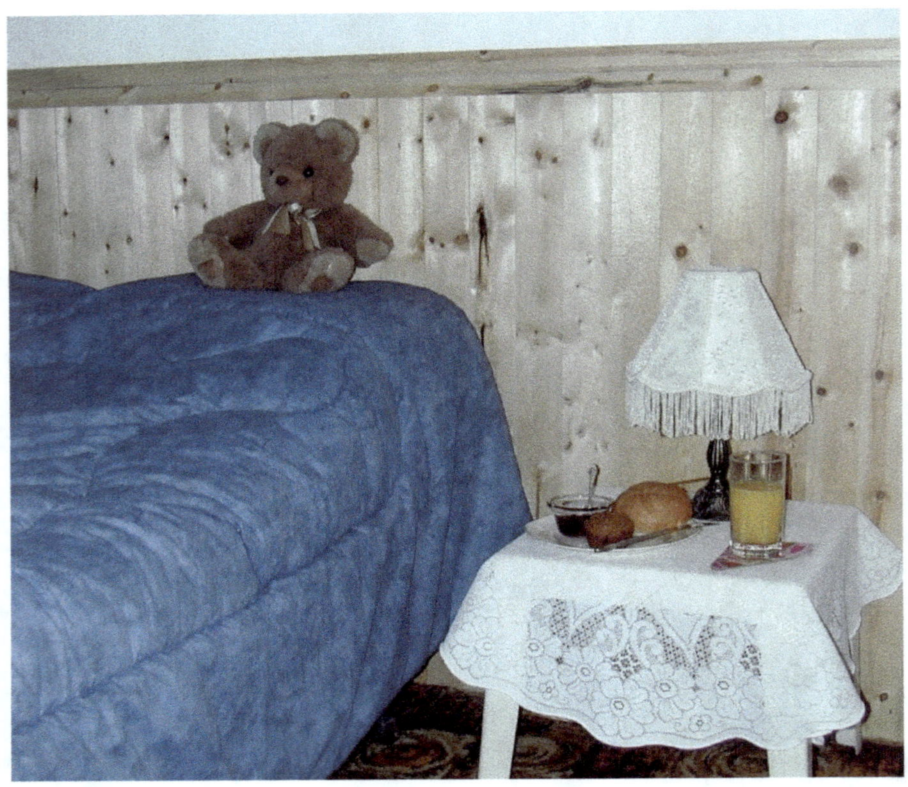

Anyone who welcomes you welcomes me, and anyone who welcomes me welcomes the one who sent me.

Bible reference: Matthew 10:40

Context: Jesus Sends Out the Twelve

Illustration ID (credit): fa_33 (author)

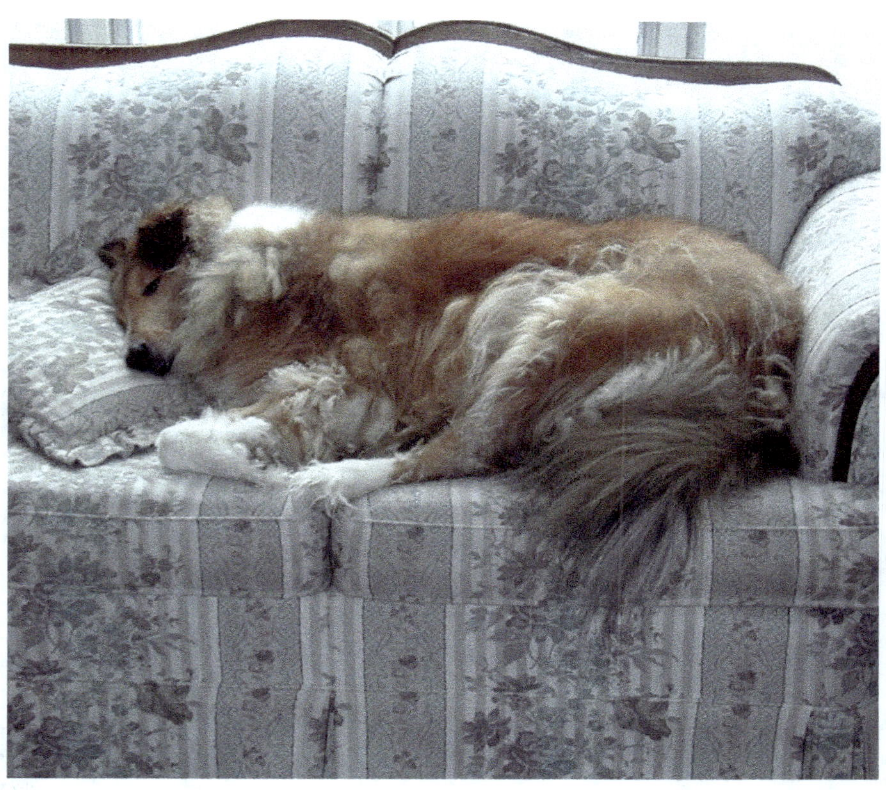

Come to me, all you who are weary and burdened, and I will give you rest.

Bible reference: Matthew 11:28

Context: Rest for the Weary

Illustration ID (credit): fx_5849 (author)

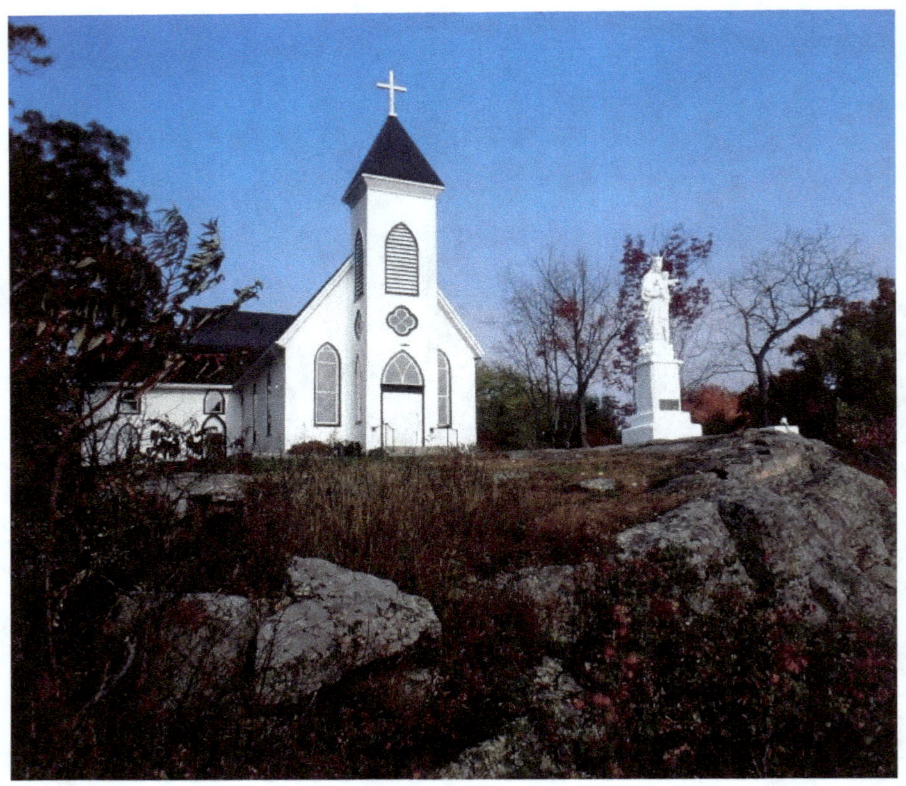

And I tell you that you are Peter, and on this rock I will build my church, and the gates of Hades will not overcome it.

Bible reference: Matthew 16:18

Context: Peter's Confession of Christ

Illustration ID (credit): fa_41 (author)

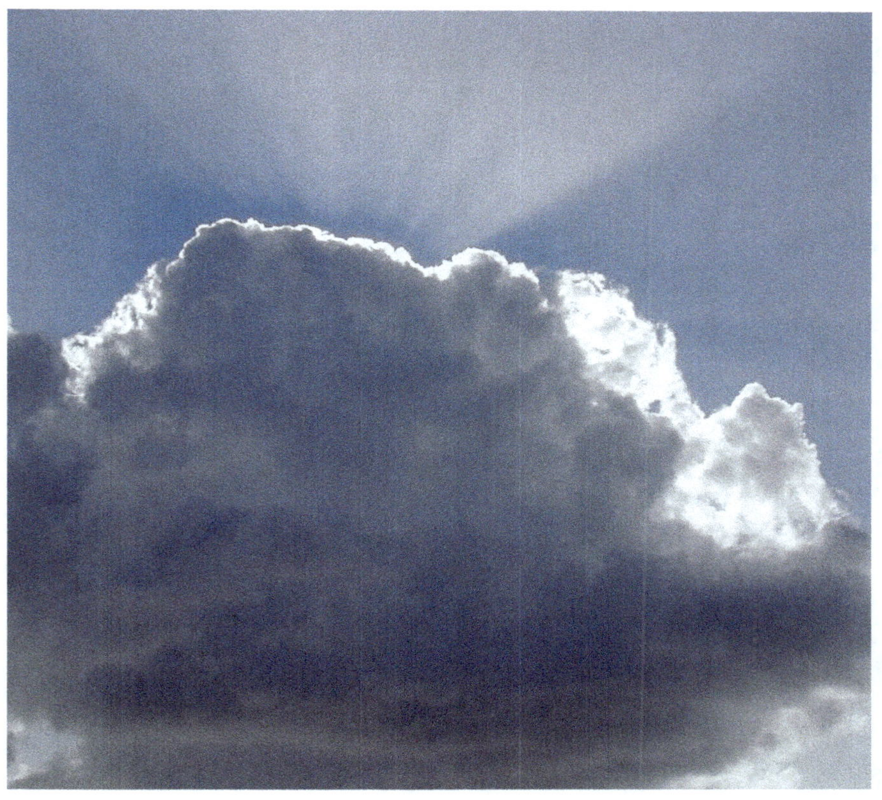

While he was still speaking, a bright cloud covered them, and a voice from the cloud said, "This is my Son, whom I love; with him I am well pleased. Listen to him!"

Bible reference: Matthew 17:5

Context: The Transfiguration

Illustration ID (credit): fx_0484 (author)

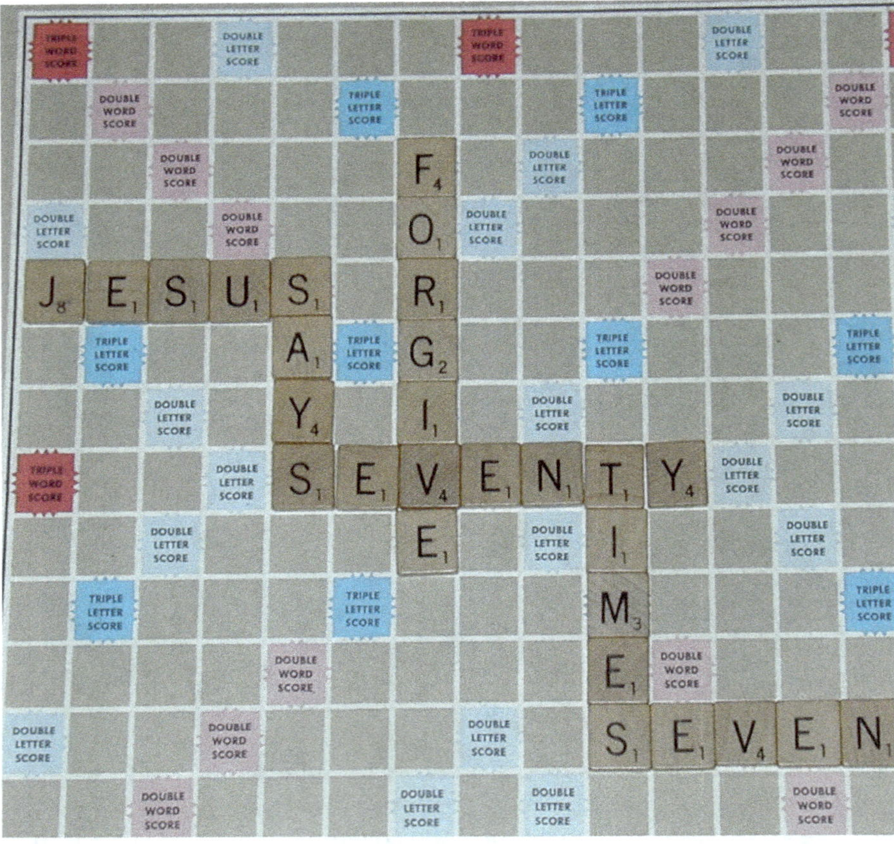

Then Peter came up and said to him, "Lord, how often shall my brother sin against me, and I forgive him? As many as seven times?" Jesus said to him, "I do not say to you seven times, but seventy times seven."

Bible reference: Matthew 18:21-22 (RSV)

Context: The Parable of the Unmerciful Servant

Illustration ID (credit): fa_44 (author)

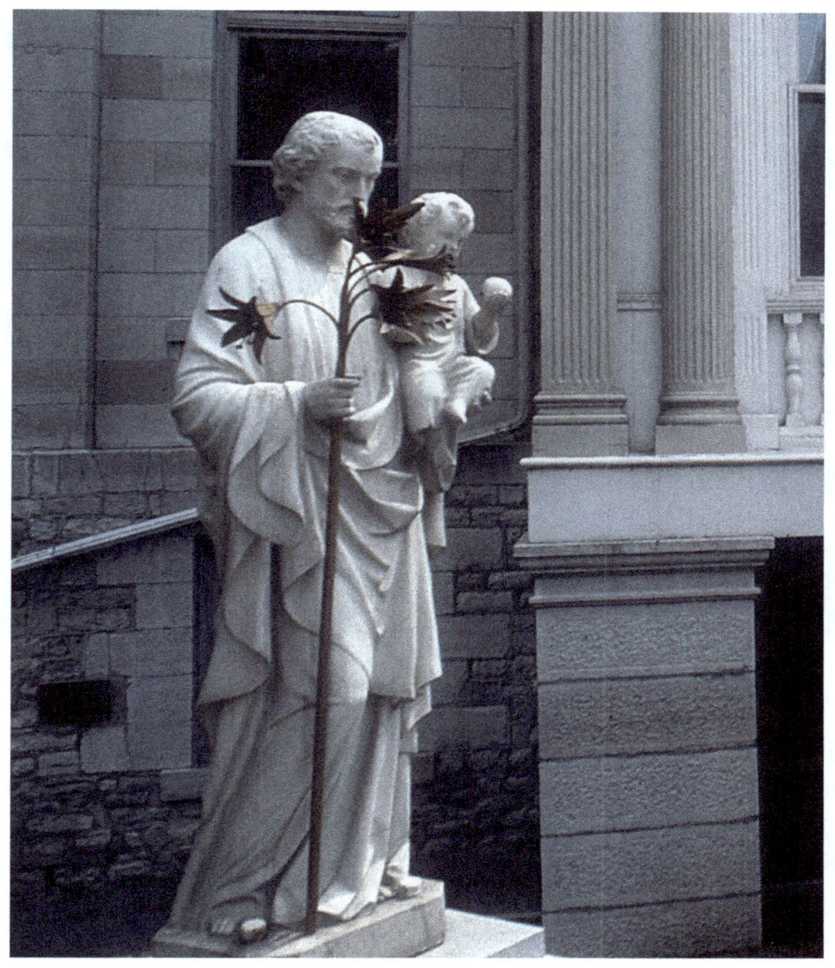

Jesus said, "Let the little children come to me, and do not hinder them, for the kingdom of heaven belongs to such as these.

Bible reference: Matthew 19:14

Context: The Little Children and Jesus

Illustration ID (credit): fs_356 (author)

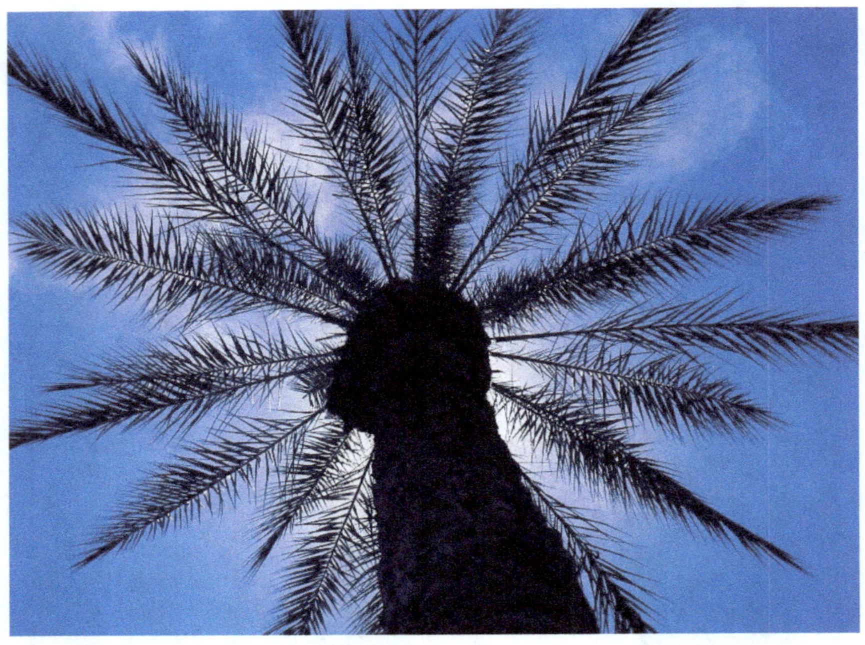

A very large crowd spread their cloaks on the road, while others cut branches from the trees and spread them on the road. The crowds that went ahead of him and those that followed shouted, "Hosanna to the Son of David!" "Blessed is he who comes in the name of the Lord!" "Hosanna in the highest heaven!"

Bible reference: Matthew 21:8-9

Context: The Triumphal Entry

Illustration ID (credit): fy_51 (author)

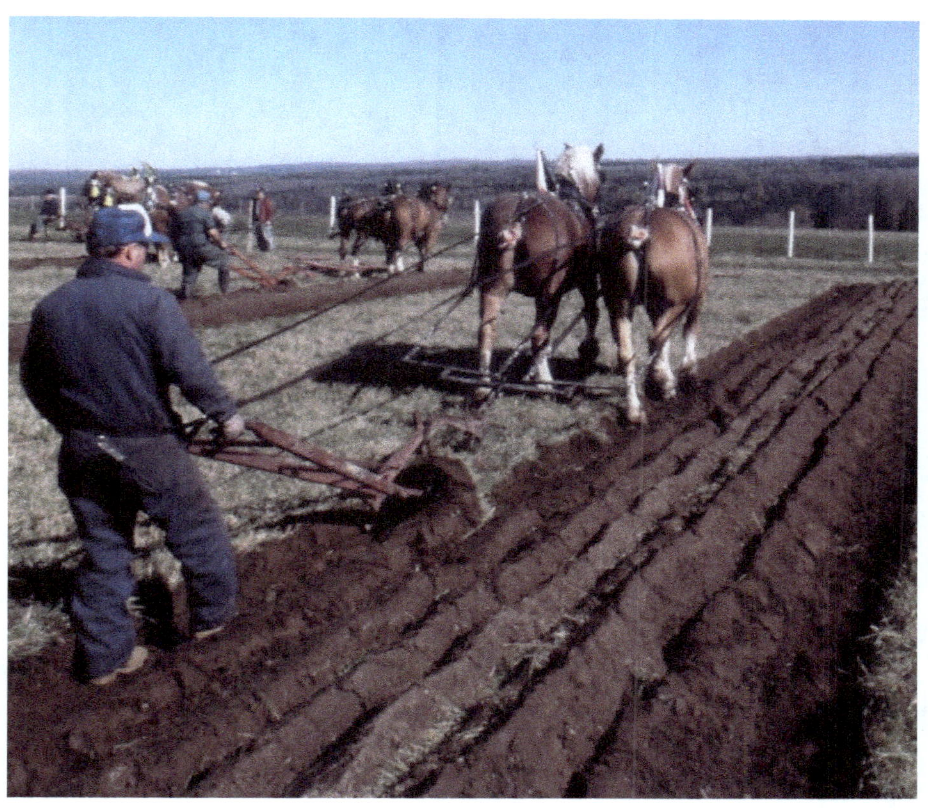

Two men will be in the field; one will be taken and the other left.

Bible reference: Matthew 24:40

Context: The Day and Hour Unknown

Illustration ID (credit): fa_01 (author)

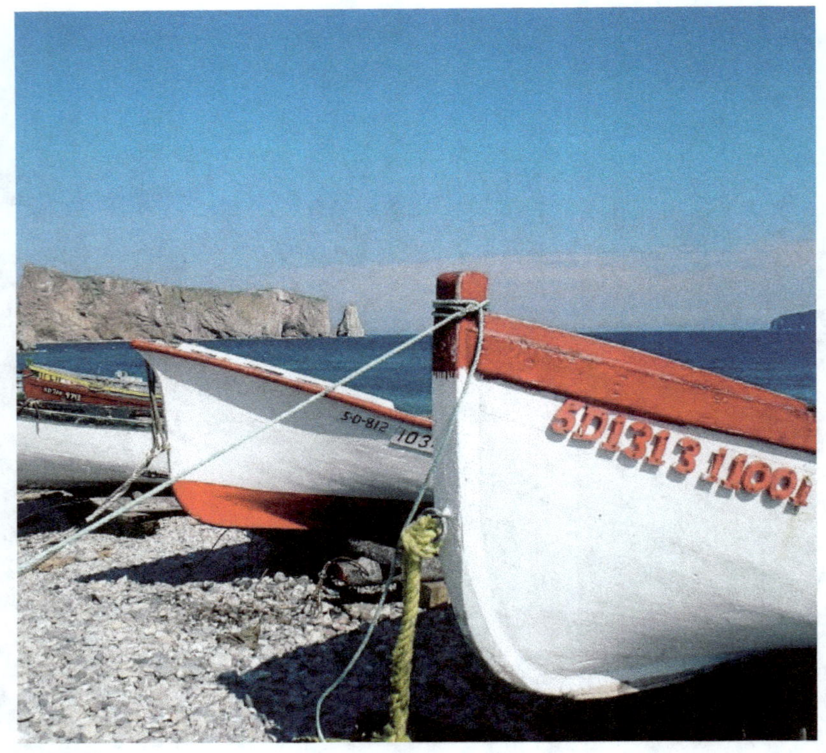

"Come, follow me," Jesus said, "and I will make you fishers of men."

Bible reference: Mark 1:17

Context: The Calling of the First Disciples

Illustration ID (credit): fa_10 (author)

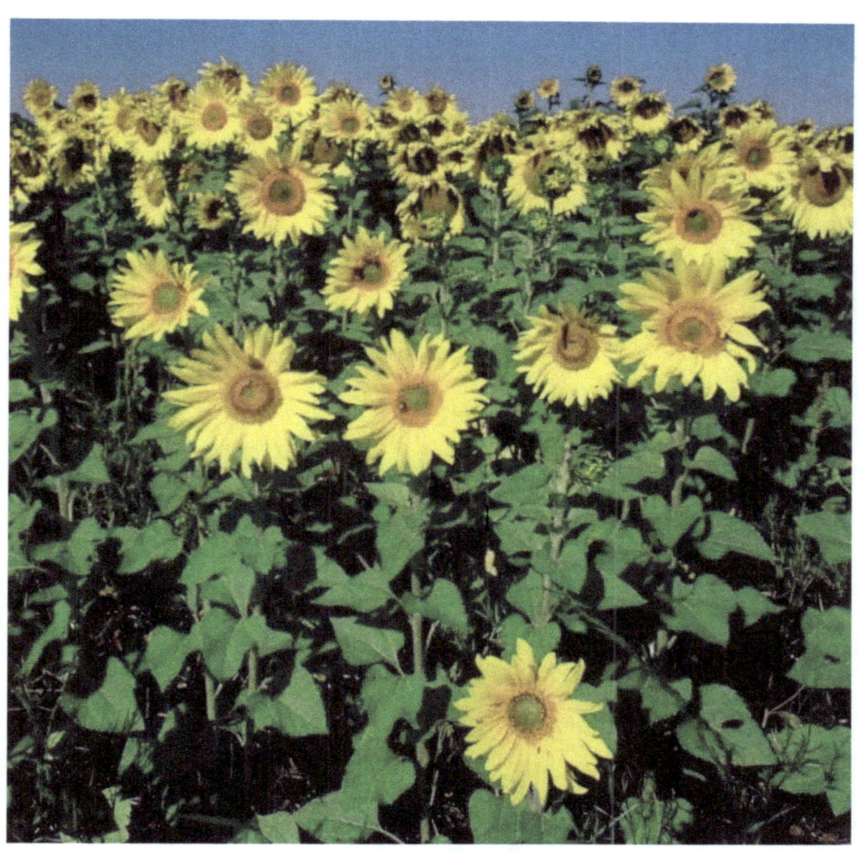

Still other seed fell on good soil. It came up, grew and produced a crop, some multiplying thirty, some sixty, some a hundred times.

Bible reference: Mark 4:8

Context: The Parable of the Sower

Illustration ID (credit): fa_35 (author)

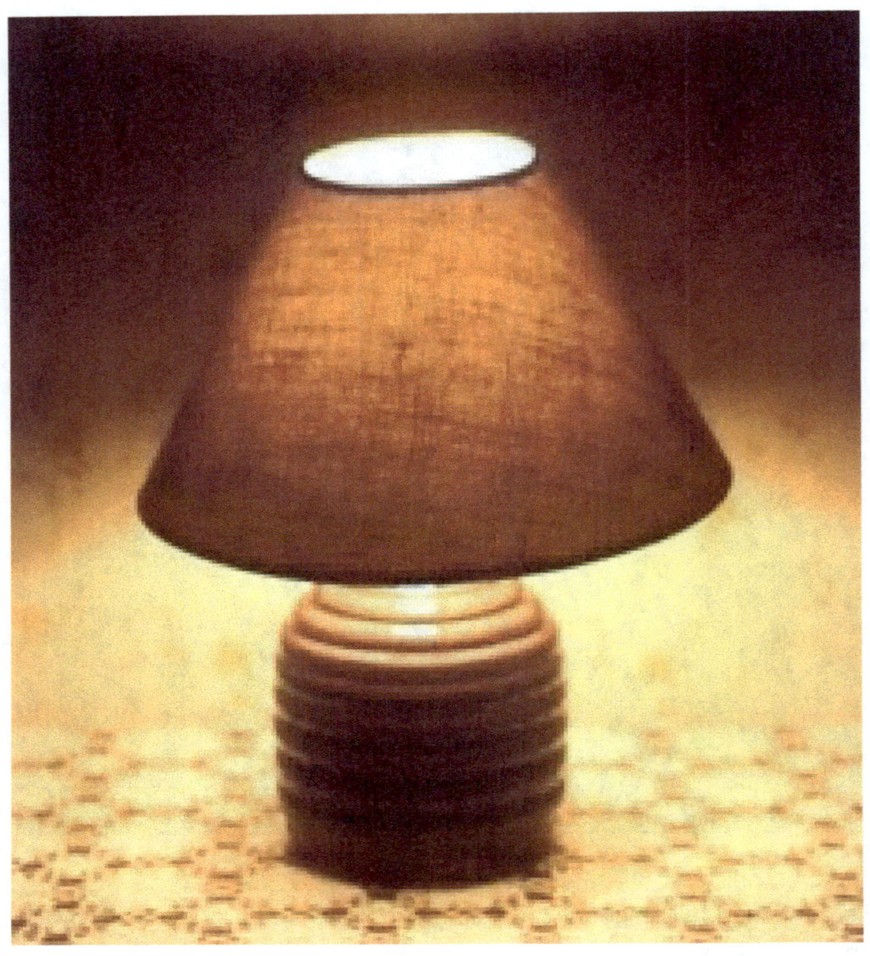

He said to them, "Do you bring in a lamp to put it under a bowl or a bed? Instead, don't you put it on its stand?"

Bible reference: Mark 4:21

Context: A Lamp on a Stand

Illustration ID (credit): fa_90001 (author)

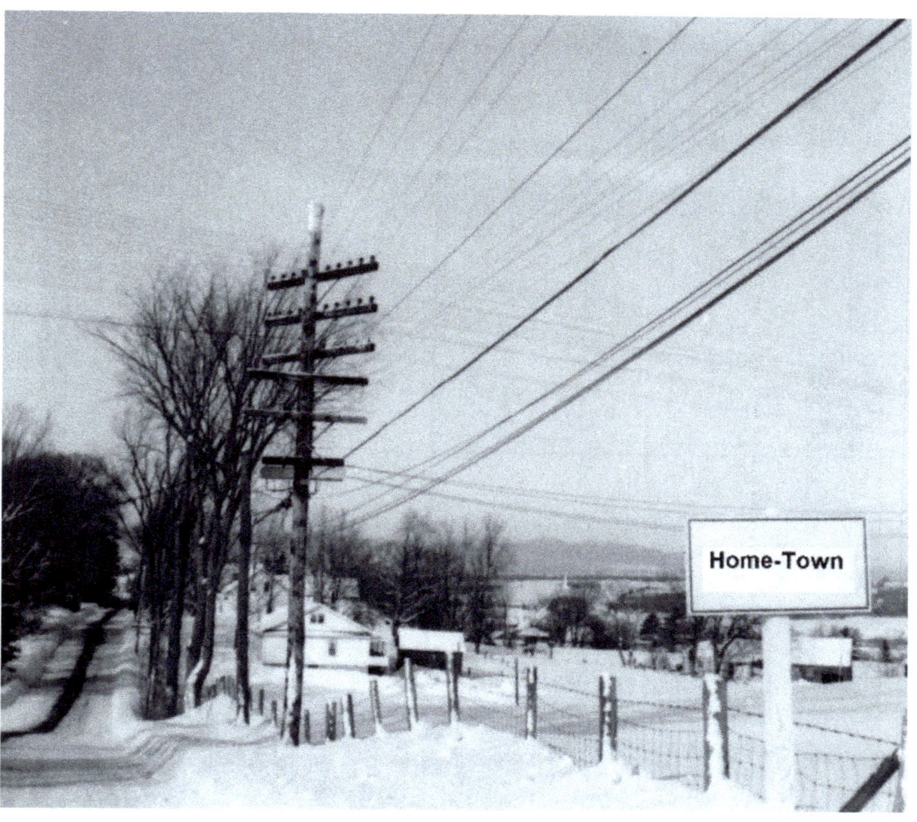

Jesus said to them, "A prophet is not without honor except in his own town, among his relatives and in his own home. . ."

Bible reference: Mark 6:4

Context: A Prophet Without Honor

Illustration ID (credit): fa_770_1140 (author)

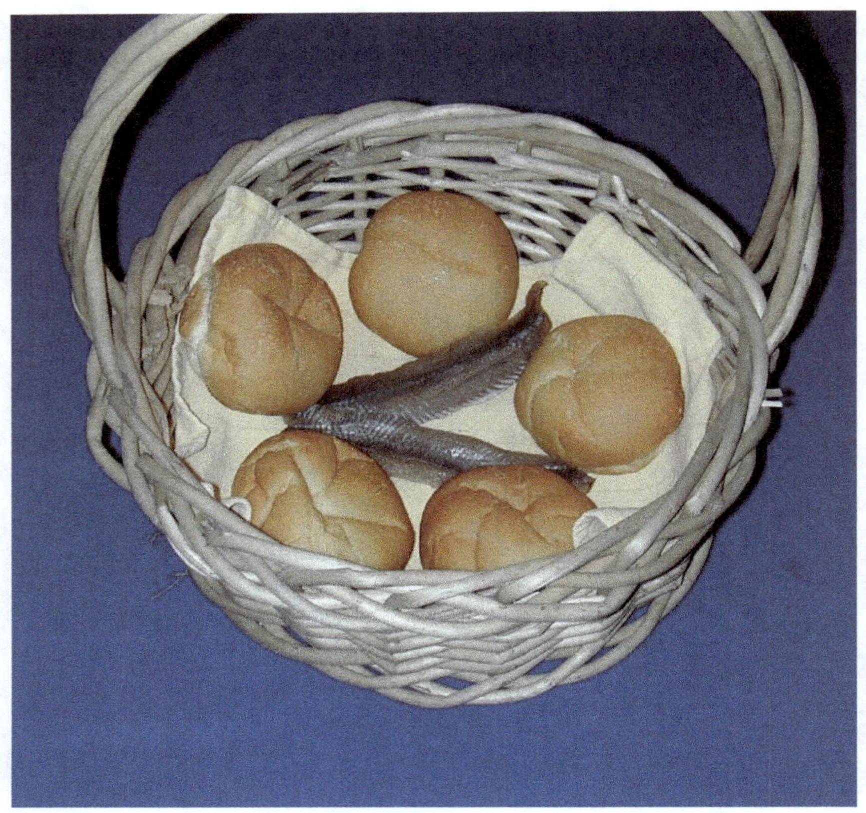

Taking the five loaves and the two fish and looking up to heaven, he gave thanks and broke the loaves. Then he gave them to his disciples to distribute to the people. He also divided the two fish among them all. They all ate and were satisfied,

Bible reference: Mark 6:41-42

Context: Jesus Feeds the Five Thousand

Illustration ID (credit): fa_38 (author)

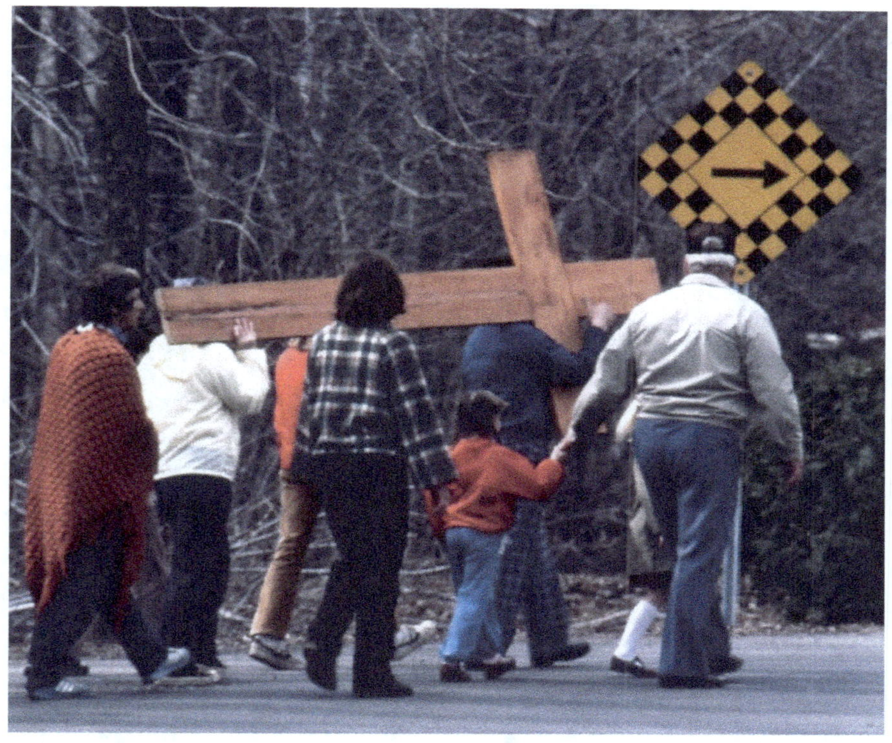

Whoever wants to be my disciple must deny themselves and take up their cross and follow me.

Bible reference: Mark 8:34

Context: Jesus Predicts His Death

Illustration ID (credit): fa_25 (author)

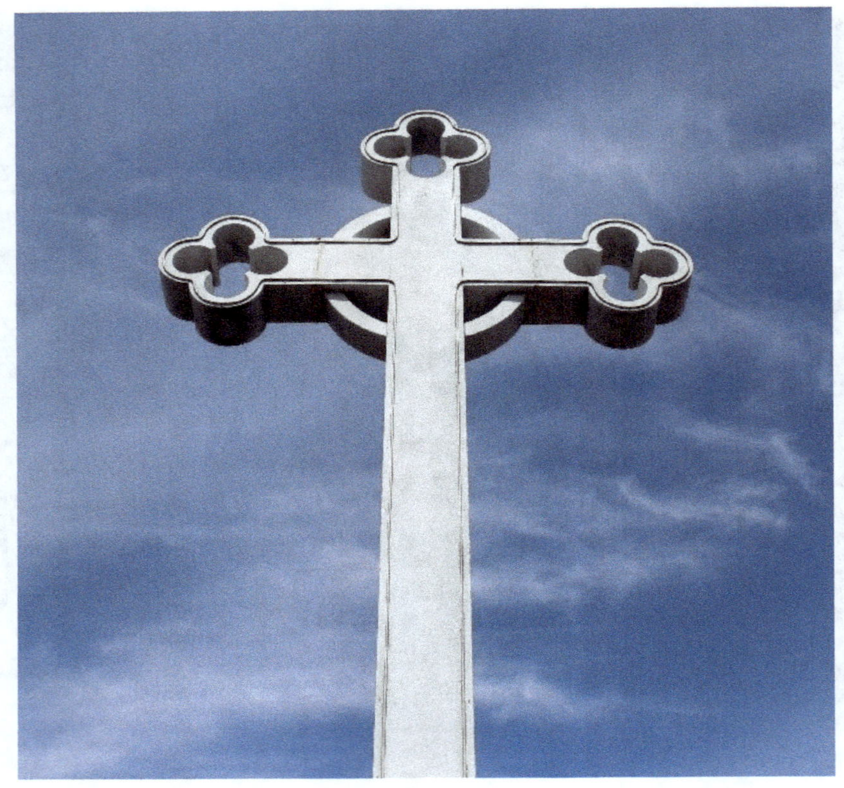

"If you can?" said Jesus. "Everything is possible for him who believes."

Bible reference: Mark 9:23-24

Context: The Healing of a Boy With an Evil Spirit

Illustration ID (credit): fc_3858 (author)

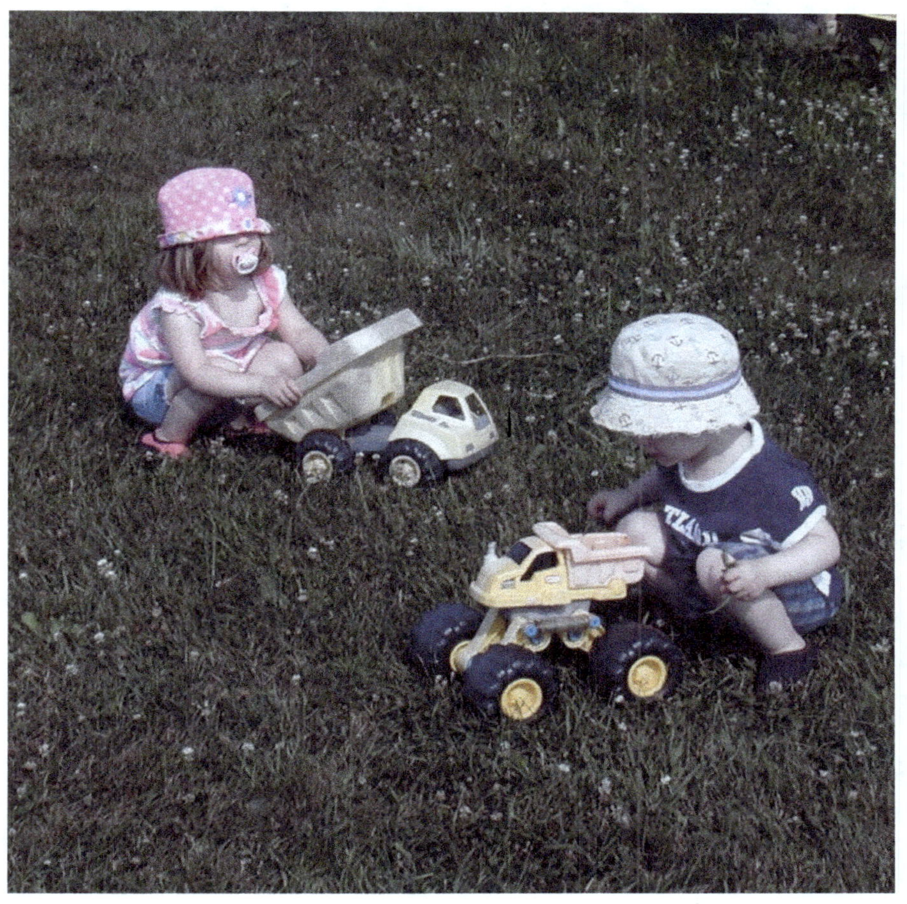

"Whoever welcomes one of these little children in my name welcomes me; and whoever welcomes me does not welcome me but the one who sent me."

Bible reference: Mark 9:37

Context: Who is the Greatest?

Illustration ID (credit): fx_0168 (author)

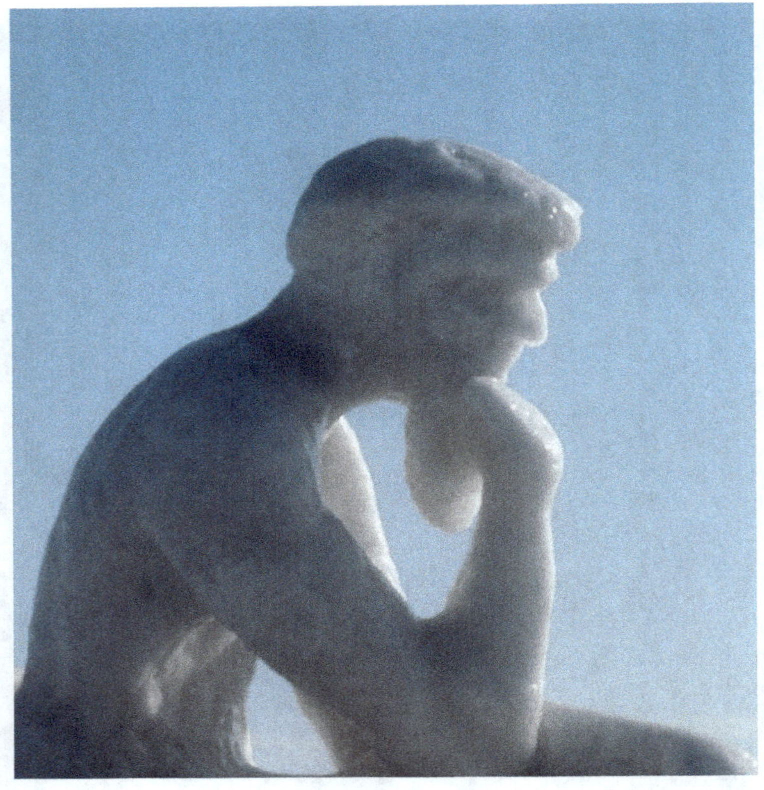

Love the Lord your God with all your heart and with all your soul and with all your mind and with all your strength.

Bible reference: Mark 12:30

Context: The Greatest Commandment

Illustration ID (credit): fs_360 (author)

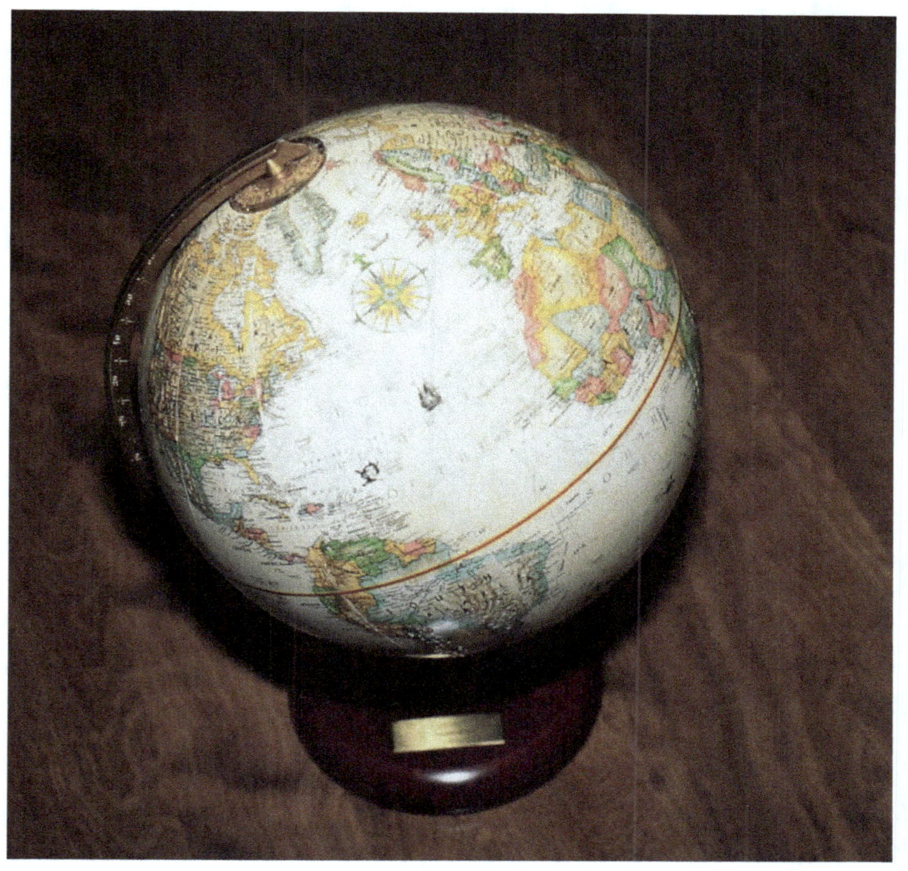

He said to them, "Go into all the world and preach the gospel to all creation."

Bible reference: Mark 16:15

Context: The Resurrection

Illustration ID (credit): fa_27 (author)

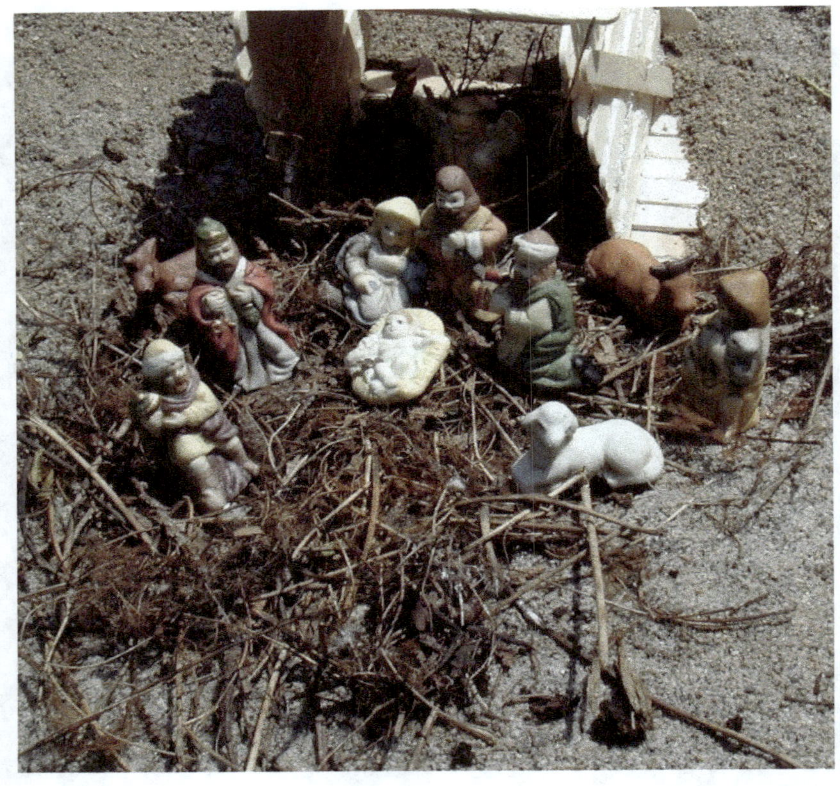

So they hurried off and found Mary and Joseph, and the baby, who was lying in the manger.

Bible reference: Luke 2:16

Context: The Shepherds and the Angels

Illustration ID (credit): fa_05 (author)

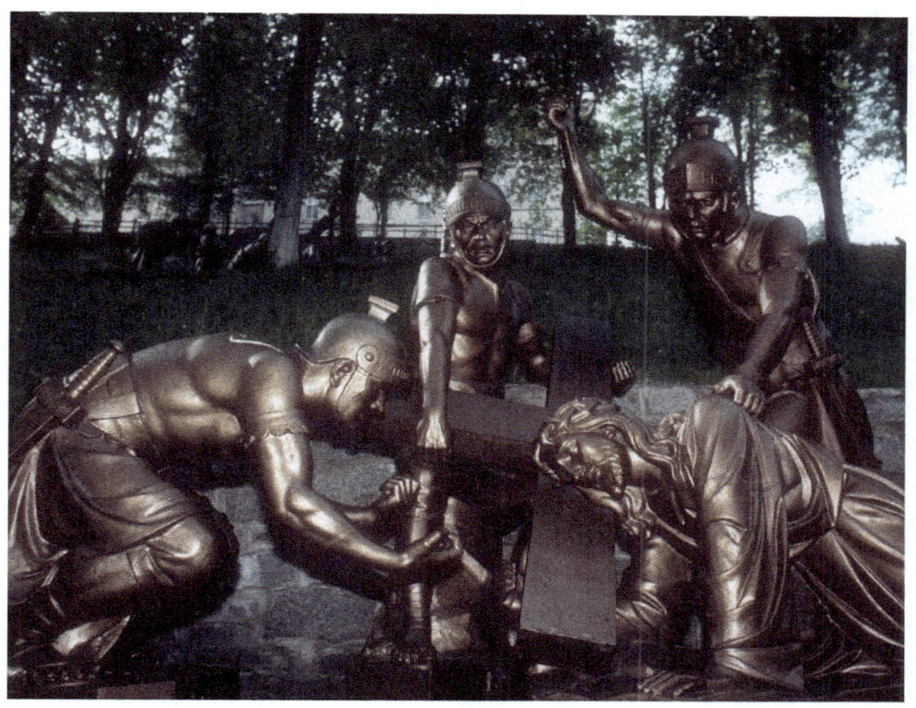

But I tell you who hear me: Love your enemies, do good to those who hate you, bless those who curse you, pray for those who mistreat you.

Bible reference: Luke 6:27-28

Context: Love for Enemies

Illustration ID (credit): fs_357 (author)

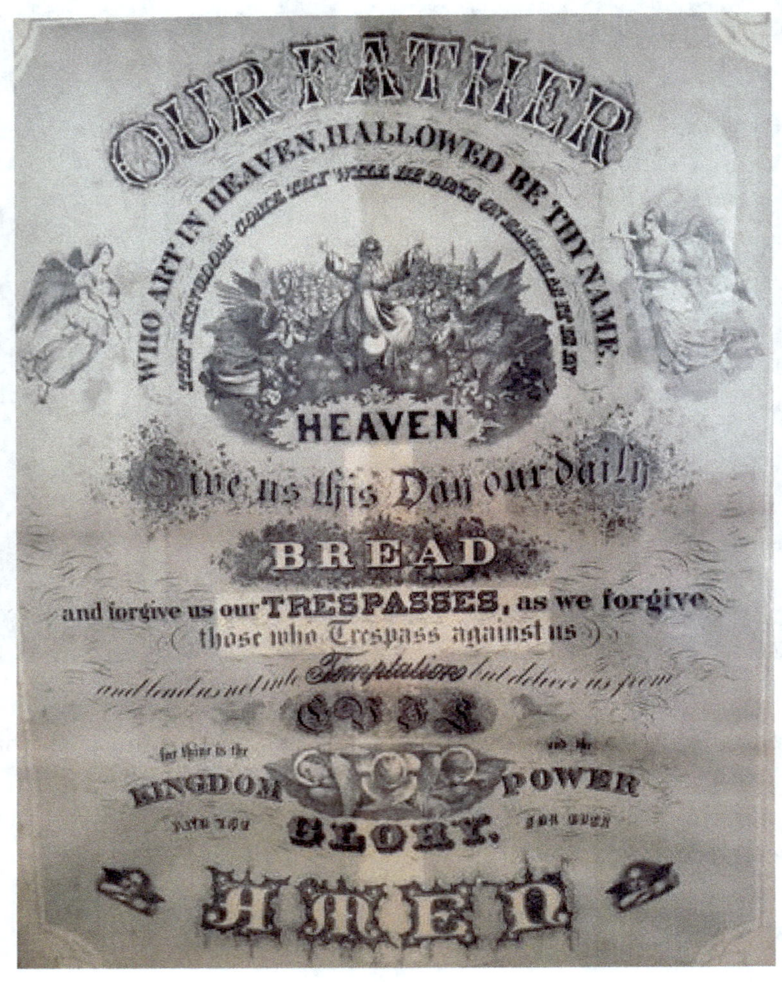

He said to them, "When you pray, say: "'Father, hallowed be your name, your kingdom come. . ."

Bible reference: Luke 11:2

Context: Jesus' Teaching on Prayer

Illustration ID (credit): fx_000 (Fraser family archive)

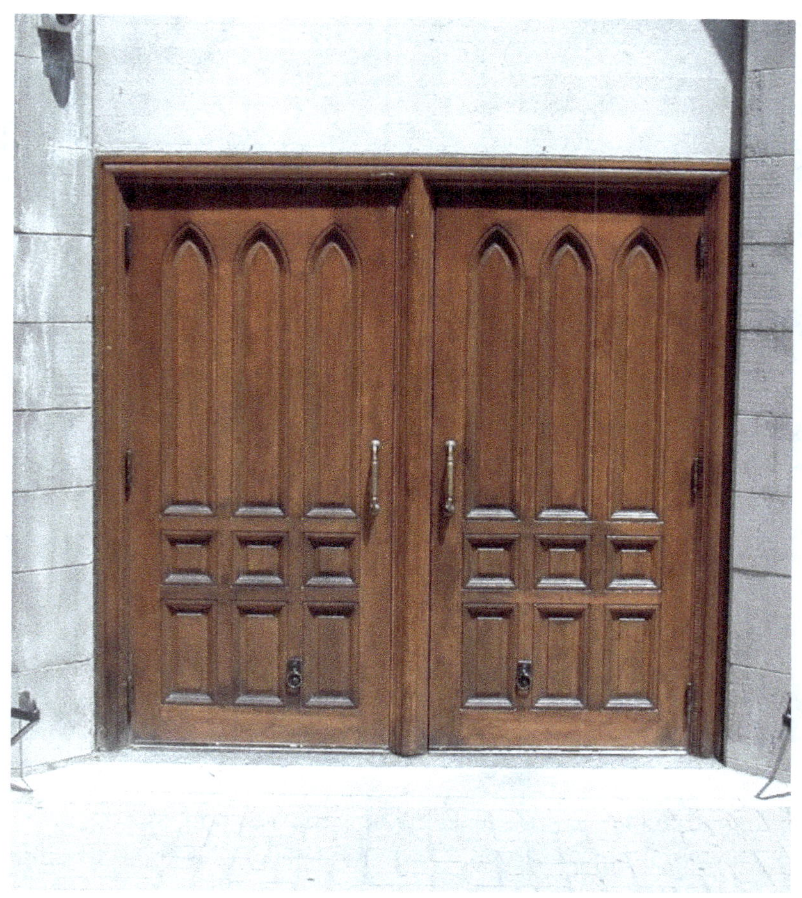

For everyone who asks receives; he who seeks finds; and to him who knocks, the door will be opened.

Bible reference: Luke 11:10

Context: Jesus' Teaching on Prayer

Illustration ID (credit): fz_15 (author)

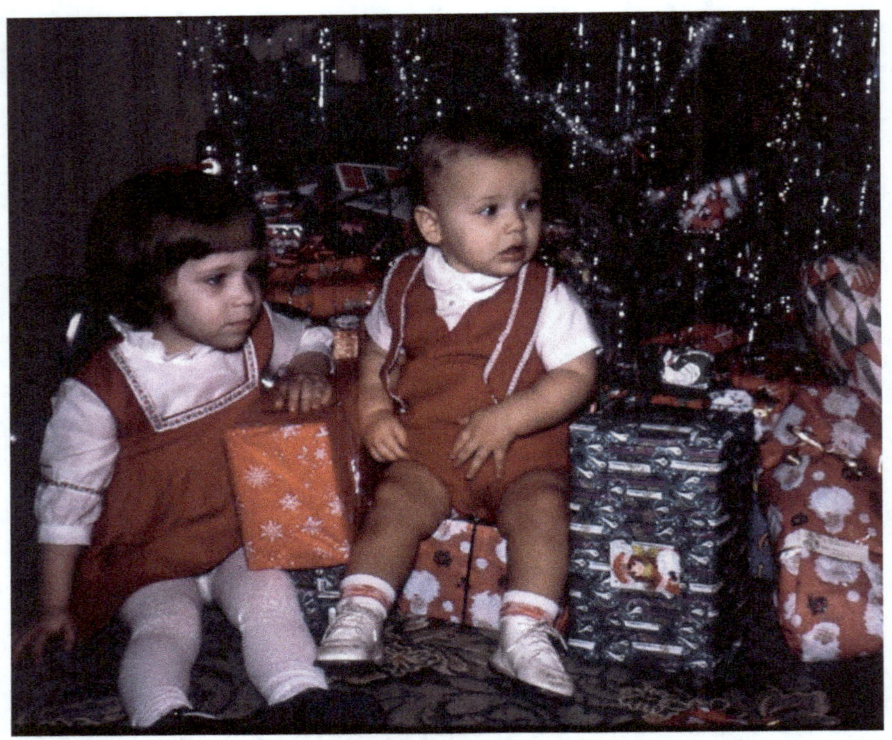

"If you then, though you are evil, know how to give good gifts to your children, how much more will your Father in heaven give the Holy Spirit to those who ask him!"

Bible reference: Luke 11:13

Context: Jesus' Teaching on Prayer

Illustration ID (credit): fa_07 (author)

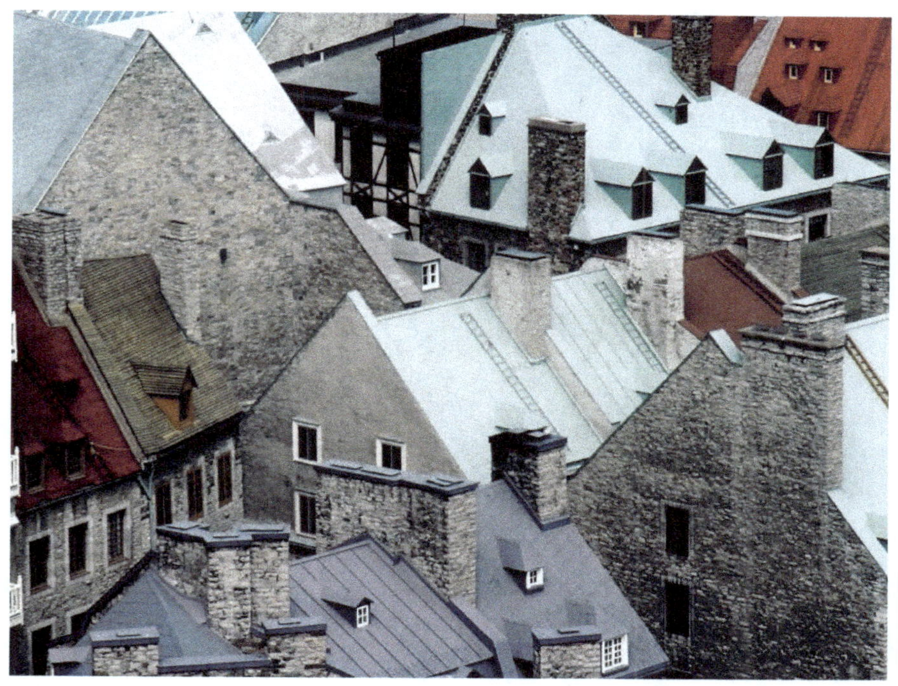

What you have said in the dark will be heard in the daylight, and what you have whispered in the ear in the inner rooms will be proclaimed from the roofs.

Bible reference: Luke 12:3

Context: Warnings and Encouragements

Illustration ID (credit): fa_32 (author)

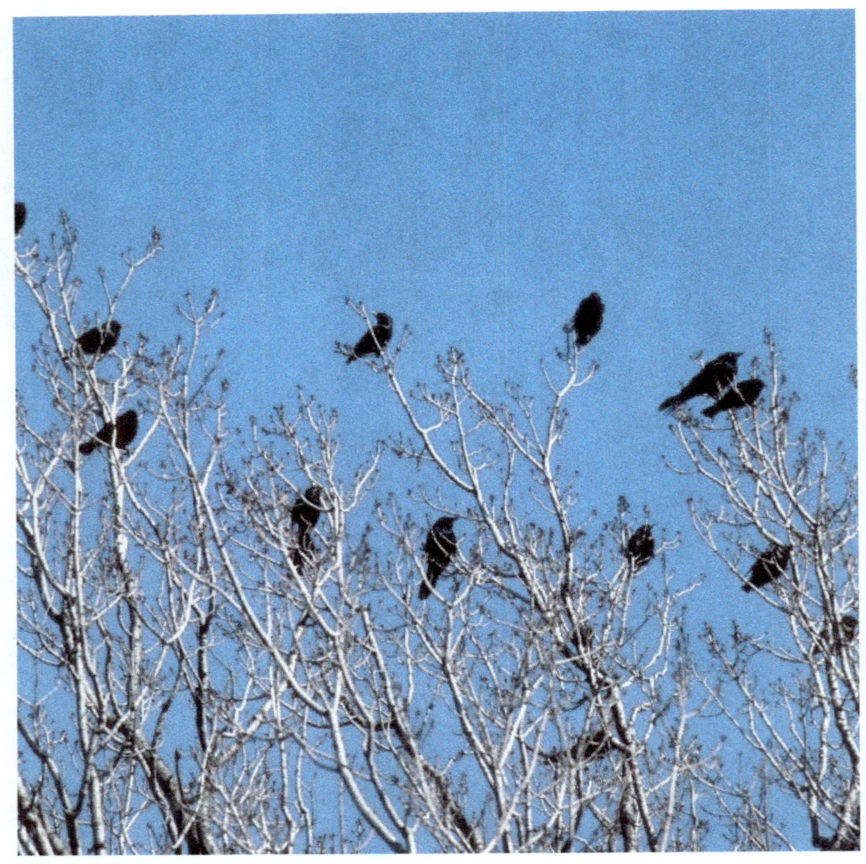

Consider the ravens: They do not sow or reap, they have no storeroom or barn; yet God feeds them. And how much more valuable you are than birds!

Bible reference: Luke 12:24

Context: The Parable of the Rich Fool

Illustration ID (credit): fy_40 (author)

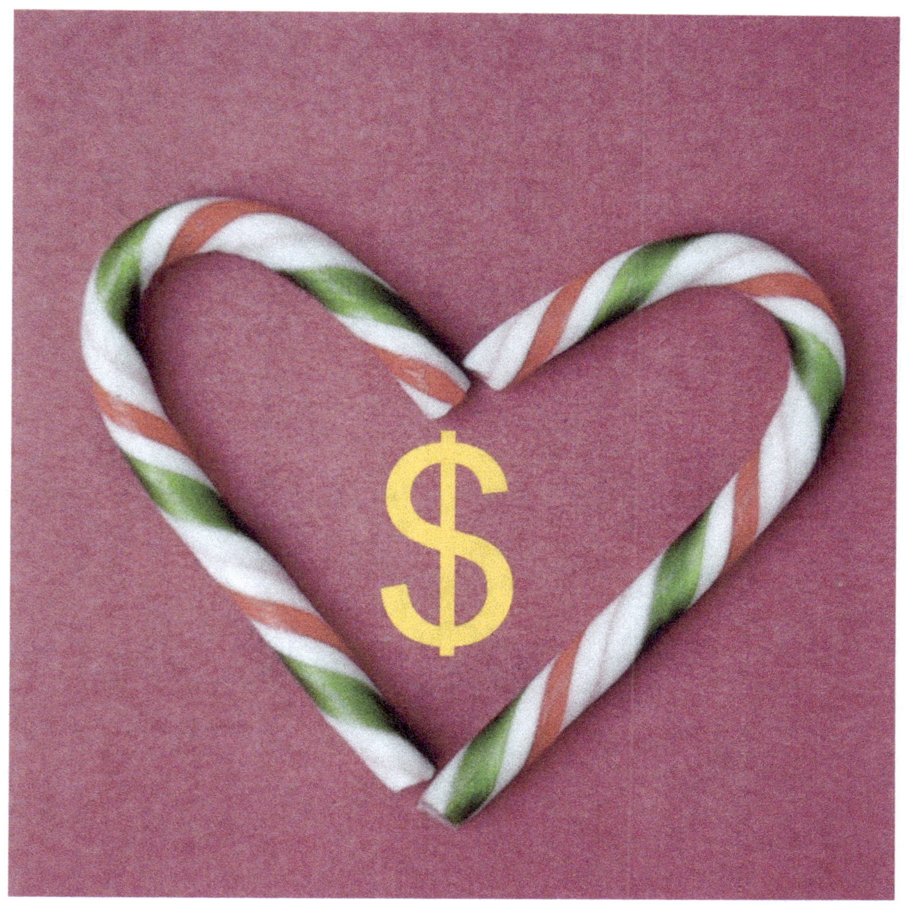

For where your treasure is, there your heart will be also.

Bible reference: Luke 12:34

Context: The Parable of the Rich Fool

Illustration ID (credit): fx_1225 (author)

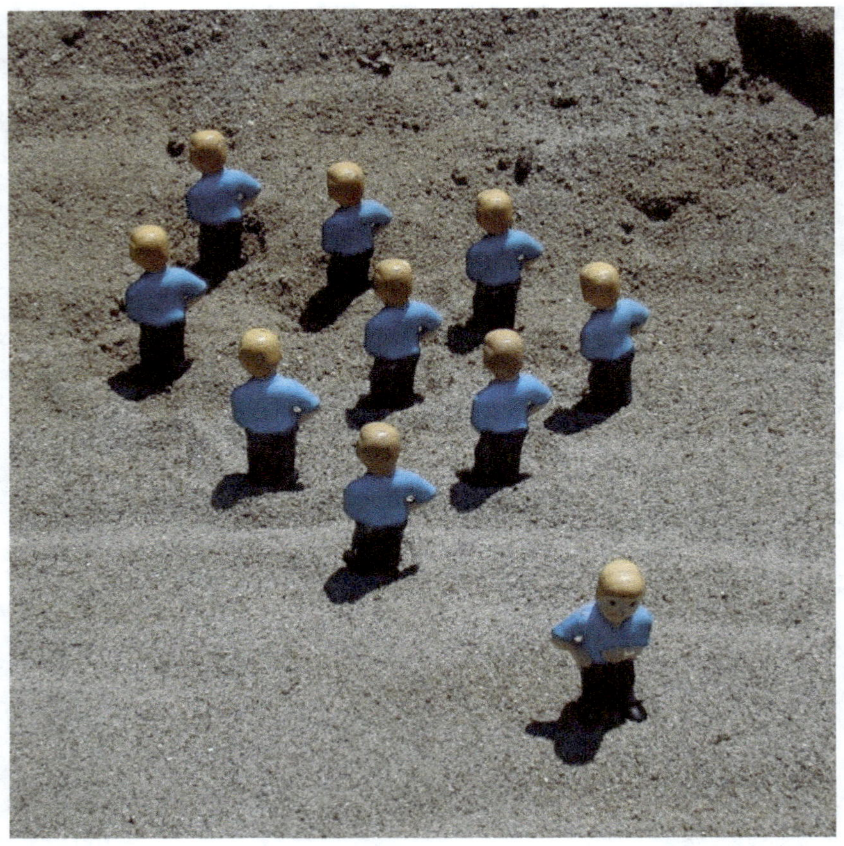

One of them, when he saw he was healed, came back, praising God in a loud voice. He threw himself at Jesus' feet and thanked him—and he was a Samaritan. Jesus asked, "Were not all ten cleansed? Where are the other nine?"

Bible reference: Luke 17:15-17

Context: Sin, Faith, Duty

Illustration ID (credit): fa_48 (author)

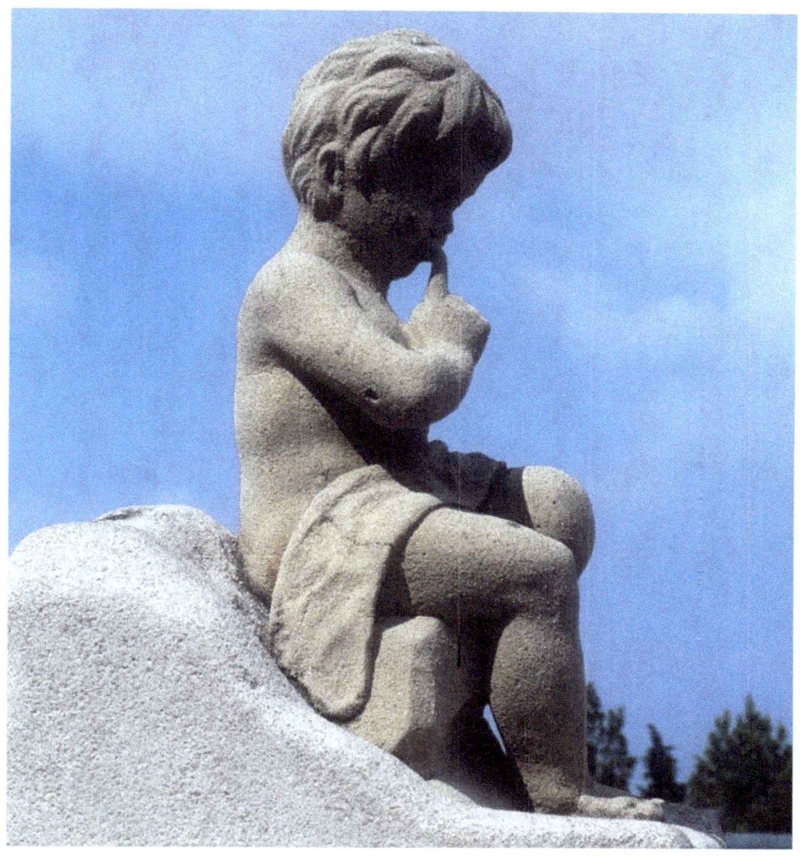

I tell you the truth, anyone who will not receive the kingdom of God like a little child will never enter it.

Bible reference: Luke 18:17

Context: The Little Children and Jesus

Illustration ID (credit): fs_346 (author)

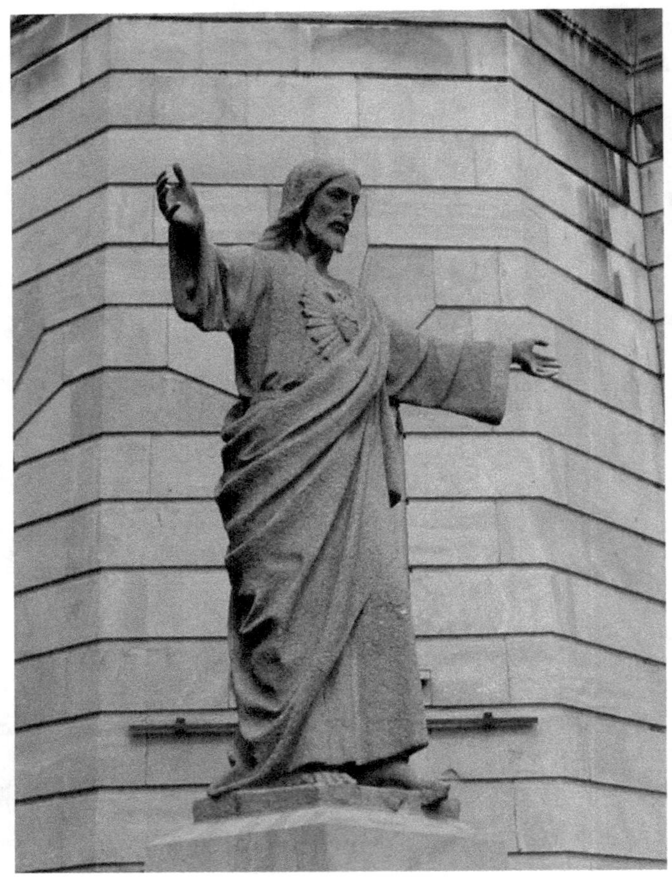

The Word became flesh and made his dwelling among us. We have seen his glory, the glory of the One and Only, who came from the Father, full of grace and truth.

Bible reference: John 1:14

Context: The Word Became Flesh

Illustration ID (credit): fx_6313 (author)

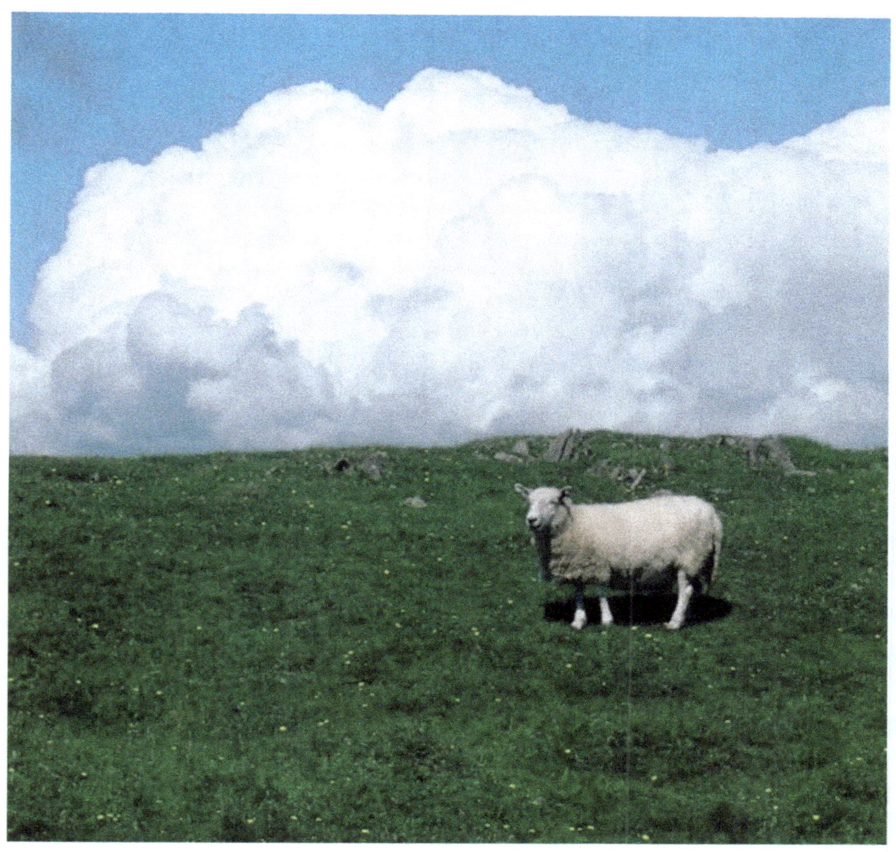

The next day John saw Jesus coming toward him and said, "Look, the Lamb of God, who takes away the sin of the world!"

Bible reference: John 1:29

Context: Jesus the Lamb of God

Illustration ID (credit): fa_31 (author)

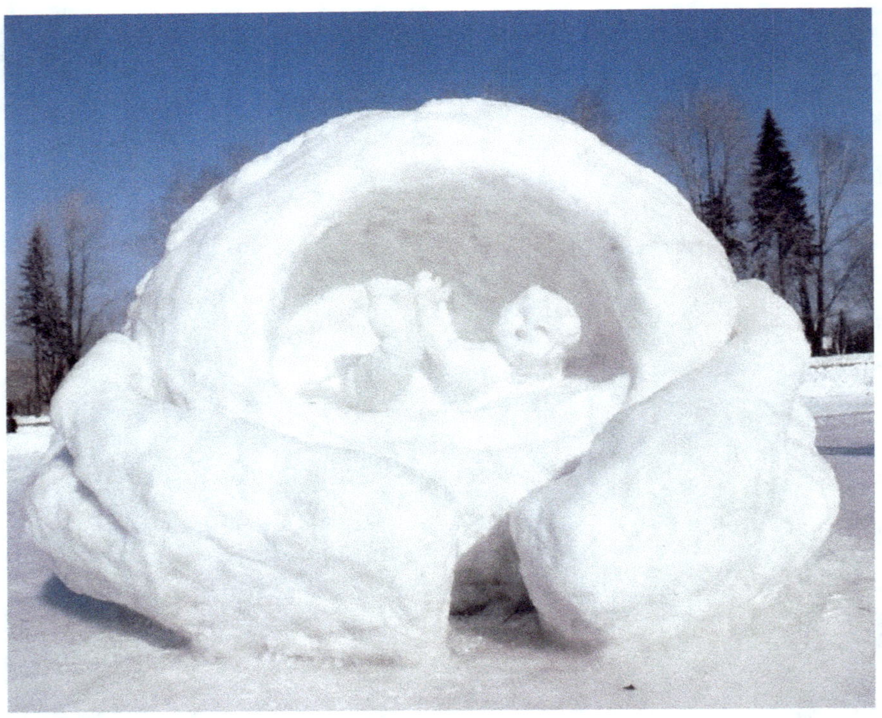

"How can someone be born when they are old?" Nicodemus asked. "Surely they cannot enter a second time into their mother's womb to be born!"

Bible reference: John 3:4

Context: Jesus Teaches Nicodemus

Illustration ID (credit): fa_13 (author)

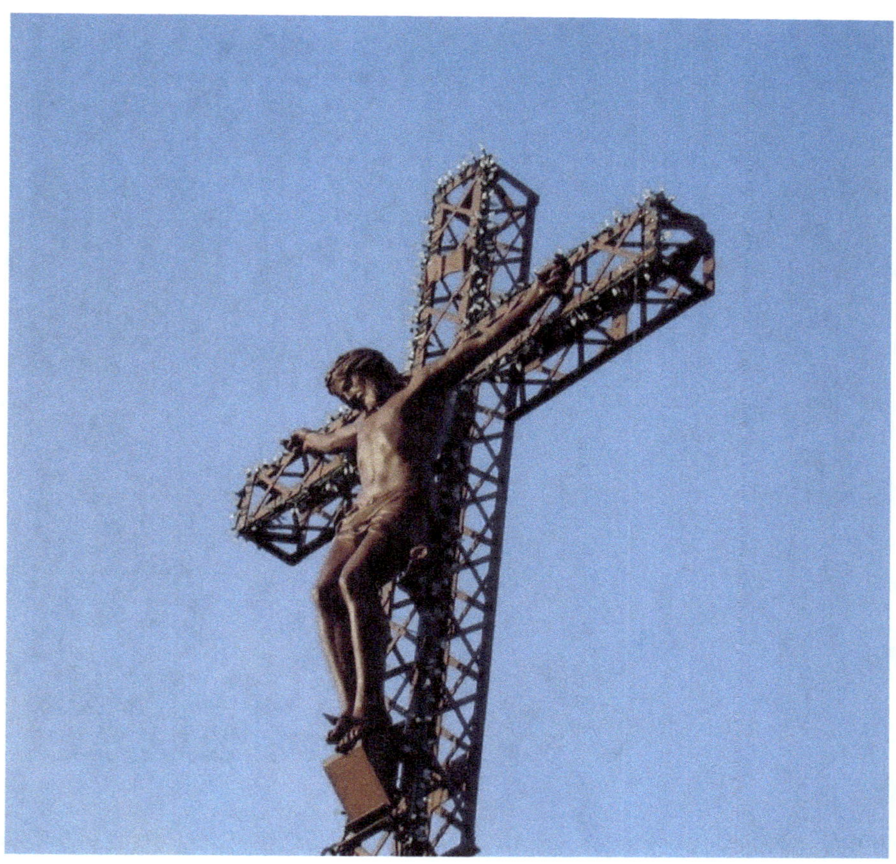

For God so loved the world that he gave his one and only Son, that whoever believes in him shall not perish but have eternal life.

Bible reference: John 3:16

Context: Jesus Teaches Nicodemus

Illustration ID (credit): fa_17 (author)

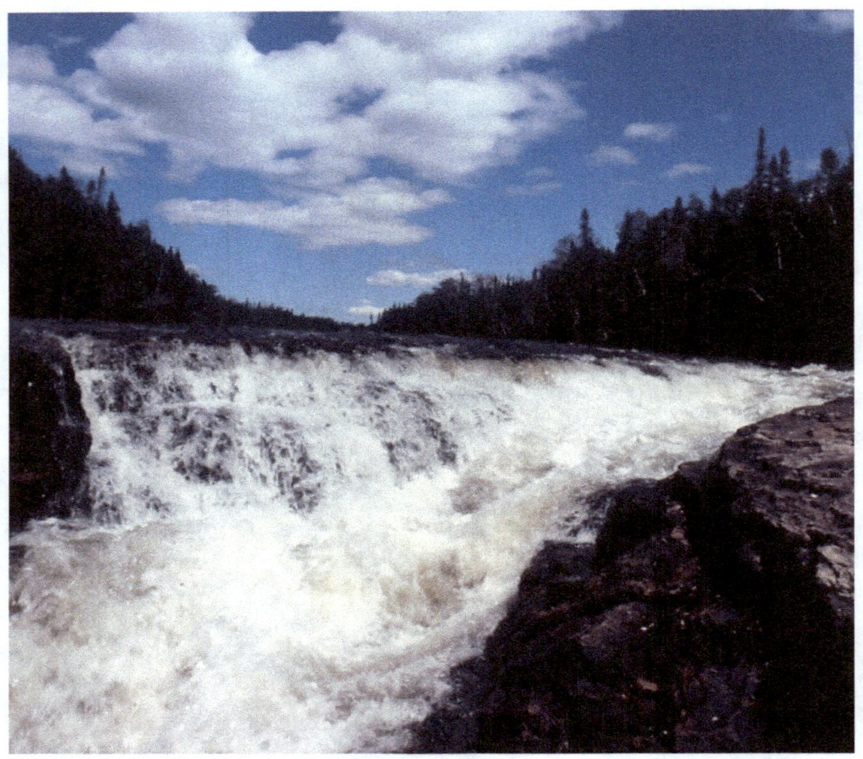

Whoever believes in me, as Scripture has said, rivers of living water will flow from within them

Bible reference: John 7:38

Context: Is Jesus the Christ?

Illustration ID (credit): fy_35 (author)

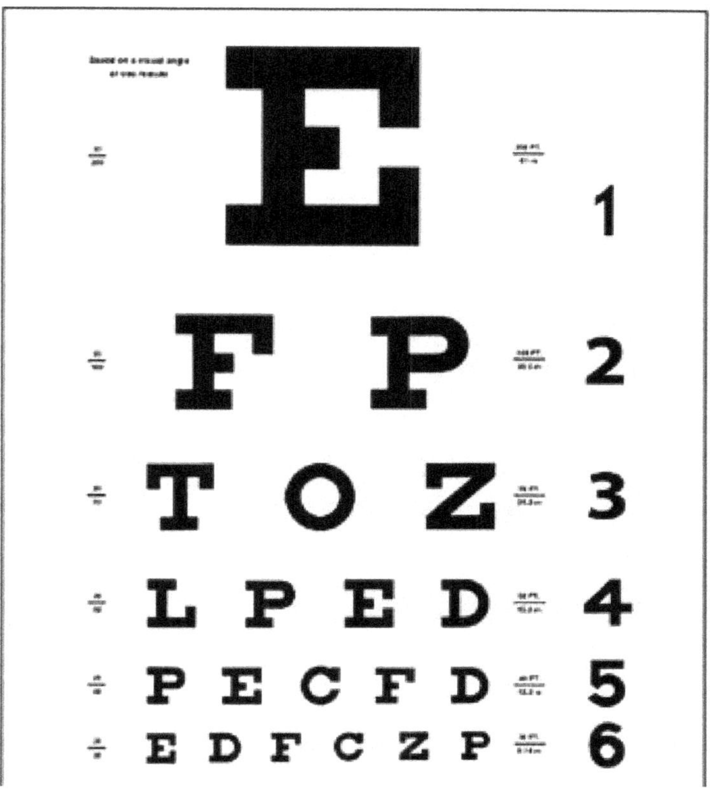

He replied, "Whether he is a sinner or not, I don't know. One thing I do know. I was blind but now I see!"

Bible reference: John 9:25

Context: The Pharisees Investigate the Healing

Illustration ID (credit): fv_017 (visioncenter.org)

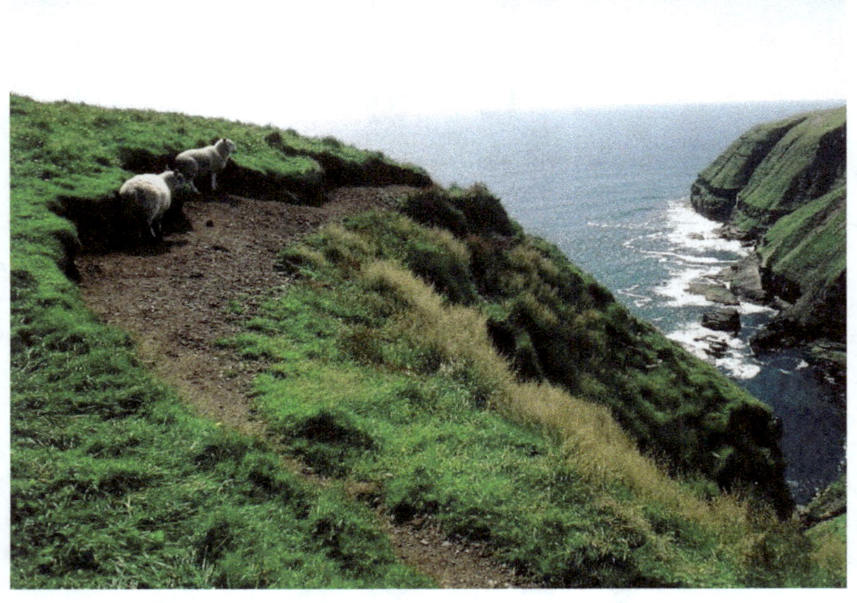

Therefore Jesus said again, "Very truly I tell you, I am the gate for the sheep . . ."

Bible reference: John 10:7

Context: The Shepherd and His Flock

Illustration ID (credit): fa_22 (author)

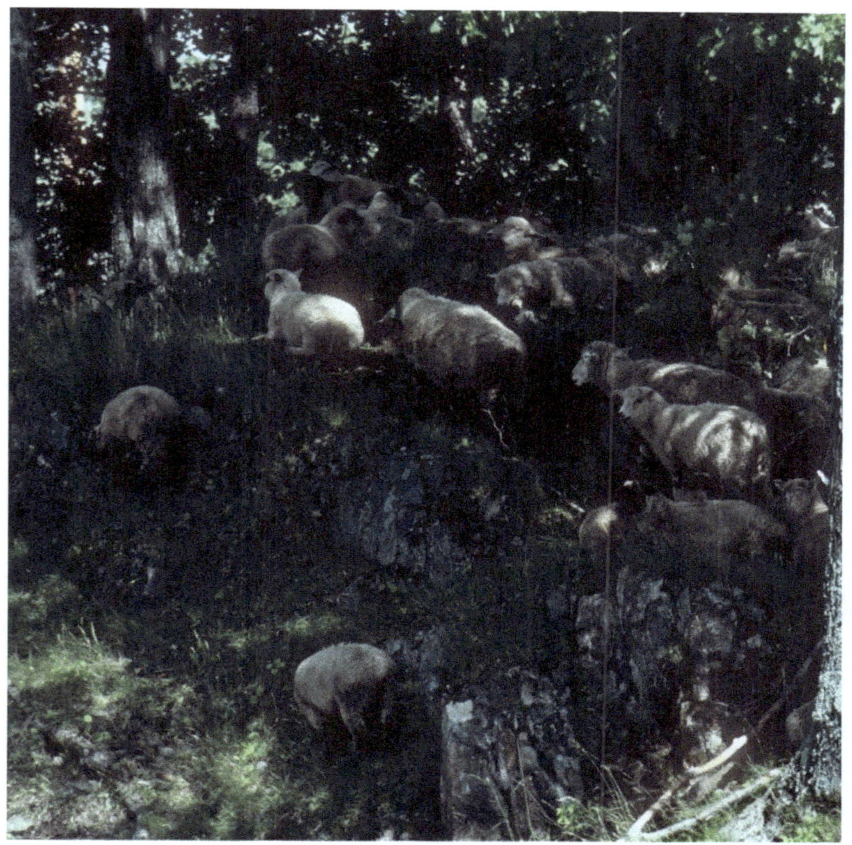

My sheep listen to my voice; I know them, and they follow me. I give them eternal life, and they shall never perish; no one can snatch them out of my hand.

Bible reference: John 10:27-28

Context: The Unbelief of the Jews

Illustration ID (credit): fs_337 (author)

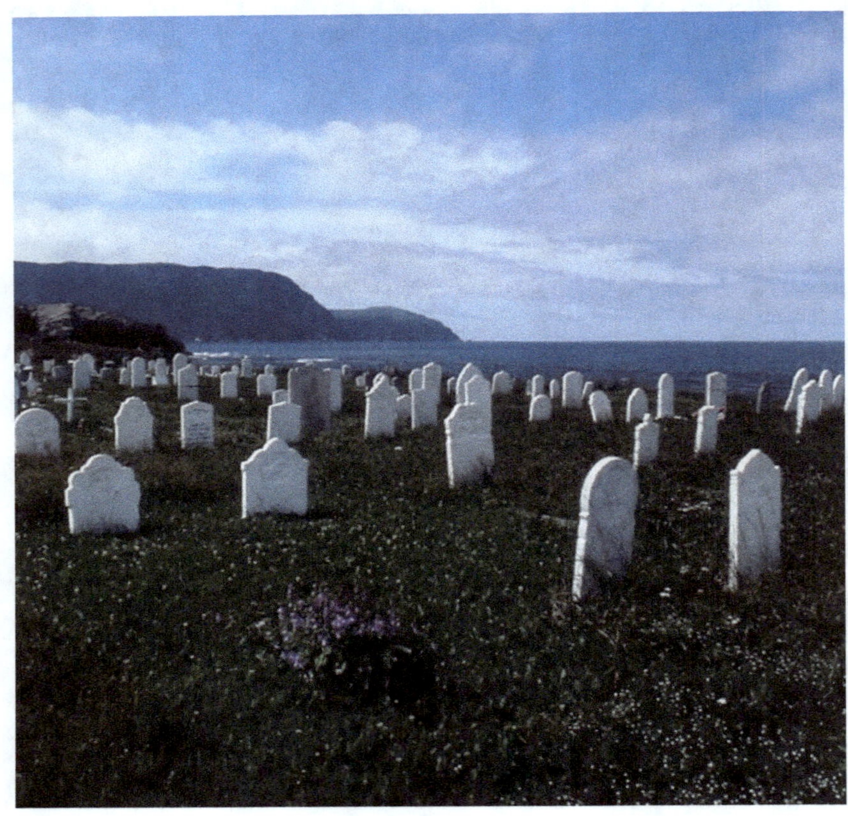

Jesus said to her, "I am the resurrection and the life. The one who believes in me will live, even though they die; and whoever lives by believing in me will never die. Do you believe this?"

Bible reference: John 11:25-26

Context: Jesus Comforts the Sisters

Illustration ID (credit): fa_16 (author)

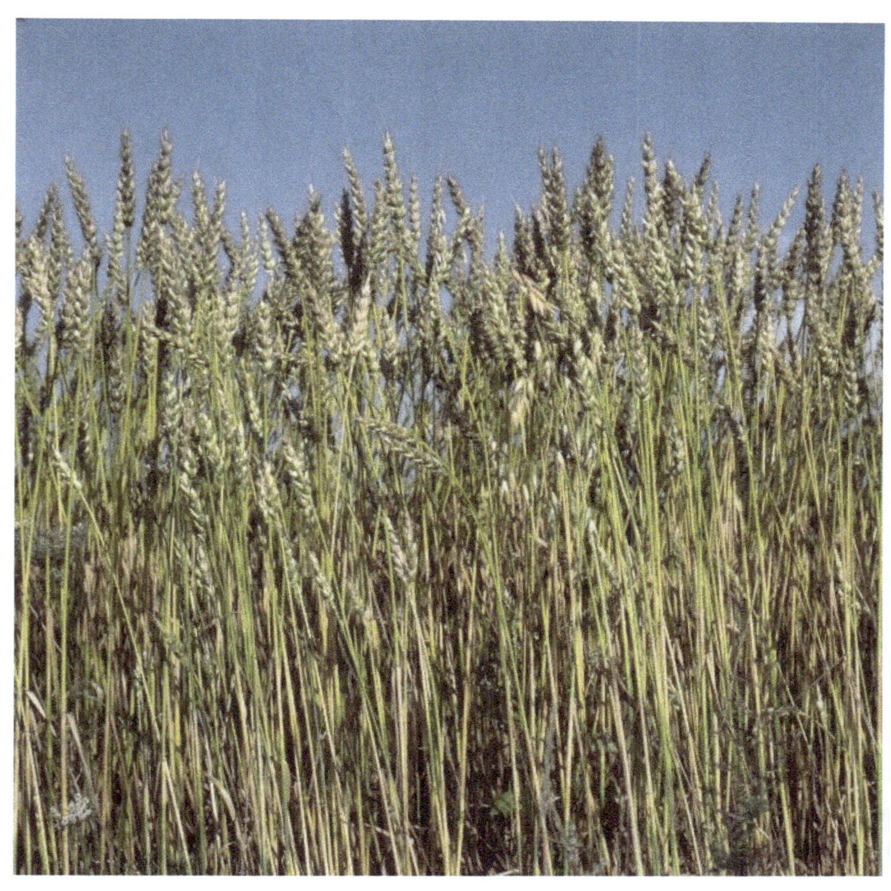

Very truly I tell you, unless a kernel of wheat falls to the ground and dies, it remains only a single seed. But if it dies, it produces many seeds.

Bible reference: John 12:24

Context: Jesus Predicts His Death

Illustration ID (credit): fa_18 (author)

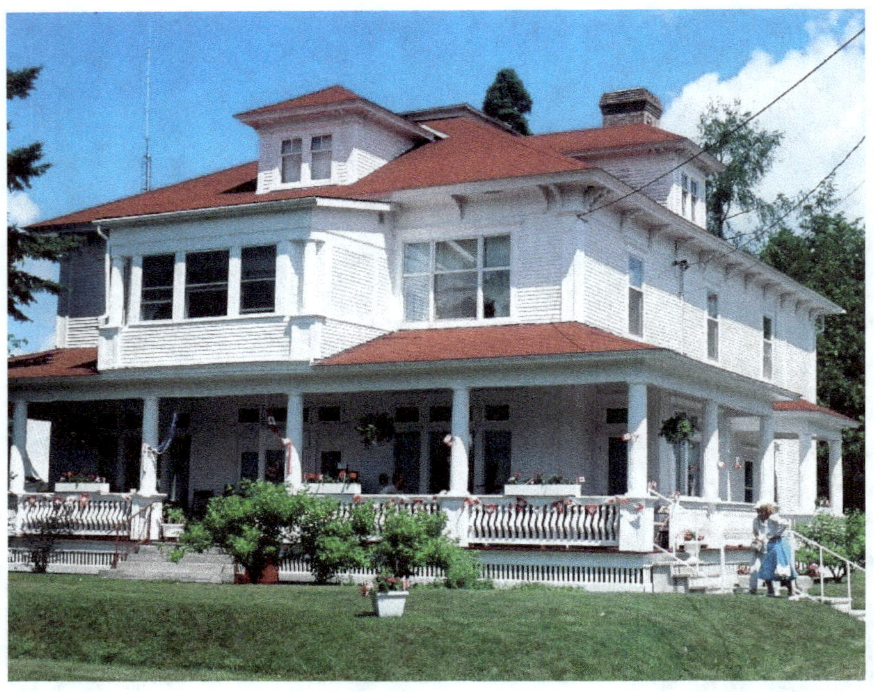

"Do not let your hearts be troubled. Trust in God; trust also in me. In my Father's house are many rooms; if it were not so, I would have told you. I am going there to prepare a place for you."

Bible reference: John 14:1-2

Context: Jesus Comforts His Disciples

Illustration ID (credit): fa_23 (author)

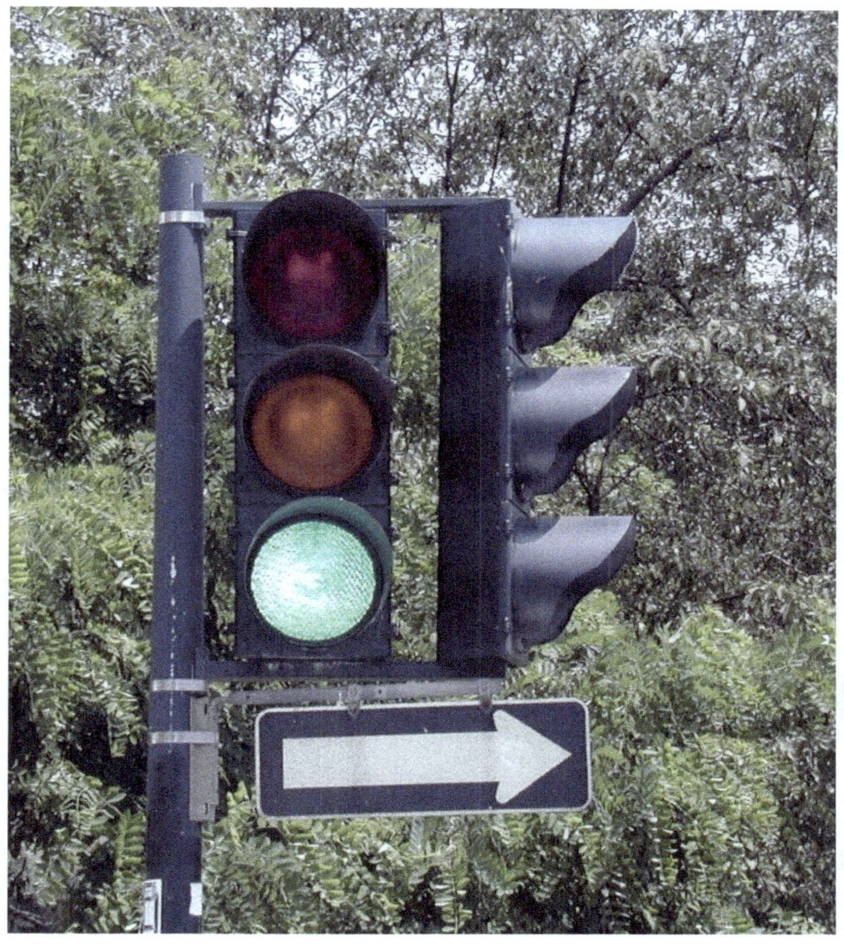

Jesus answered, "I am the way and the truth and the life. No one comes to the Father except through me."

Bible reference: John 14:6

Context: Jesus the Way to the Father

Illustration ID (credit): fa_04 (author)

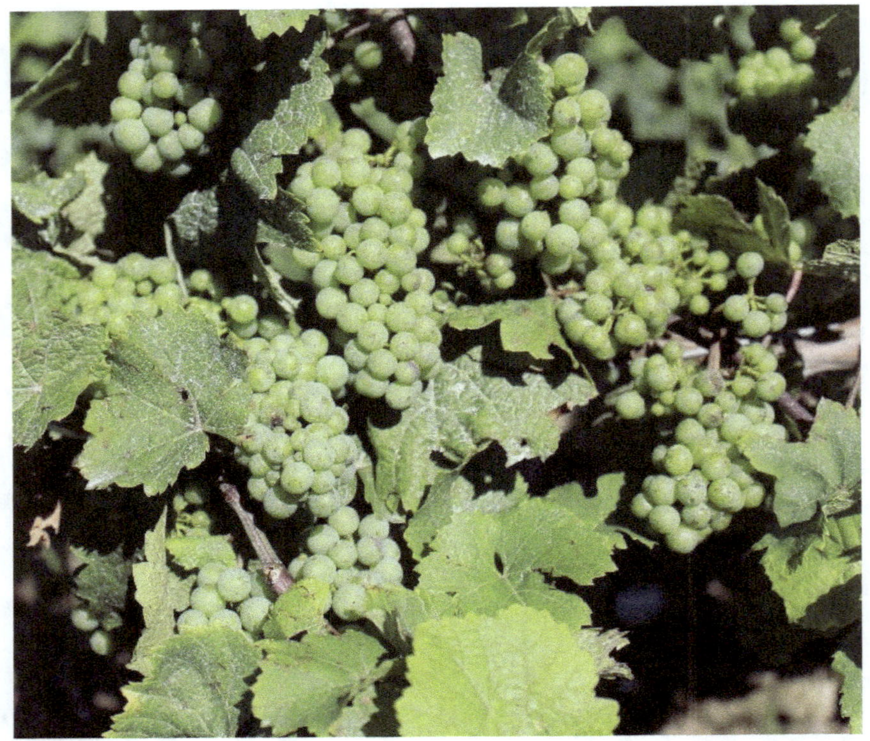

I am the vine; you are the branches. If a man remains in me and I in him, he will bear much fruit; apart from me you can do nothing

Bible reference: John 15:5

Context: The Vine and the Branches

Illustration ID (credit): fy_10 (author)

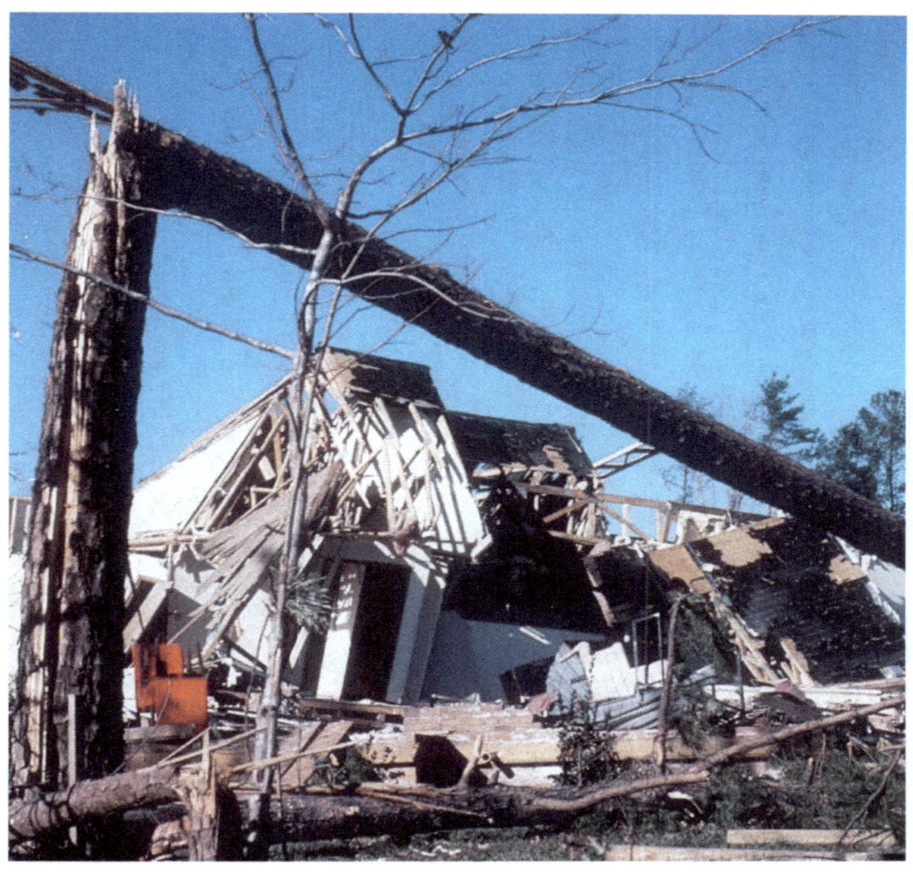

"I have told you these things, so that in me you may have peace. In this world you will have trouble. But take heart! I have overcome the world."

Bible reference: John 16:33

Context: The Disciples' Grief Will Turn to Joy

Illustration ID (credit): fv_016 (author)

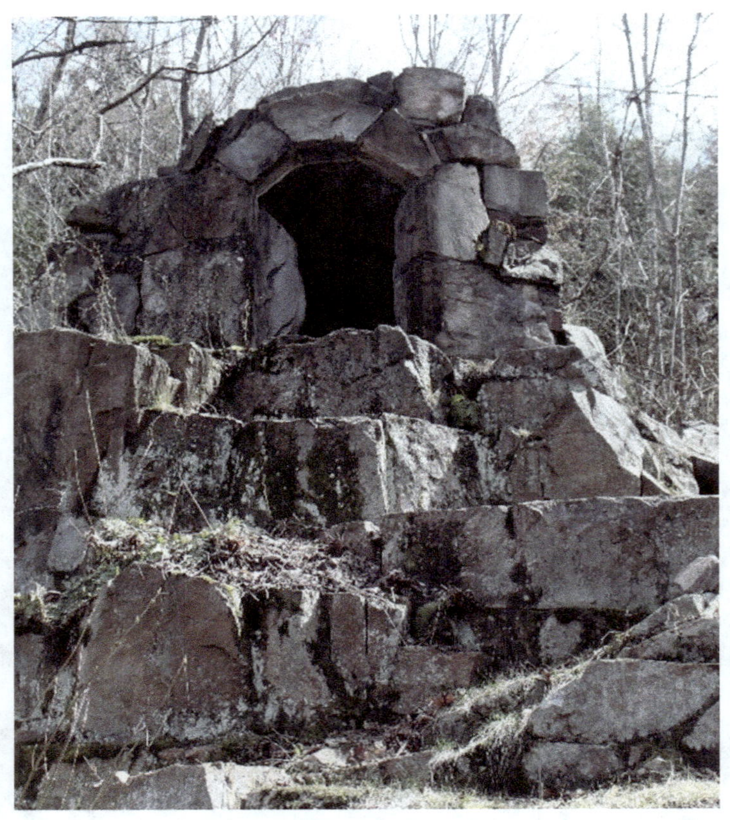

Early on the first day of the week, while it was still dark, Mary Magdalene went to the tomb and saw that the stone had been removed from the entrance. So she came running to Simon Peter and the other disciple, the one Jesus loved, and said, "They have taken the Lord out of the tomb, and we don't know where they have put him!"

Bible reference: John 20:1-2

Context: The Empty Tomb

Illustration ID (credit): fc_3861 (author)

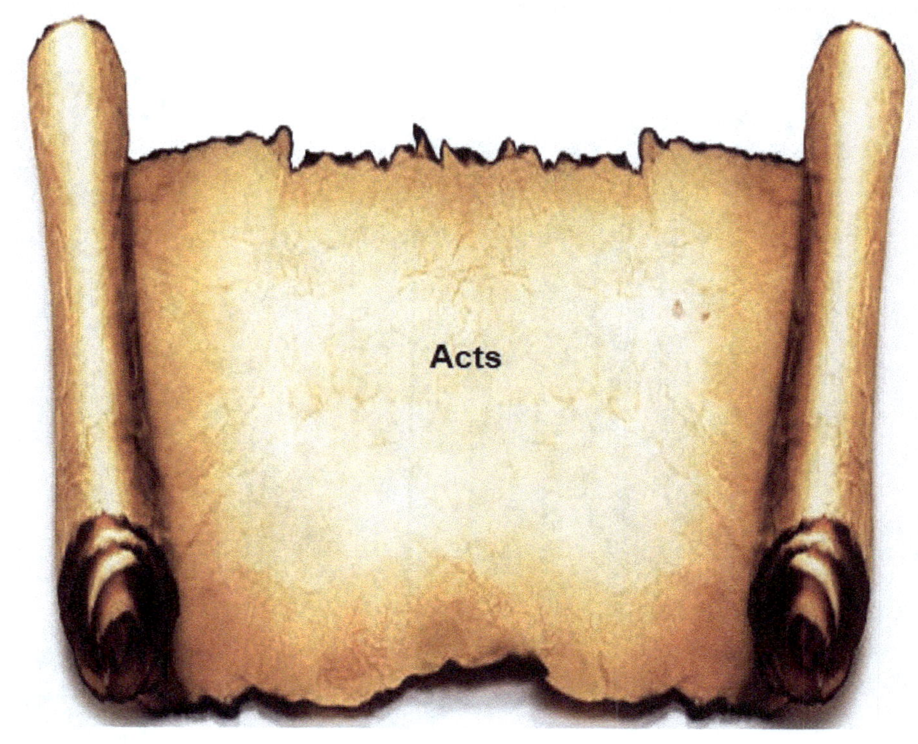
Acts

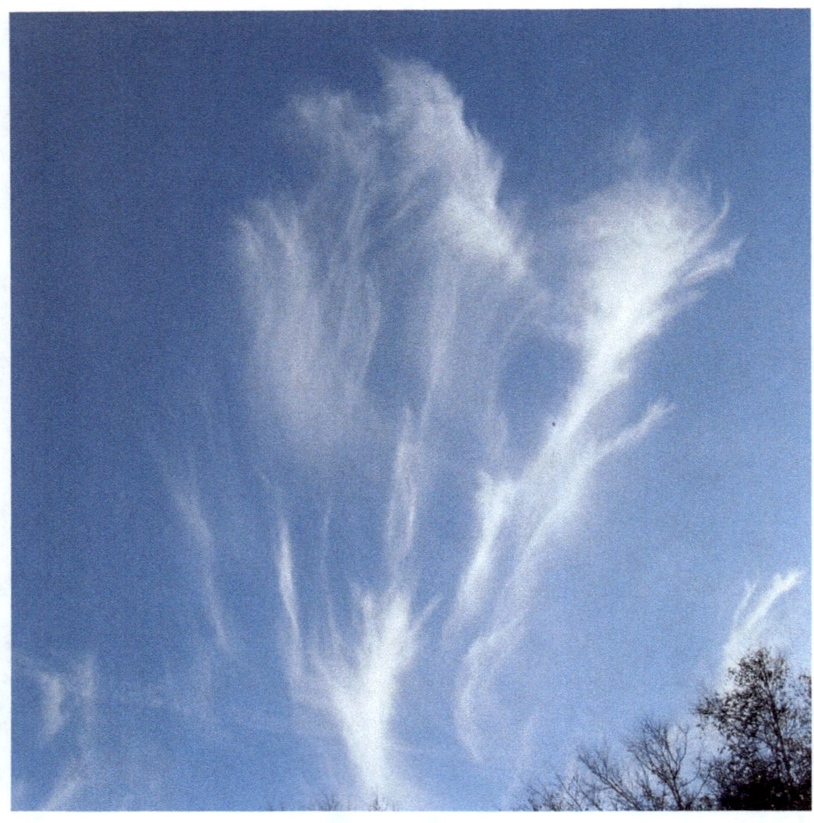

"But you will receive power when the Holy Spirit comes upon you. And you will be my witnesses, telling people about me everywhere — in Jerusalem, throughout Judea, in Samaria, and to the ends of the earth." After saying this, he was taken up into a cloud while they were watching, and they could no longer see him.

Bible reference: Acts 1:8-9

Context: Jesus Taken Up Into Heaven

Illustration ID (credit): fv_89 (Warren Fraser)

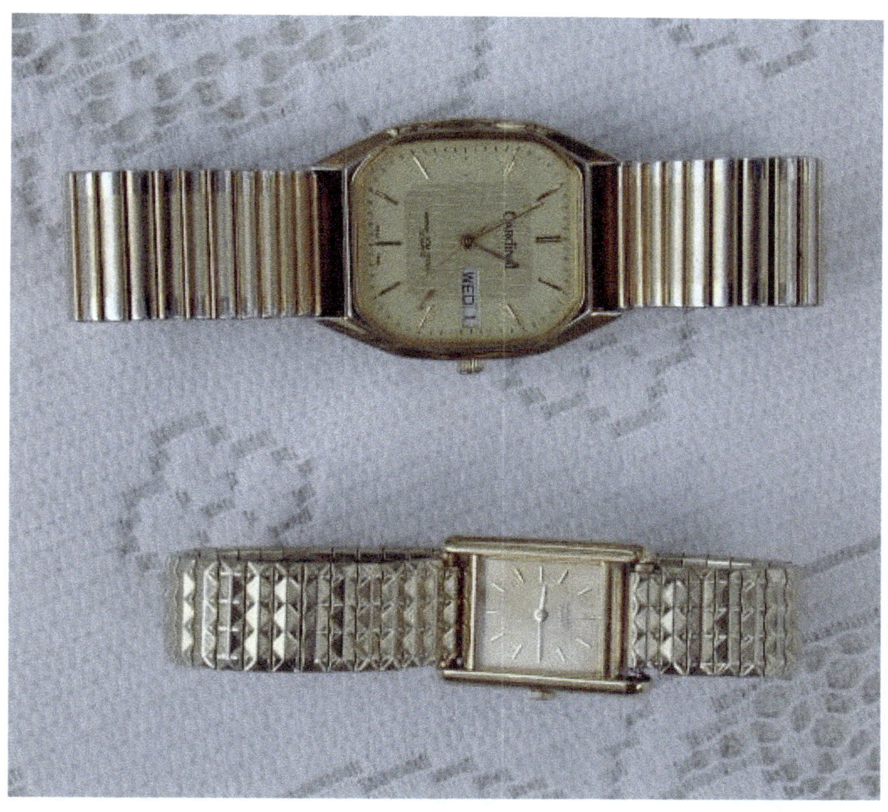

Then Peter said, "Silver or gold I do not have, but what I have I give you. In the name of Jesus Christ of Nazareth, walk."

Bible reference: Acts 3:6

Context: Peter Heals the Crippled Beggar

Illustration ID (credit): fx_0609 (author)

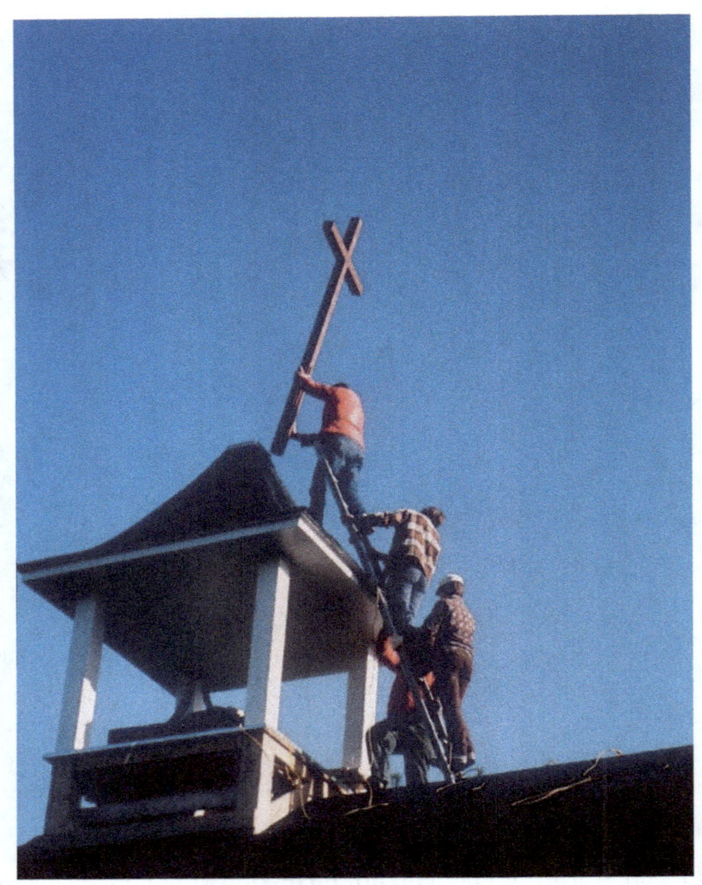

Salvation is found in no one else, for there is no other name under heaven given to men by which we must be saved.

Bible reference: Acts 4:12-13

Context: Peter and John Before the Sanhedrin

Illustration ID (credit): fs_364 (author)

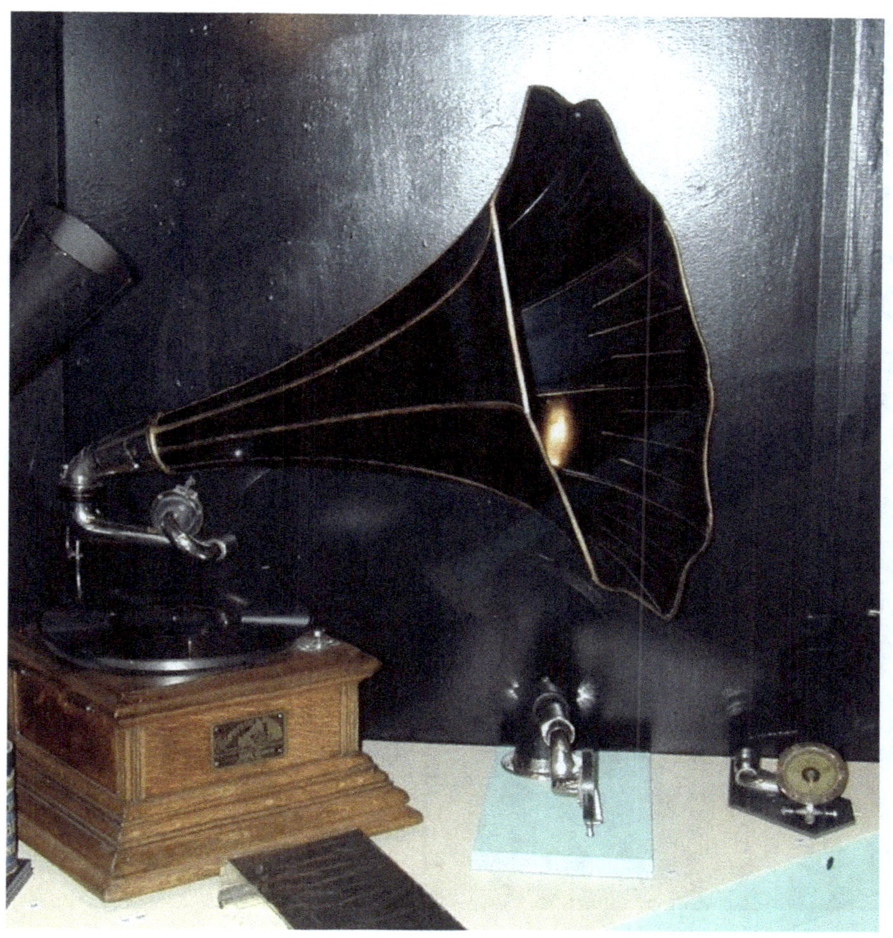

After they prayed, the place where they were meeting was shaken. And they were all filled with the Holy Spirit and spoke the word of God boldly.

Bible reference: Acts 4:31

Context: The Believers' Prayer

Illustration ID (credit): fy_33 (author)

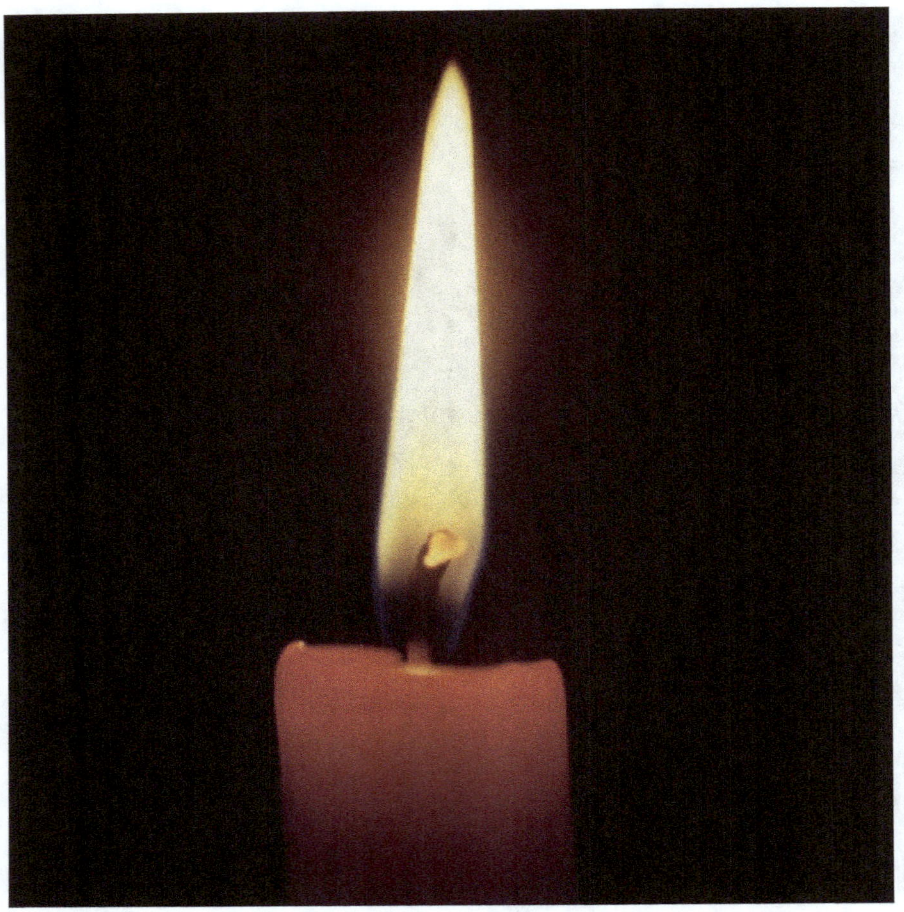

For this is what the Lord has commanded us: "I have made you a light for the Gentiles, that you may bring salvation to the ends of the earth.'"

Bible reference: Acts 13:47

Context: In Pisidian Antioch

Illustration ID (credit): fy_91 (author)

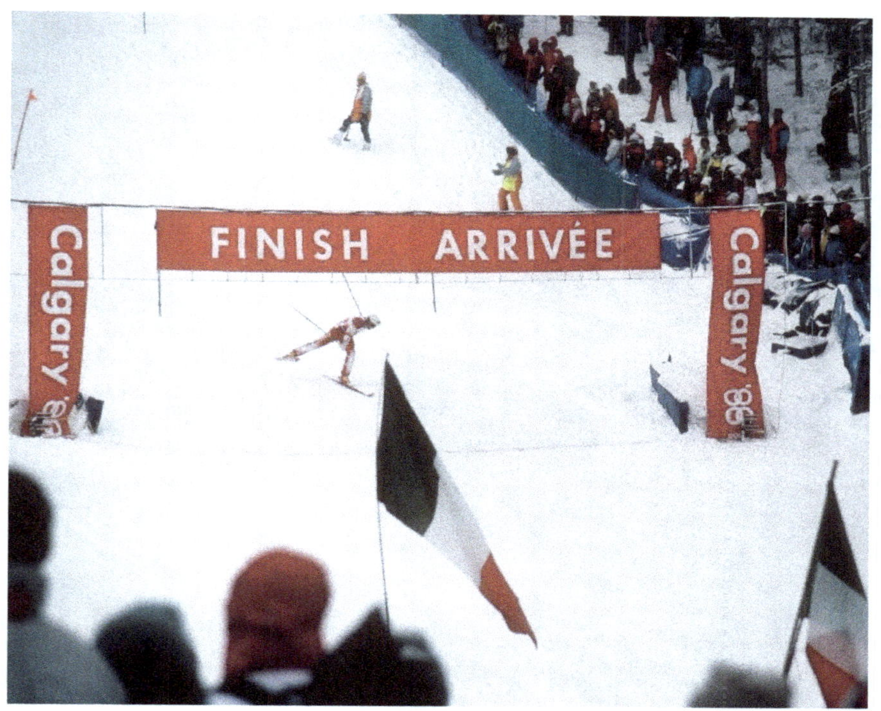

However, I consider my life worth nothing to me, if only I may finish the race and complete the task the Lord Jesus has given me--the task of testifying to the gospel of God's grace.

Bible reference: Acts 20:24

Context: Eutychus Raised From the Dead at Troas

Illustration ID (credit): fv_002 (author)

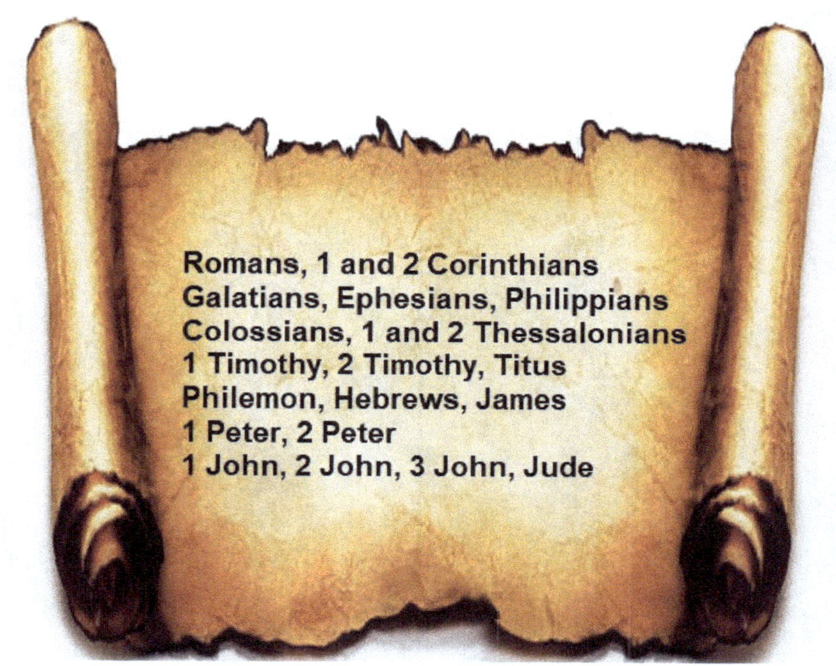
Romans, 1 and 2 Corinthians
Galatians, Ephesians, Philippians
Colossians, 1 and 2 Thessalonians
1 Timothy, 2 Timothy, Titus
Philemon, Hebrews, James
1 Peter, 2 Peter
1 John, 2 John, 3 John, Jude

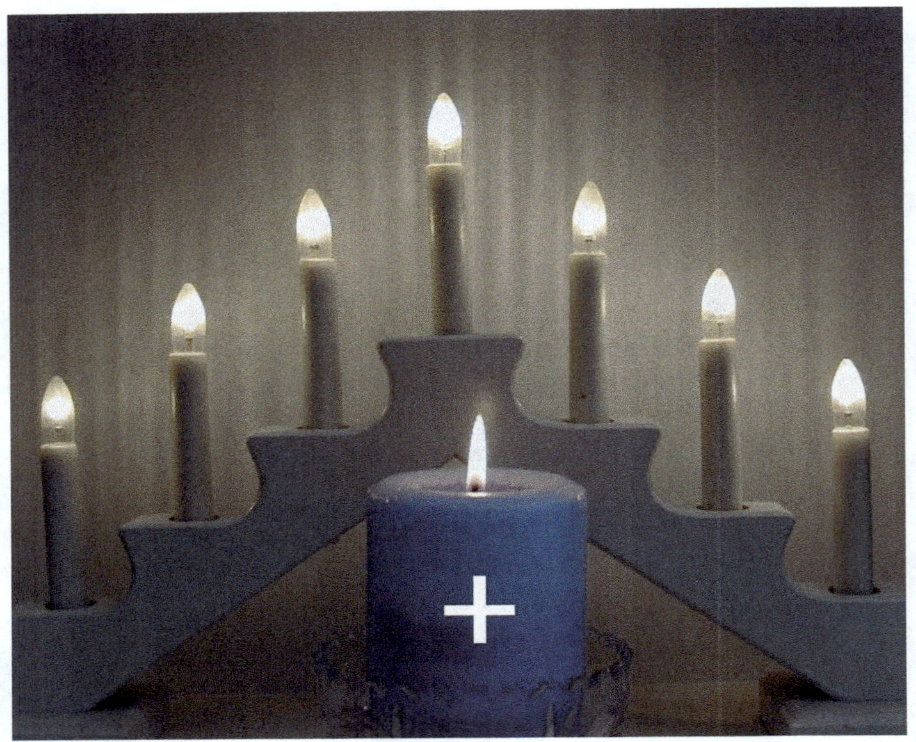

I am not ashamed of the gospel, because it is the power of God for the salvation of everyone who believes: first for the Jew, then for the Gentile.

Bible reference: Romans 1:16

Context: Paul's Longing to Visit Rome

Illustration ID (credit): fy_88 (author)

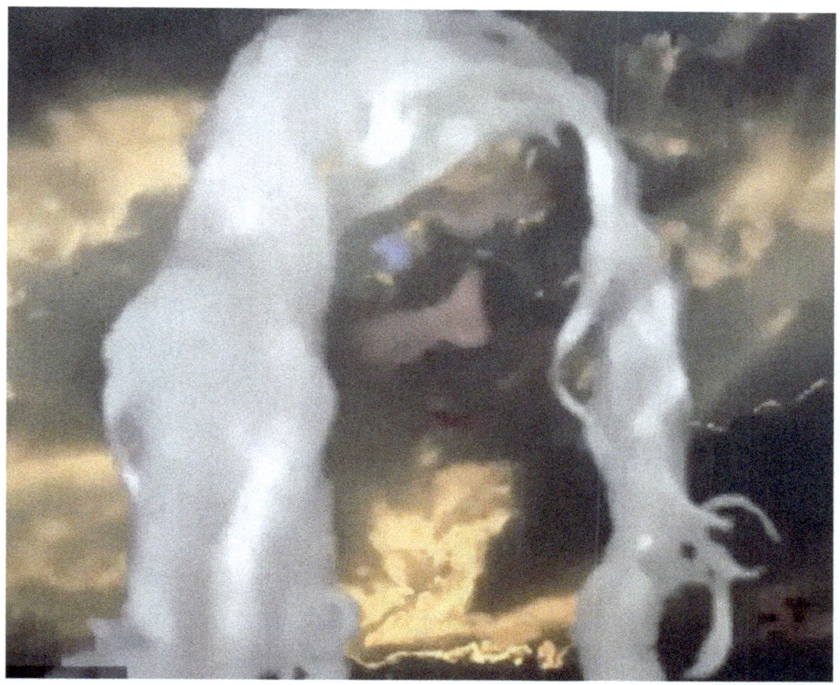

The wrath of God is being revealed from heaven against all the godlessness and wickedness of people, who suppress the truth by their wickedness,

Bible reference: Romans 1:18

Context: God's Wrath Against Mankind

Illustration ID (credit): fs_2020 (Elaine Fraser)

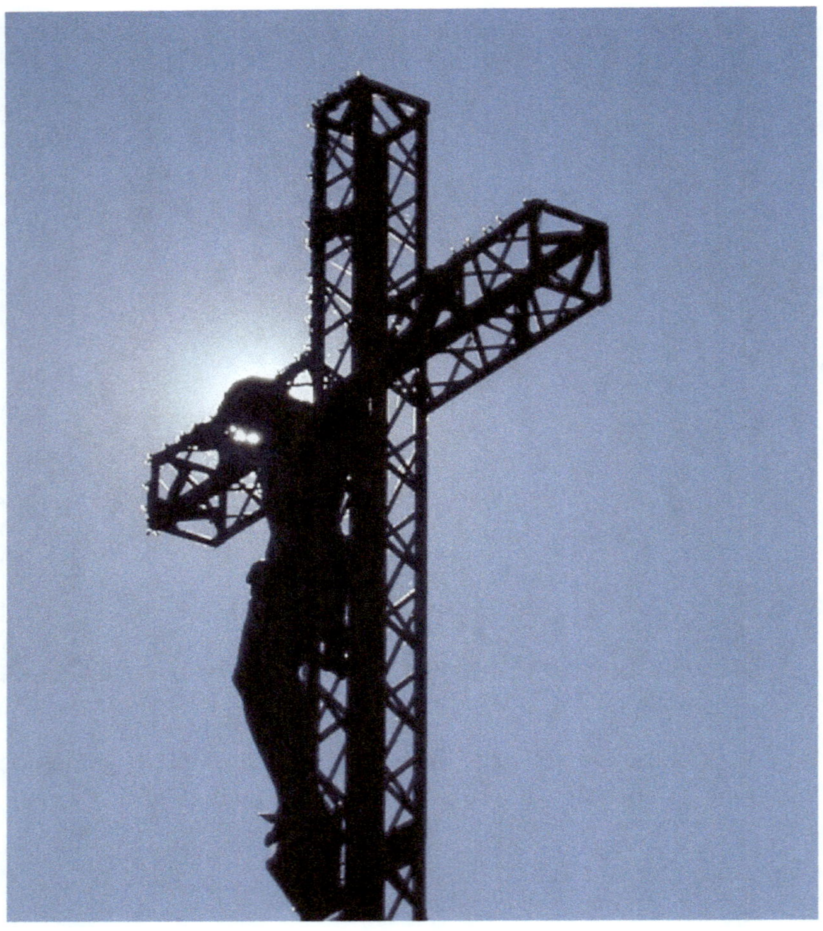

But God demonstrates his own love for us in this: While we were still sinners, Christ died for us.

Bible reference: Romans 5:8

Context: Peace and Joy

Illustration ID (credit): fc_691 (author)

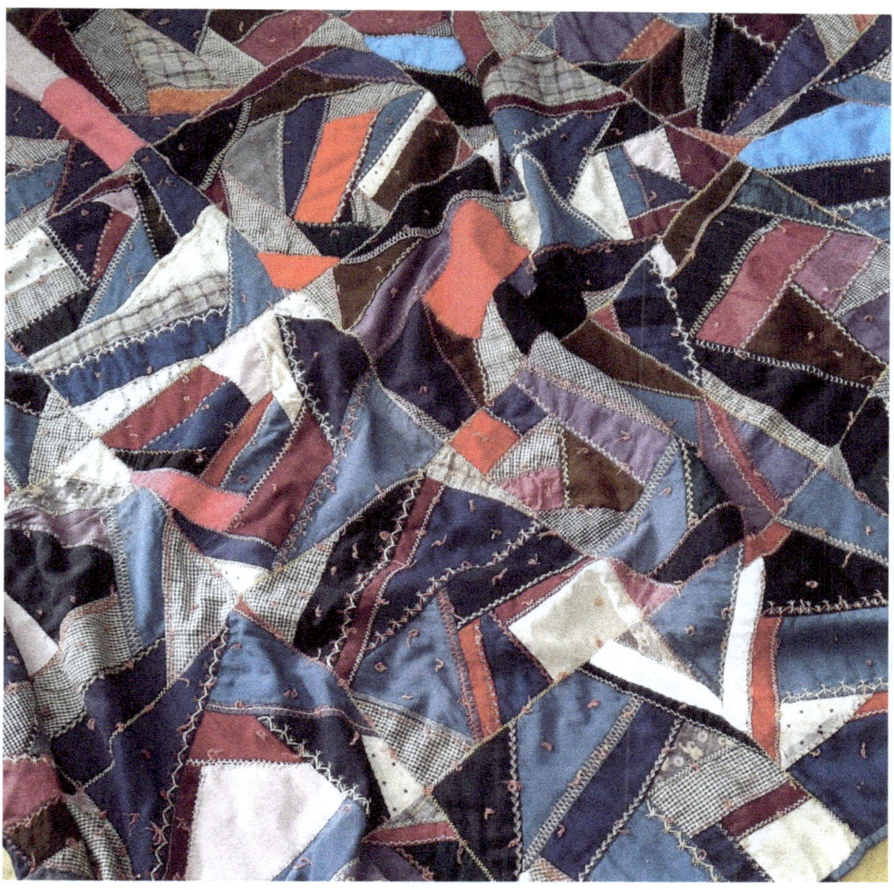

Do not conform any longer to the pattern of this world, but be transformed by the renewing of your mind. Then you will be able to test and approve what God's will is--his good, pleasing and perfect will.

Bible reference: Romans 12:2

Context: Living Sacrifices

Illustration ID (credit): fz_454 (author)

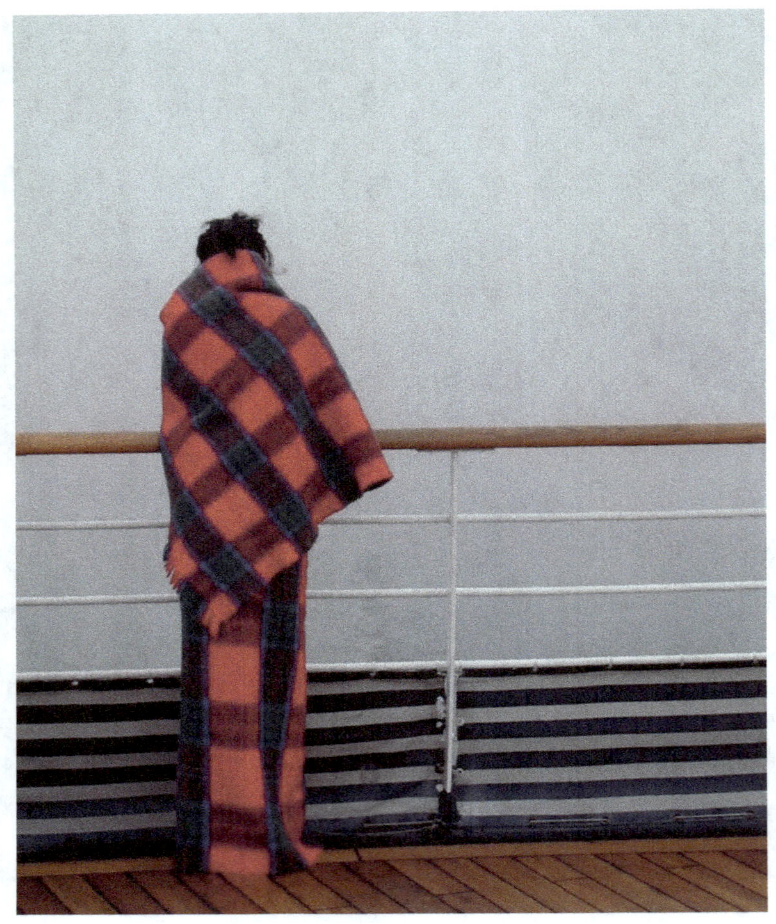

Rather, clothe yourselves with the Lord Jesus Christ, and do not think about how to gratify the desires of the flesh.

Bible reference: Romans 13:14

Context: Love, for the Day Is Near

Illustration ID (credit): fx_4503 (author)

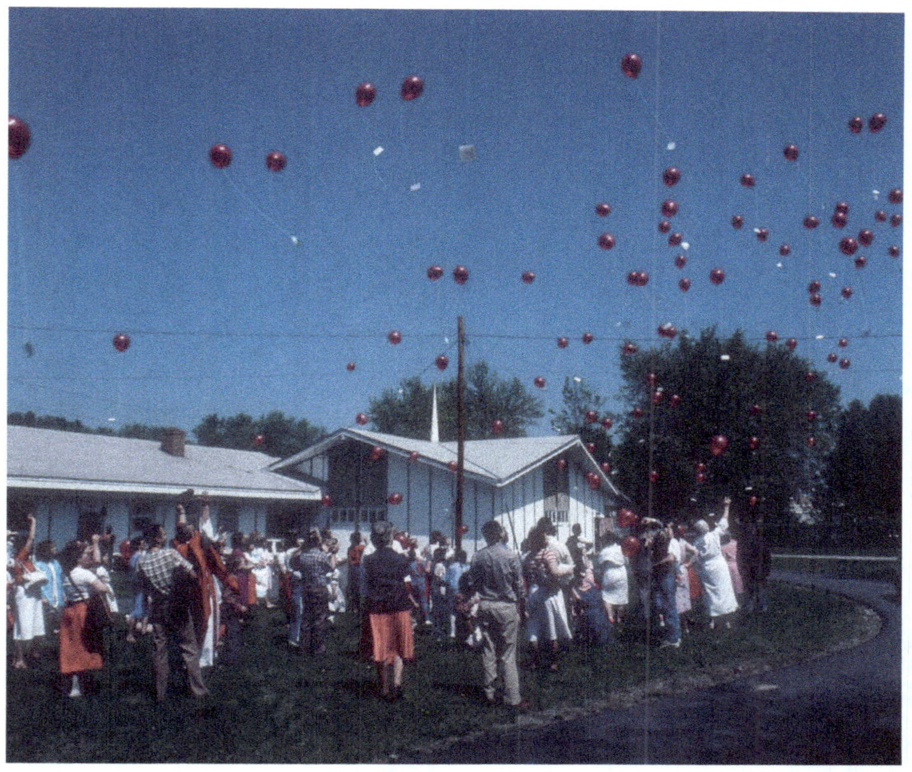

May the God of hope fill you with all joy and peace as you trust in him, so that you may overflow with hope by the power of the Holy Spirit.

Bible reference: Romans 15:13

Context: The Weak and the Strong

Illustration ID (credit): fv_11012 (author)

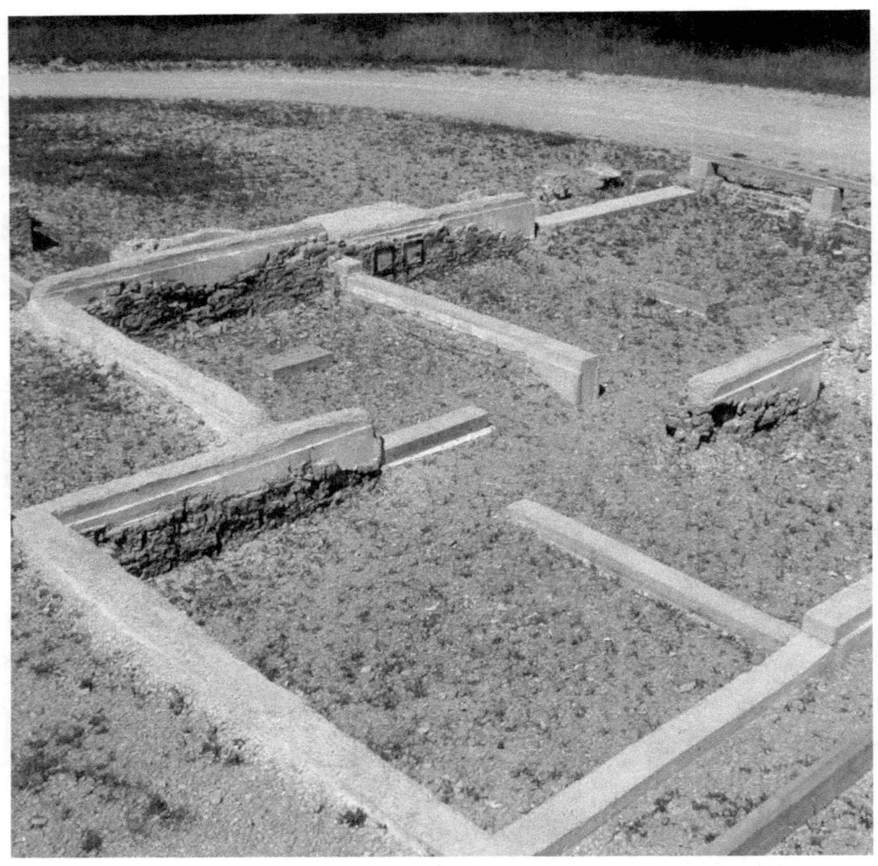

For no one can lay any foundation other than the one already laid, which is Jesus Christ.

Bible reference: 1 Corinthians 3:11

Context: On Divisions in the Church

Illustration ID (credit): fx_4985 (author)

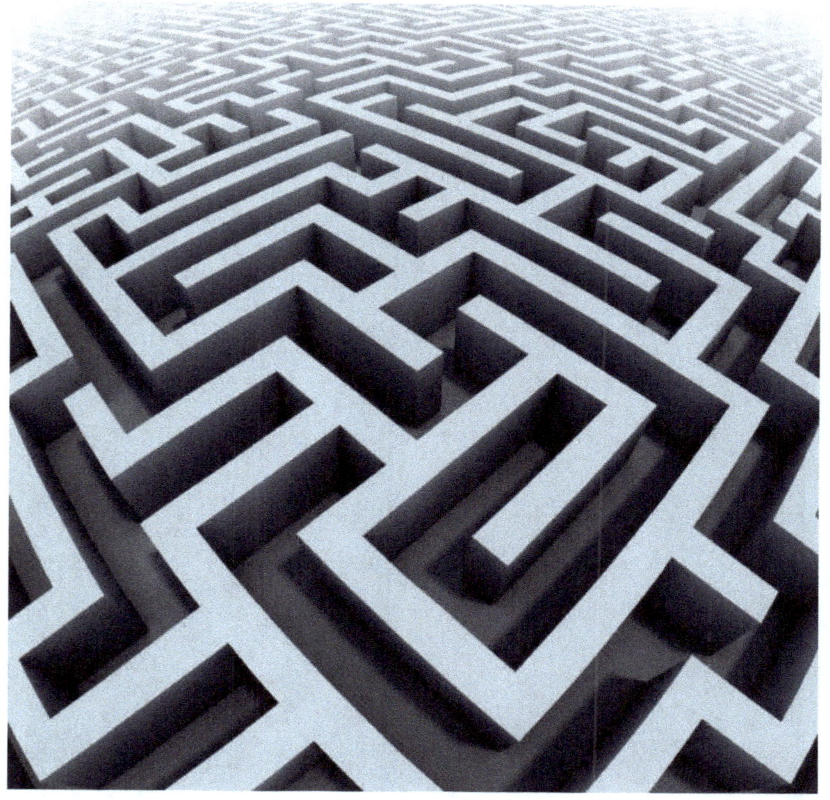

No temptation has seized you except what is common to man. And God is faithful; he will not let you be tempted beyond what you can bear. But when you are tempted, he will also provide a way out so that you can stand up under it.

Bible reference: 1 Corinthians 10:13

Context: Warnings From Israel's History

Illustration ID (credit): fs_88957314 (istockphoto)

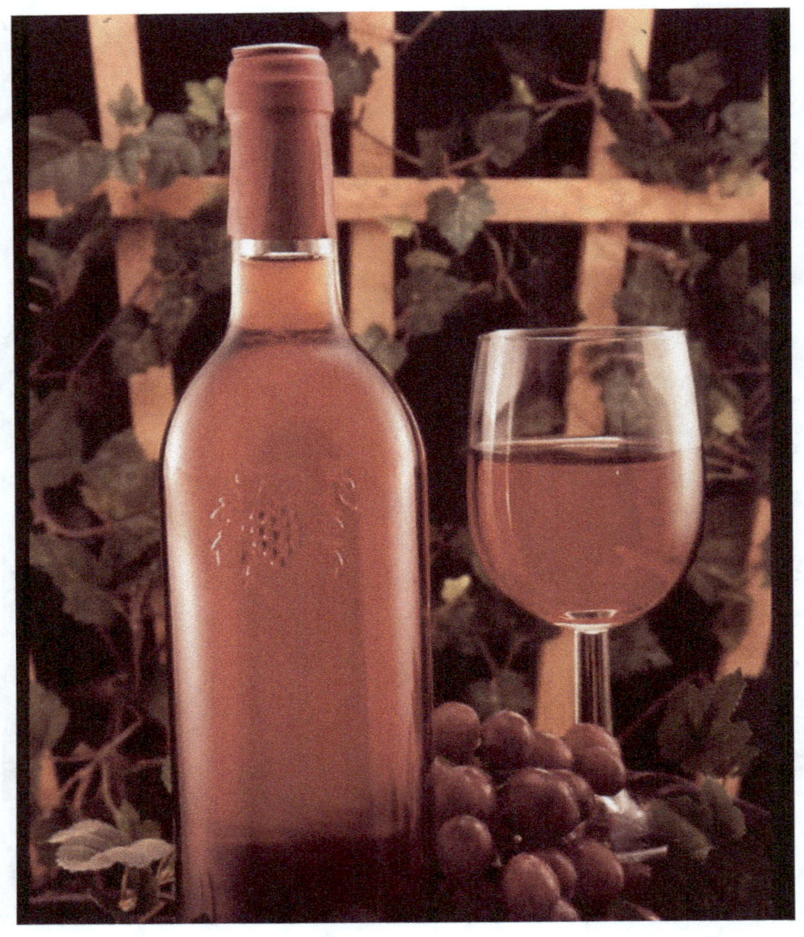

So whether you eat or drink or whatever you do, do it all for the glory of God.

Bible reference: 1 Corinthians 10:31

Context: The Believer's Freedom

Illustration ID (credit): fy_92 (Greg Beck)

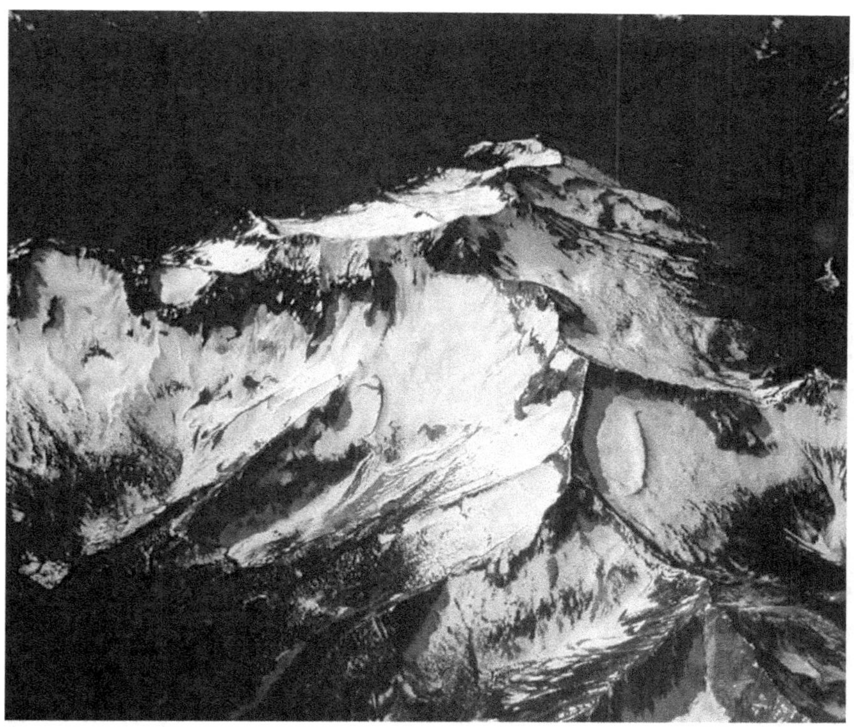

If I have the gift of prophecy and can fathom all mysteries and all knowledge, and if I have a faith that can move mountains, but do not have love, I am nothing.

Bible reference: 1 Corinthians 13:2

Context: Love

Illustration ID (credit): fx_4458 (author)

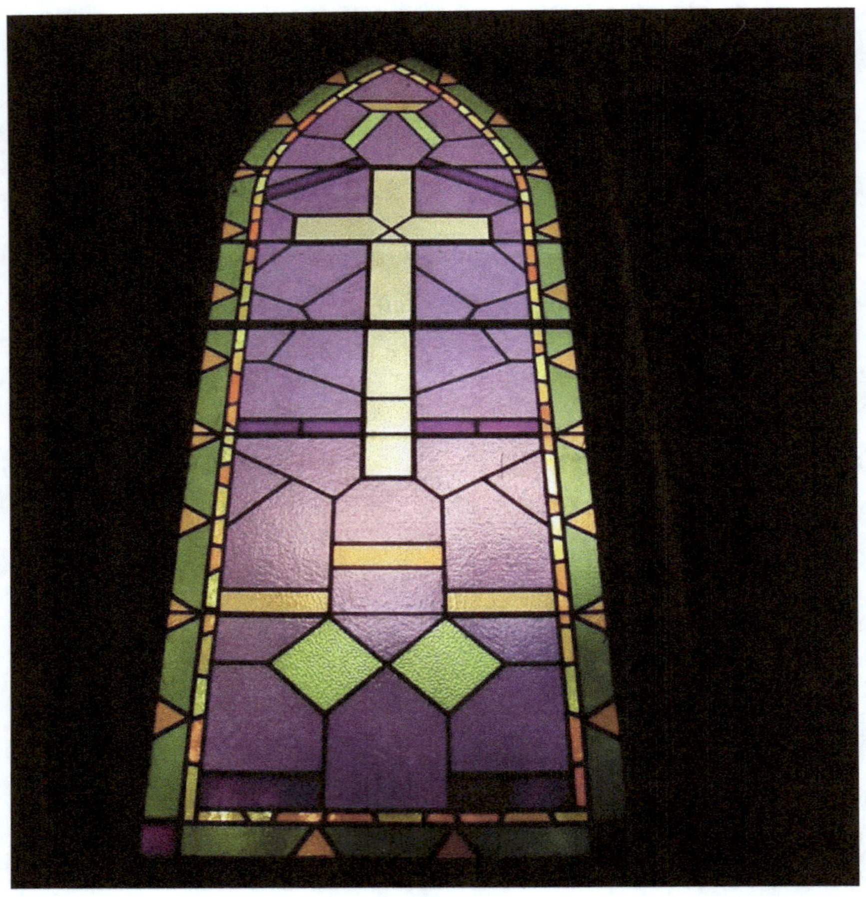

Therefore, my dear brothers, stand firm. Let nothing move you. Always give yourselves fully to the work of the Lord, because you know that your labor in the Lord is not in vain.

Bible reference: 1 Corinthians 15:58

Context: The Resurrection Body

Illustration ID (credit): fv_018 (author)

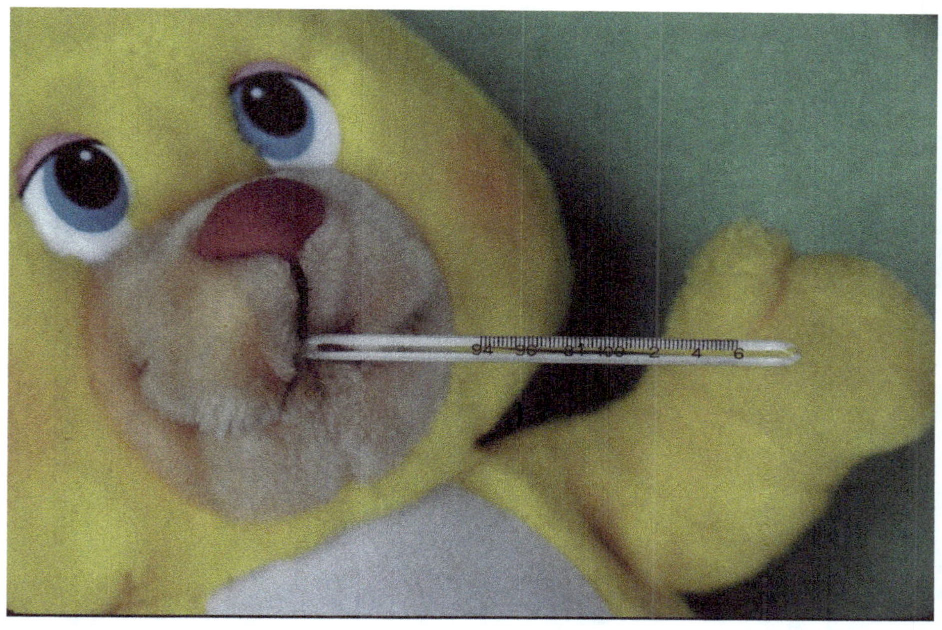

Praise be to the God and Father of our Lord Jesus Christ, the Father of compassion and the God of all comfort, who comforts us in all our troubles, so that we can comfort those in any trouble with the comfort we ourselves have received from God.

Bible reference: 2 Corinthians 1:3-4

Context: The God of All Comfort

Illustration ID (credit): fy_37 (author)

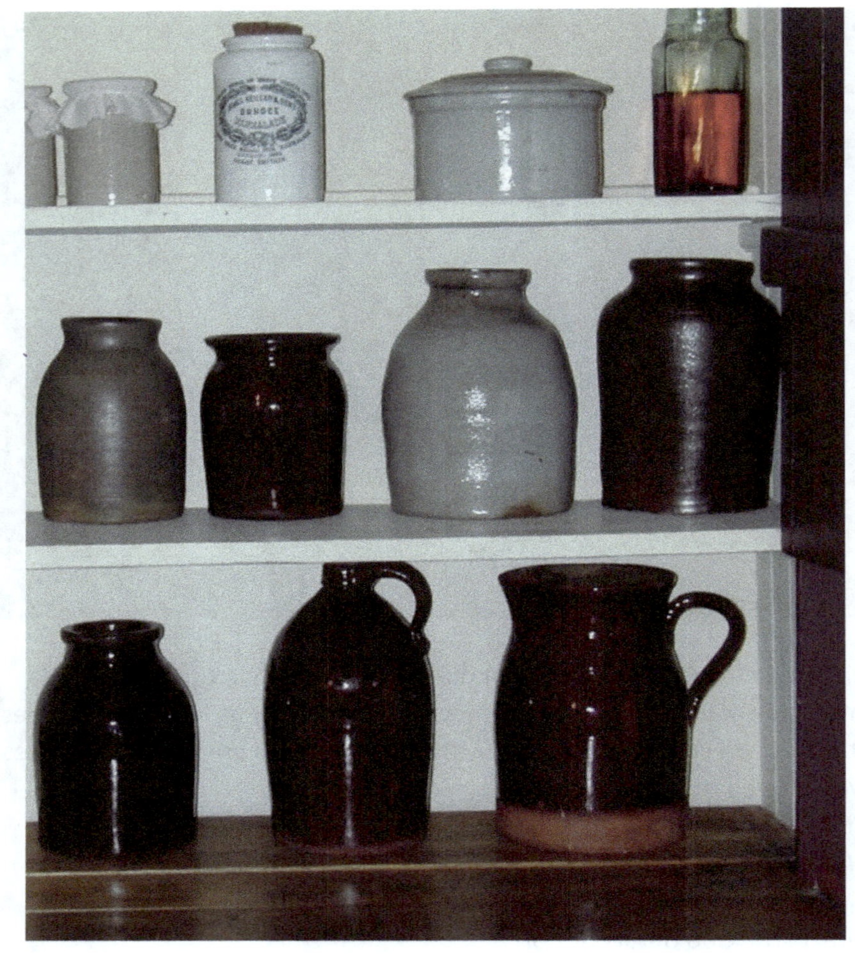

But we have this treasure in jars of clay to show that this all-surpassing power is from God and not from us.

Bible reference: 2 Corinthians 4:7

Context: Treasures in Jars of Clay

Illustration ID (credit): fx_3820 (author)

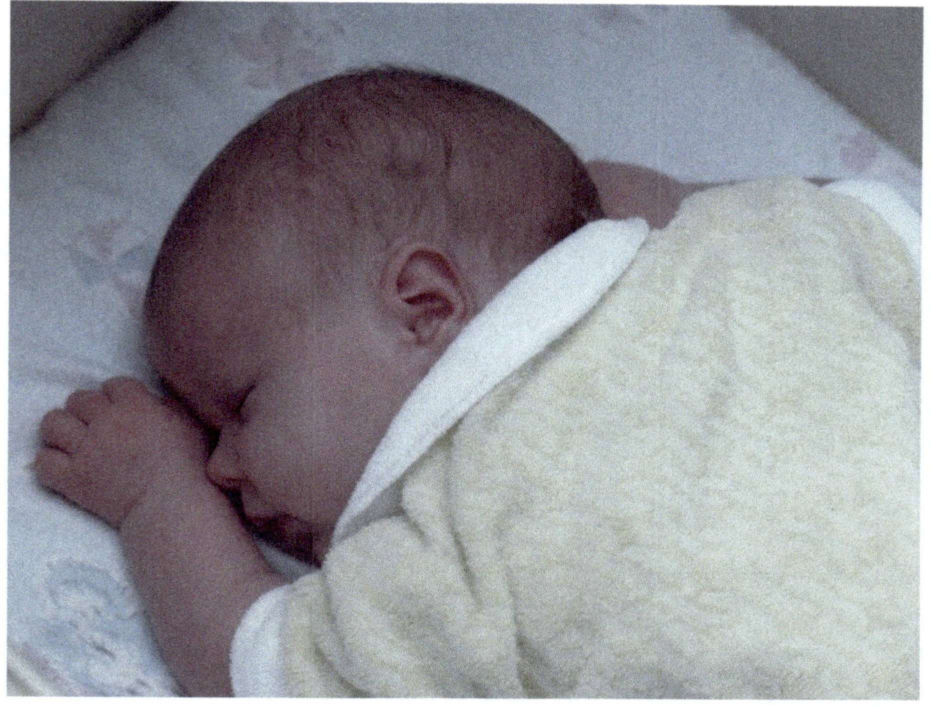

Therefore, if anyone is in Christ, he is a new creation; the old has gone, the new has come!

Bible reference: 2 Corinthians 5:17

Context: The Ministry of Reconciliation

Illustration ID (credit): fs_1055-27 (author)

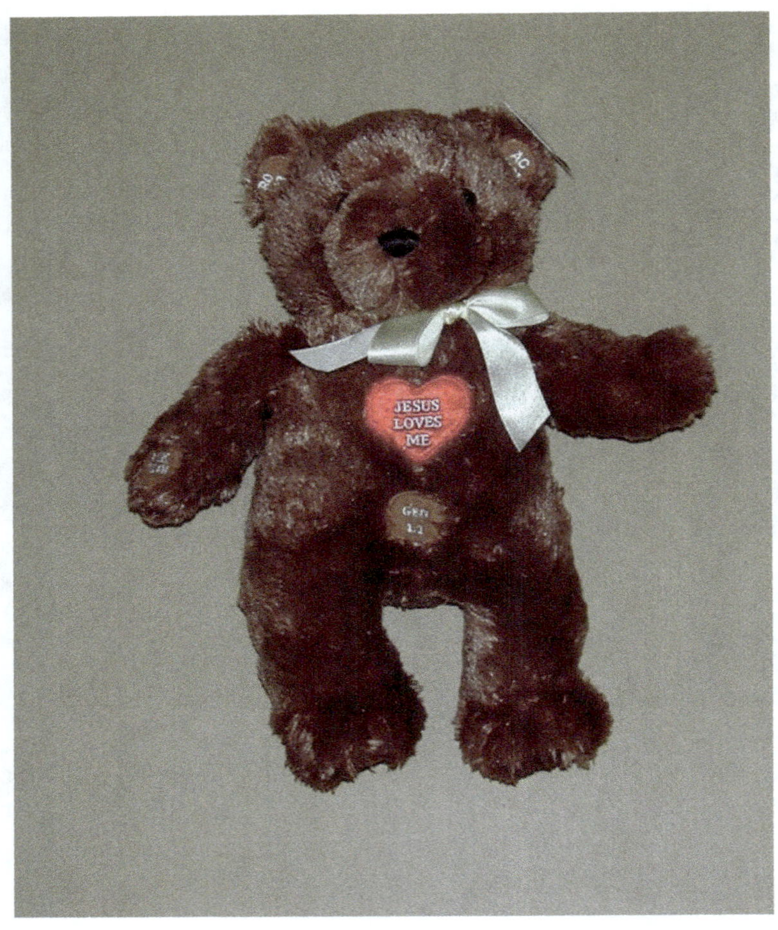

I have been crucified with Christ and I no longer live, but Christ lives in me. The life I live in the body, I live by faith in the Son of God, who loved me and gave himself for me.

Bible reference: Galatians 2:20

Context: Paul Opposes Peter

Illustration ID (credit): fx_4049 (author)

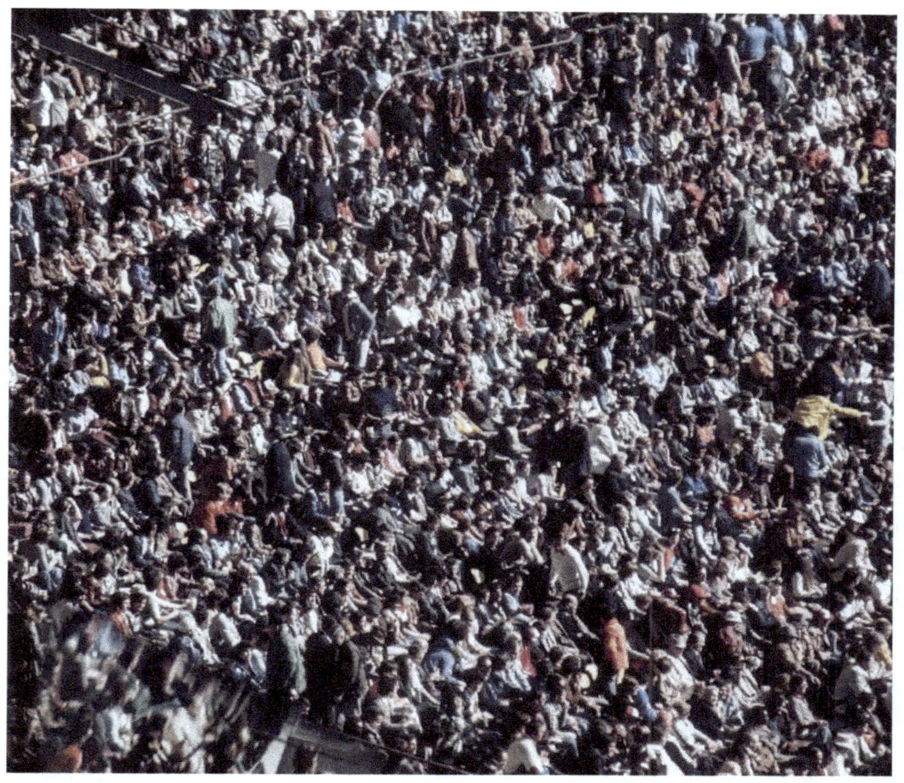

There is neither Jew nor Greek, slave nor free, male nor female, for you are all one in Christ Jesus.

Bible reference: Galatians 3:28

Context: Sons of God

Illustration ID (credit): fy_65 (author)

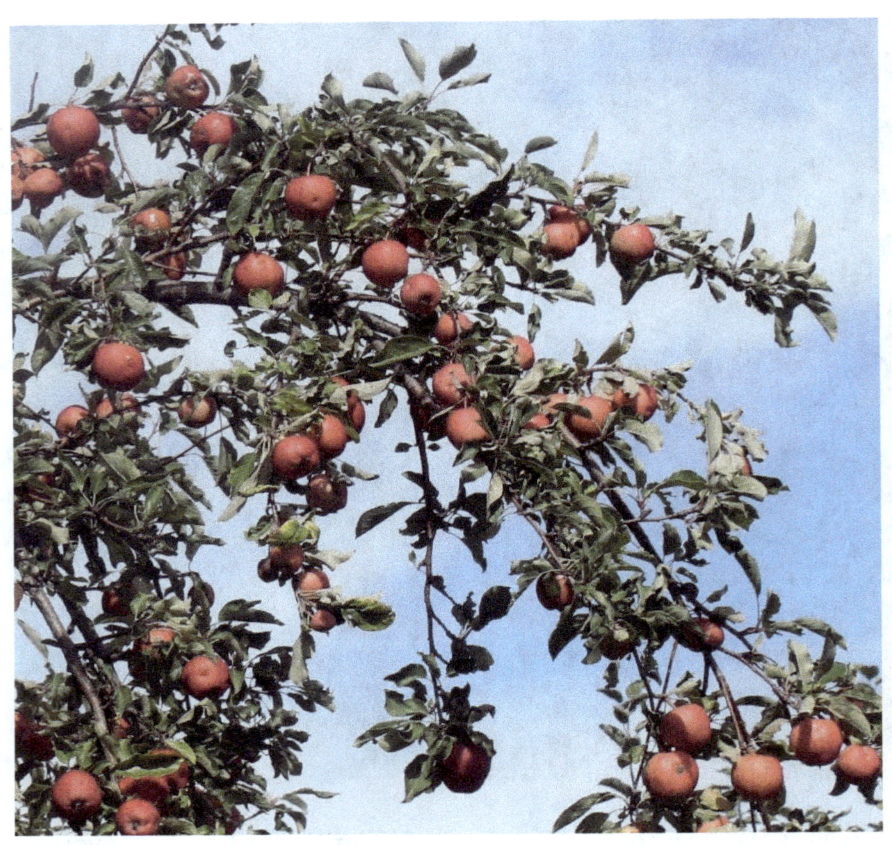

But the fruit of the Spirit is love, joy, peace, patience, kindness, goodness, faithfulness, gentleness and self-control. Against such things there is no law.

Bible reference: Galatians 5:22-23

Context: Hagar and Sarah

Illustration ID (credit): fy_13 (author)

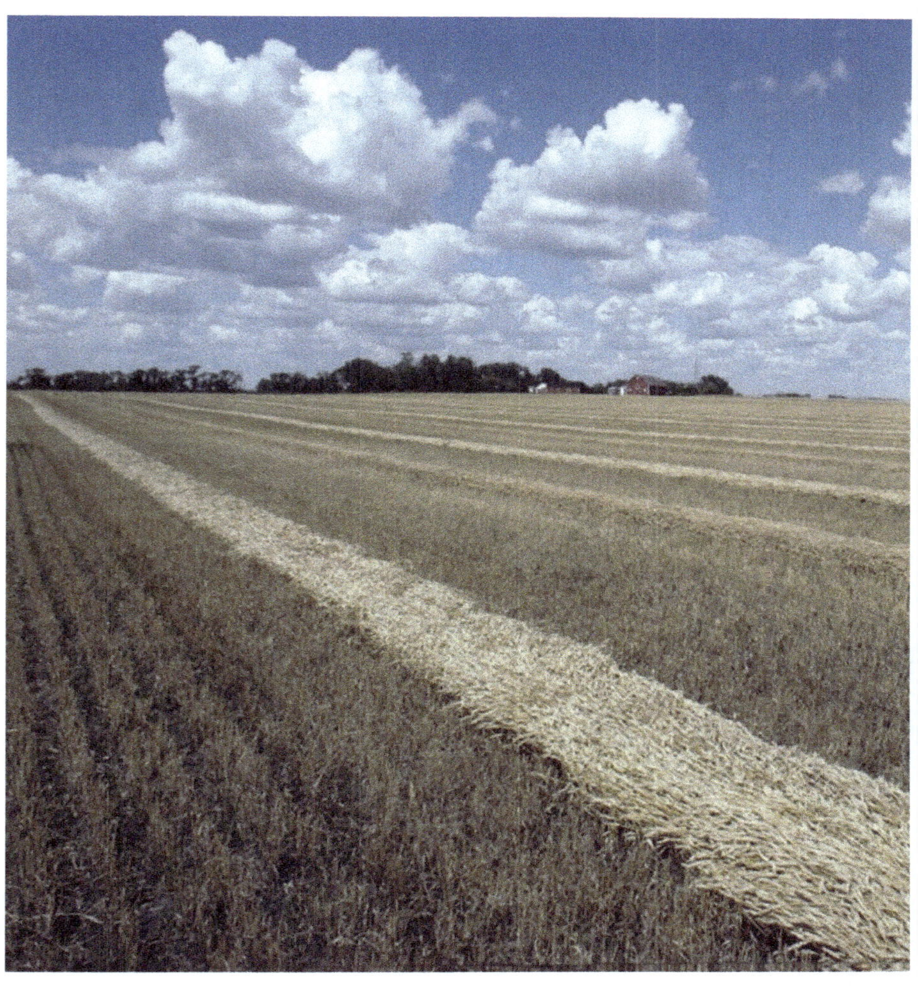

Do not be deceived: God cannot be mocked. A man reaps what he sows.

Bible reference: Galatians 6:7

Context: Doing Good to All

Illustration ID (credit): fv_011 (author)

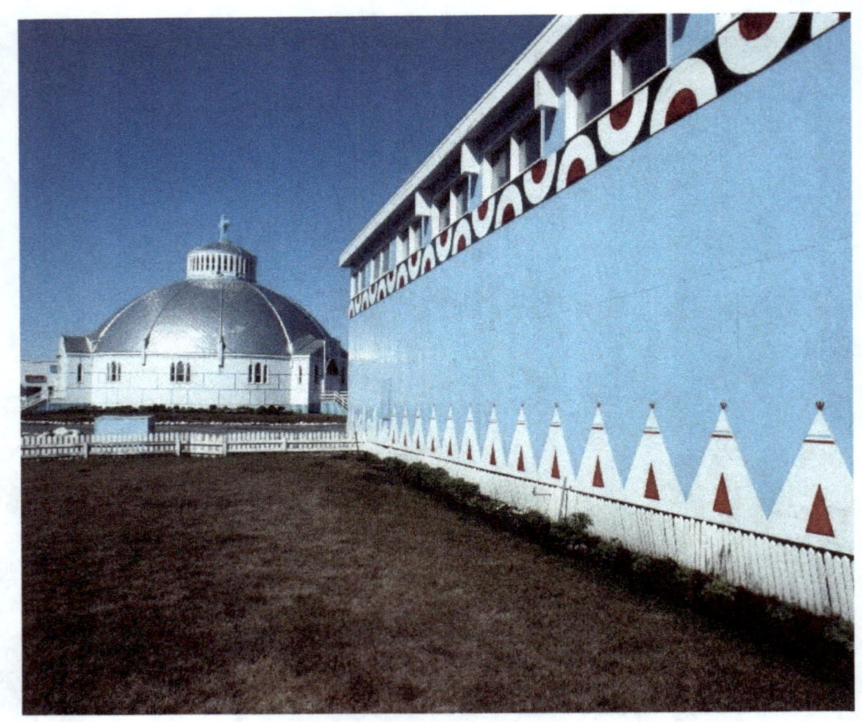

Now to him who is able to do immeasurably more than all we ask or imagine, according to his power that is at work within us, to him be glory in the church and in Christ Jesus throughout all generations, for ever and ever! Amen.

Bible reference: Ephesians 3:20-21

Context: A Prayer for the Ephesians

Illustration ID (credit): fy_84 (author)

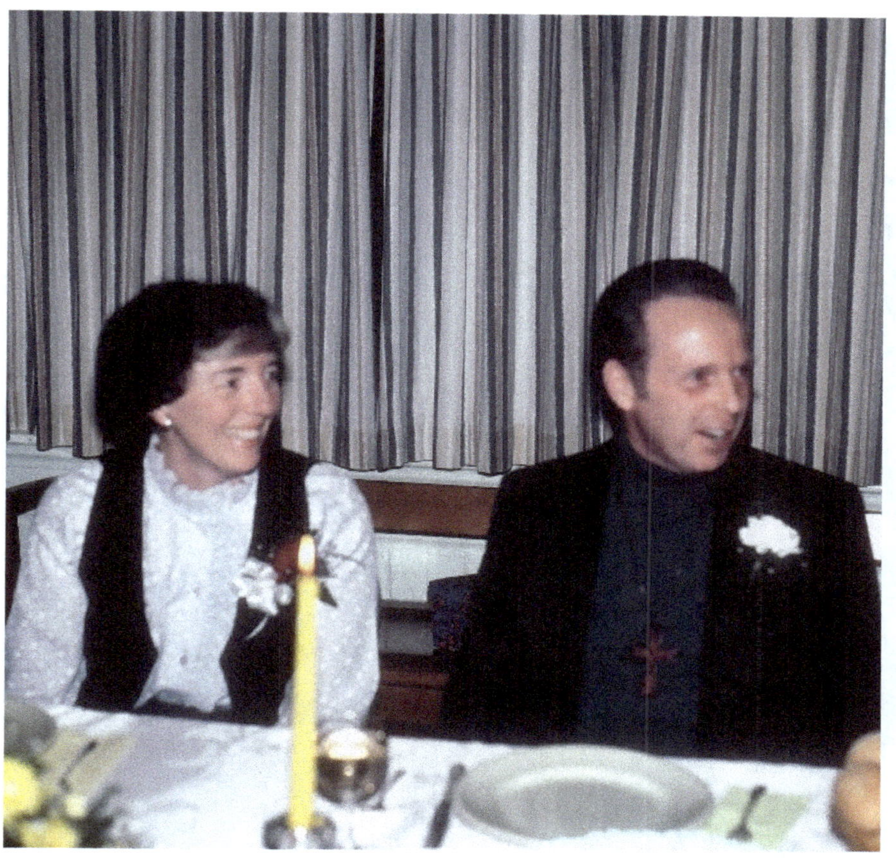

It was he who gave some to be apostles, some to be prophets, some to be evangelists, and some to be pastors and teachers, to prepare God's people for works of service, so that the body of Christ may be built up

Bible reference: Ephesians 4:11-12

Context: Unity in the Body of Christ

Illustration ID (credit): fs_363 (author)

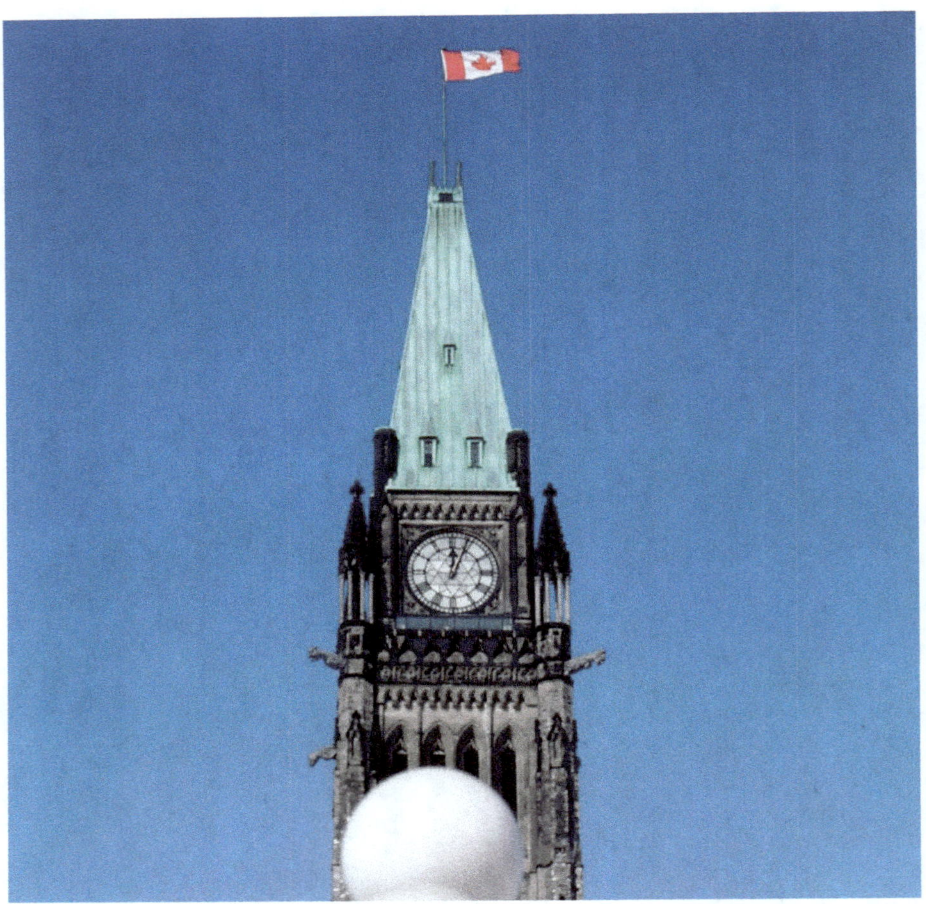

For our struggle is not against flesh and blood, but against the rulers, against the authorities, against the powers of this dark world and against the spiritual forces of evil in the heavenly realms.

Bible reference: Ephesians 6:12

Context: The Armor of God

Illustration ID (credit): fa_49 (author)

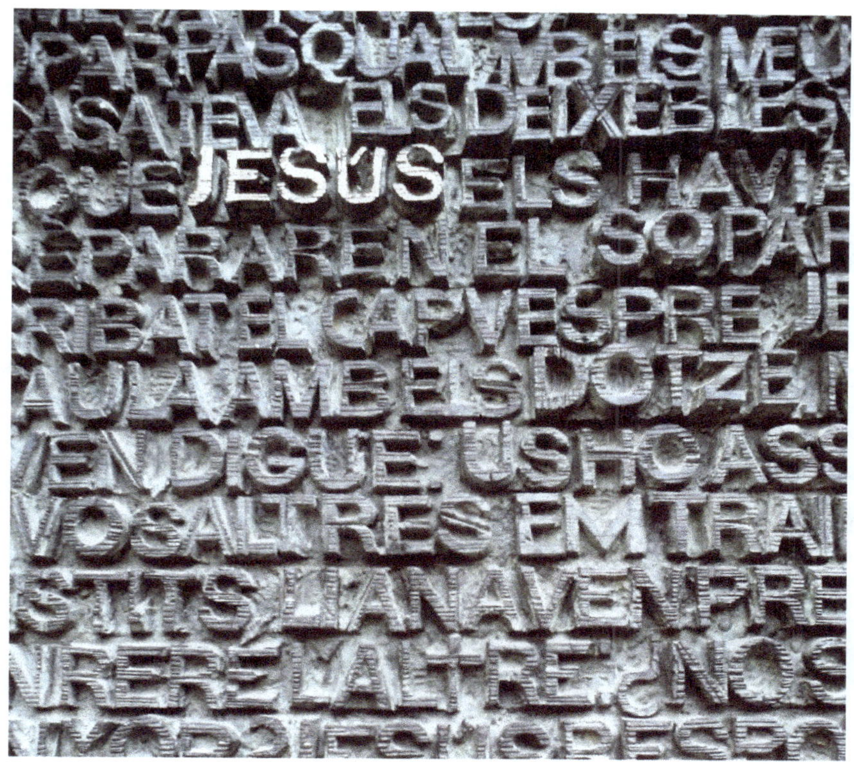

Therefore God exalted Him to the highest place and gave Him the name above all names, that at the name of Jesus every knee should bow, in heaven and on earth and under the earth, and every tongue confess that Jesus Christ is Lord

Bible reference: Phil 2:9-11

Context: Imitating Christ's Humility

Illustration ID (credit): fa_200 (author)

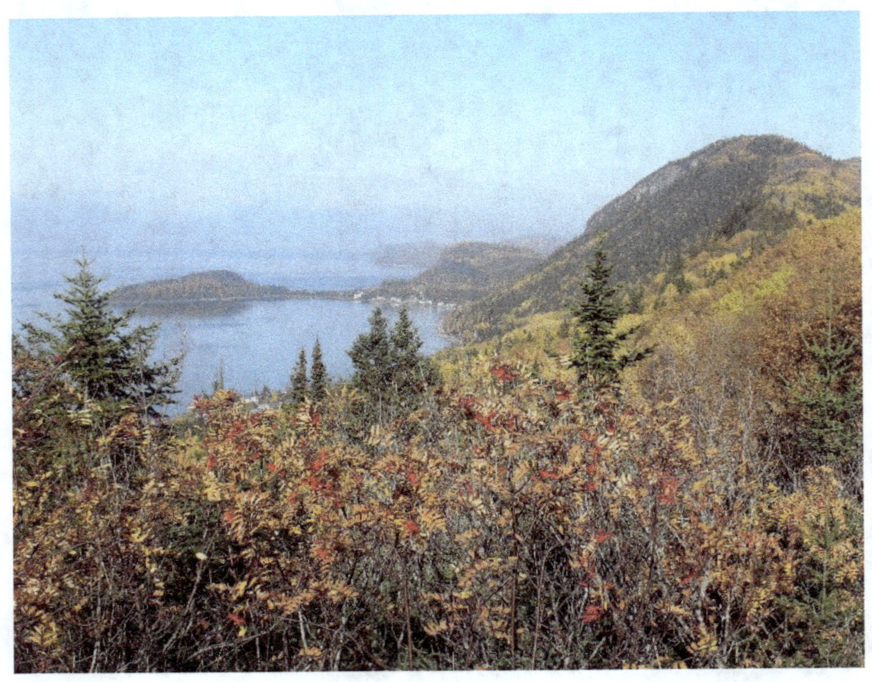

Finally, brothers, whatever is true, whatever is noble, whatever is right, whatever is pure, whatever is lovely, whatever is admirable — if anything is excellent or praiseworthy — think about such things.

Bible reference: Philippians 4:8

Context: Exhortations

Illustration ID (credit): fx_3531 (author)

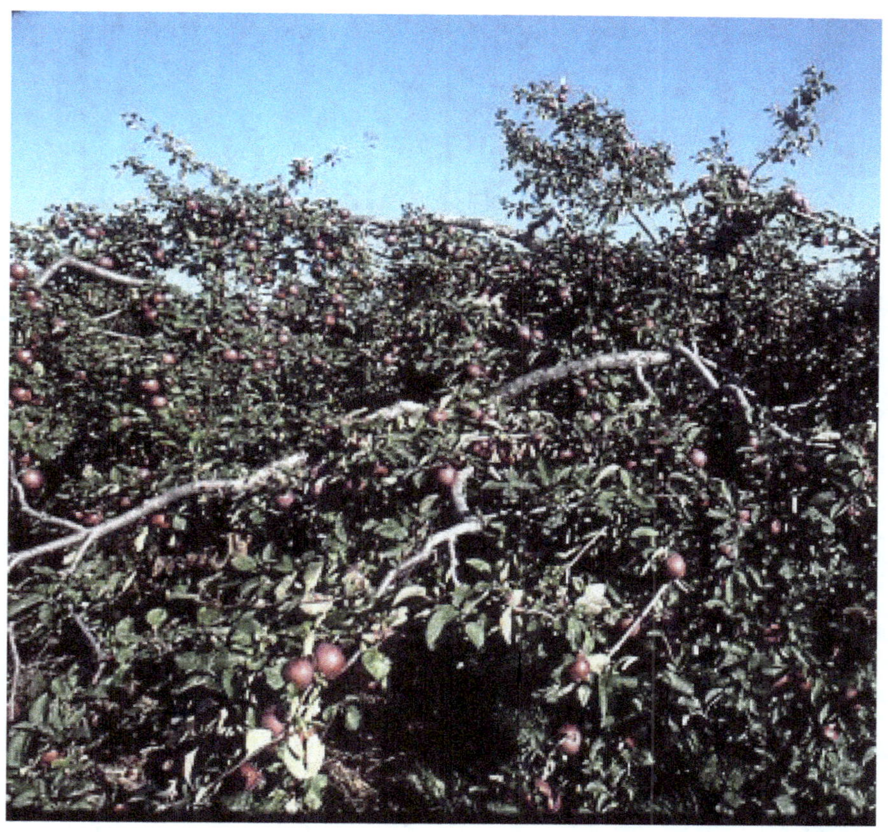

And we pray this in order that you may live a life worthy of the Lord and may please him in every way: bearing fruit in every good work, growing in the knowledge of God,

Bible reference: Colossians 1:10

Context: Thanksgiving and Prayer

Illustration ID (credit): fv_021 (author)

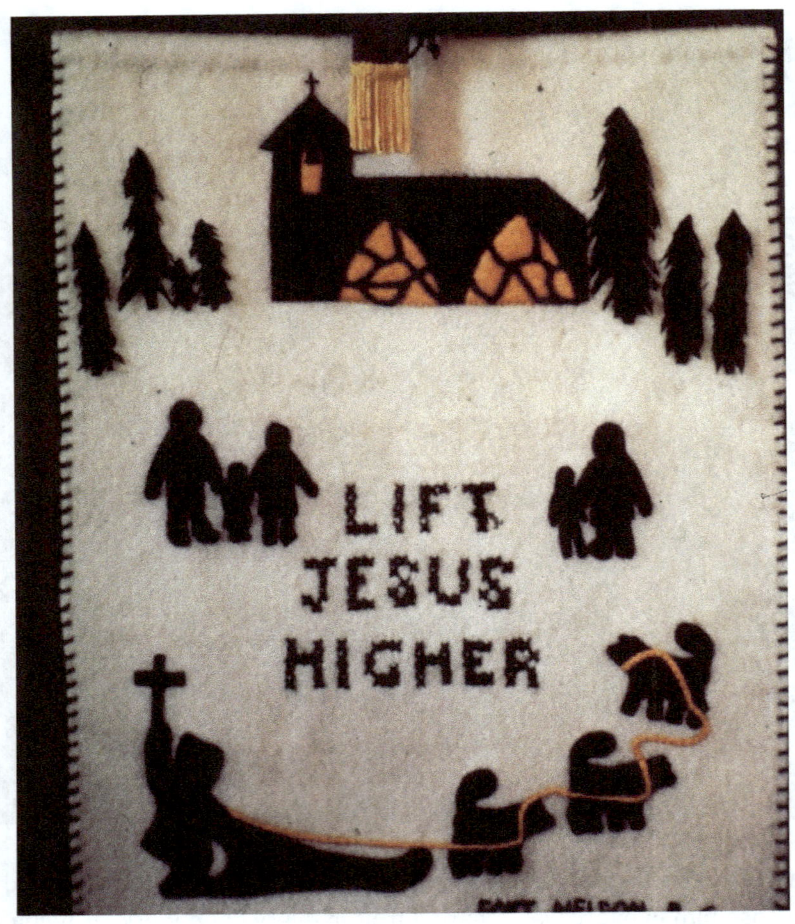

And whatever you do, whether in word or deed, do it all in the name of the Lord Jesus, giving thanks to God the Father through him.

Bible reference: Colossians 3:17

Context: Rules for Holy Living

Illustration ID (credit): fs_351 (author)

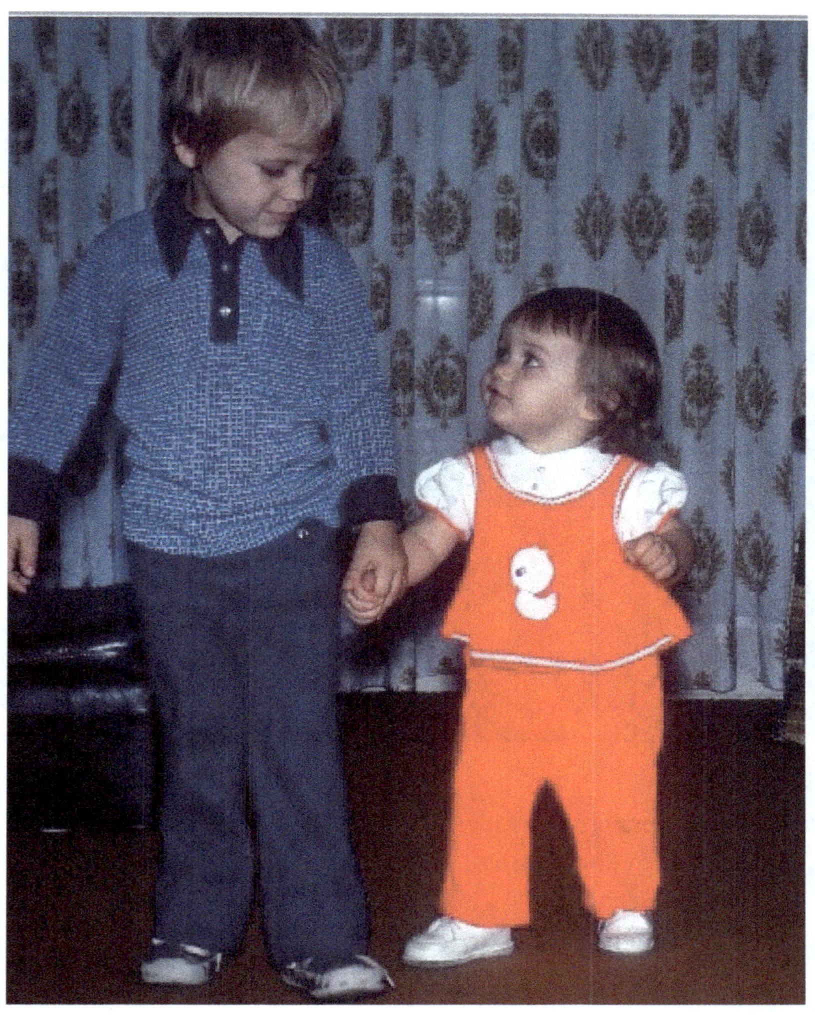

Therefore encourage one another and build each other up . . .

Bible reference: 1 Thessalonians 5:11a

Context: The Coming of the Lord

Illustration ID (credit): fx_ccfelf (author)

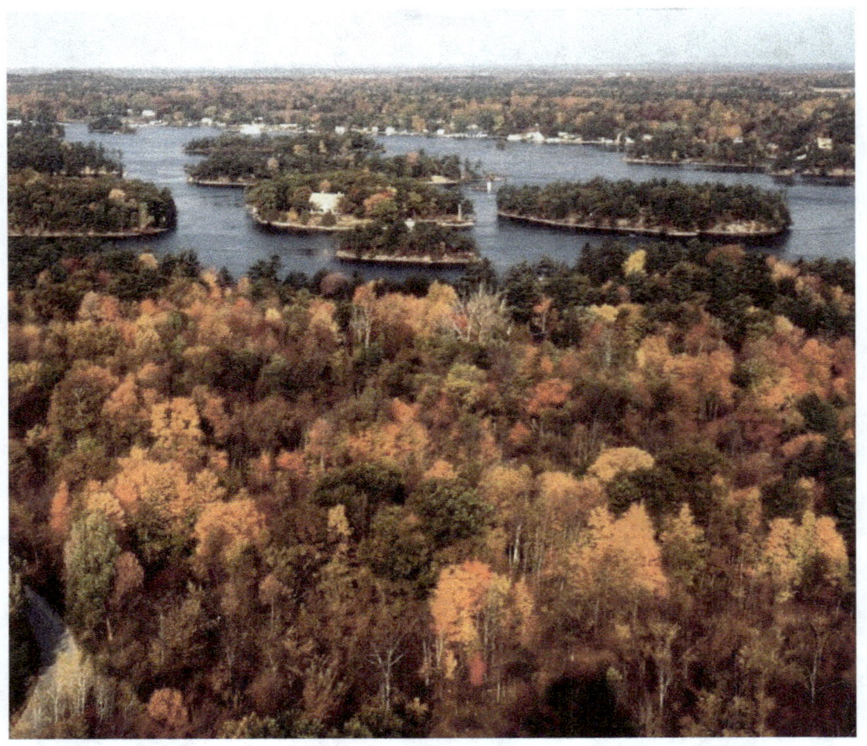

Be joyful always; pray continually; give thanks in all circumstances, for this is God's will for you in Christ Jesus.

Bible reference: 1 Thessalonians 5:16-18

Context: Final Instructions

Illustration ID (credit): fx_1026 (author)

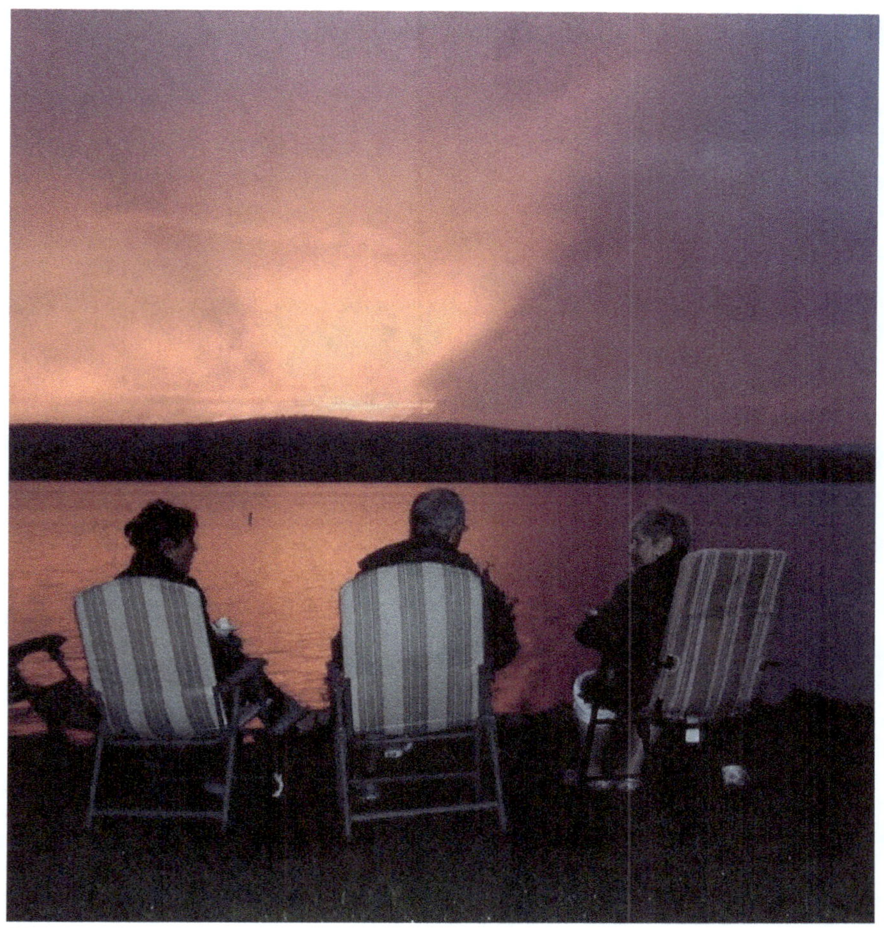

Now may the Lord of peace himself give you peace at all times and in every way. The Lord be with all of you.

Bible reference: 2 Thessalonians 3:16

Context: Final Greetings

Illustration ID (credit): fx_8837 (author)

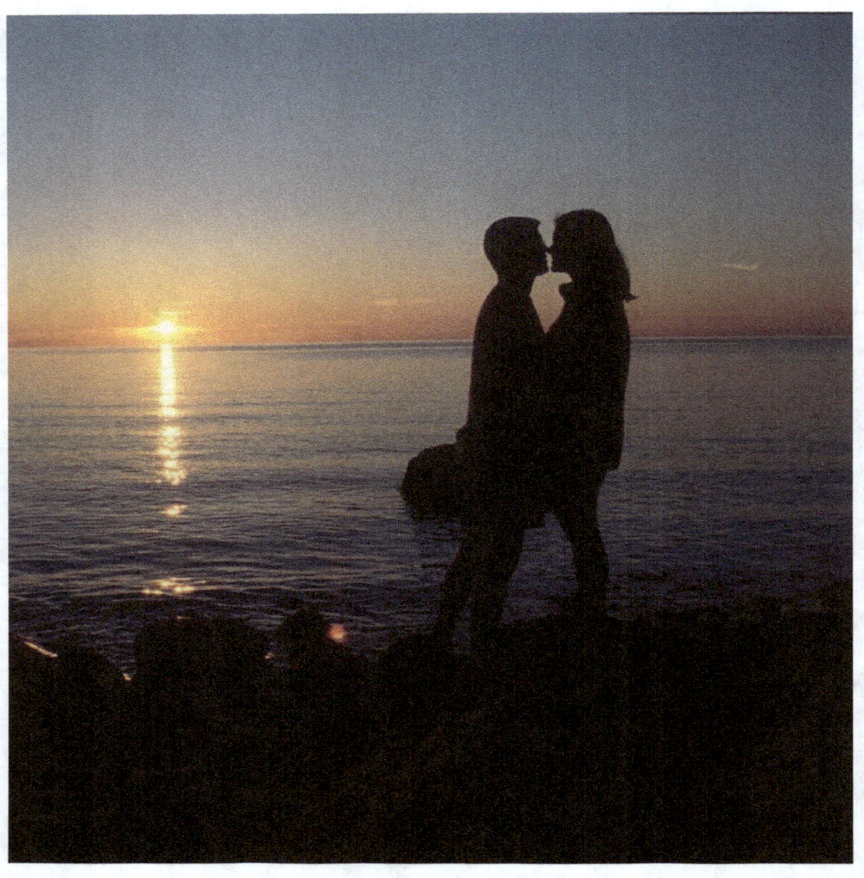

Don't let anyone look down on you because you are young, but set an example for the believers in speech, in life, in love, in faith and in purity.

Bible reference: 1 Timothy 4:12

Context: Instructions to Timothy

Illustration ID (credit): fs_348 (author)

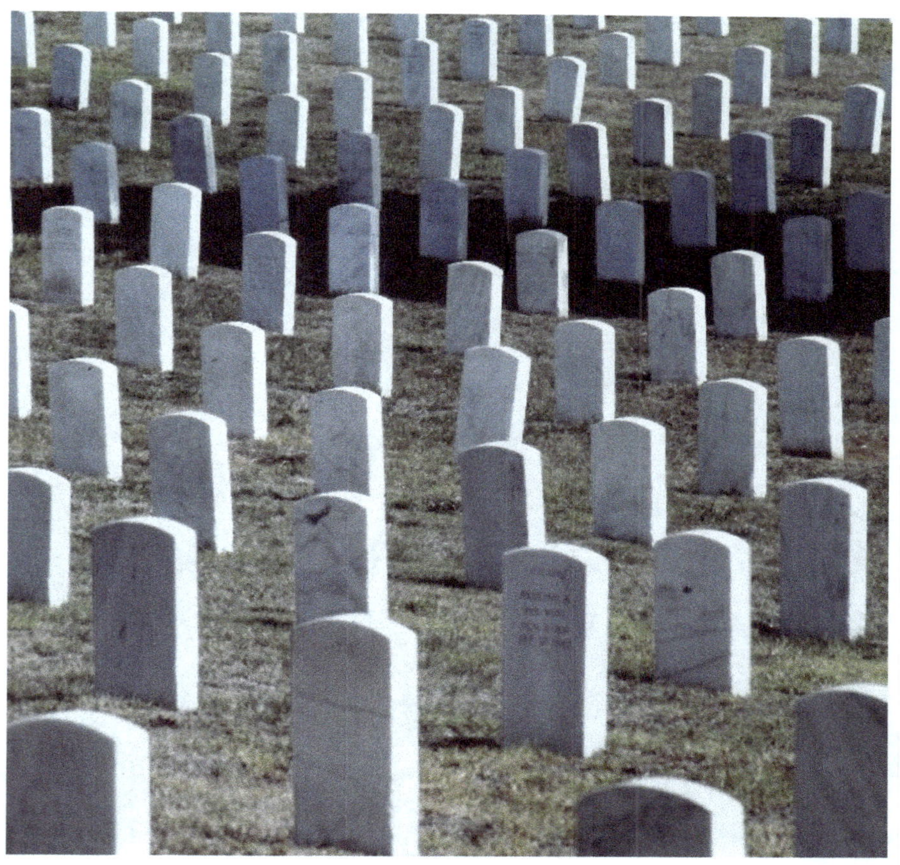

For we brought nothing into the world, and we can take nothing out of it.

Bible reference: 1 Timothy 6:7

Context: Love of Money

Illustration ID (credit): fv_022 (author)

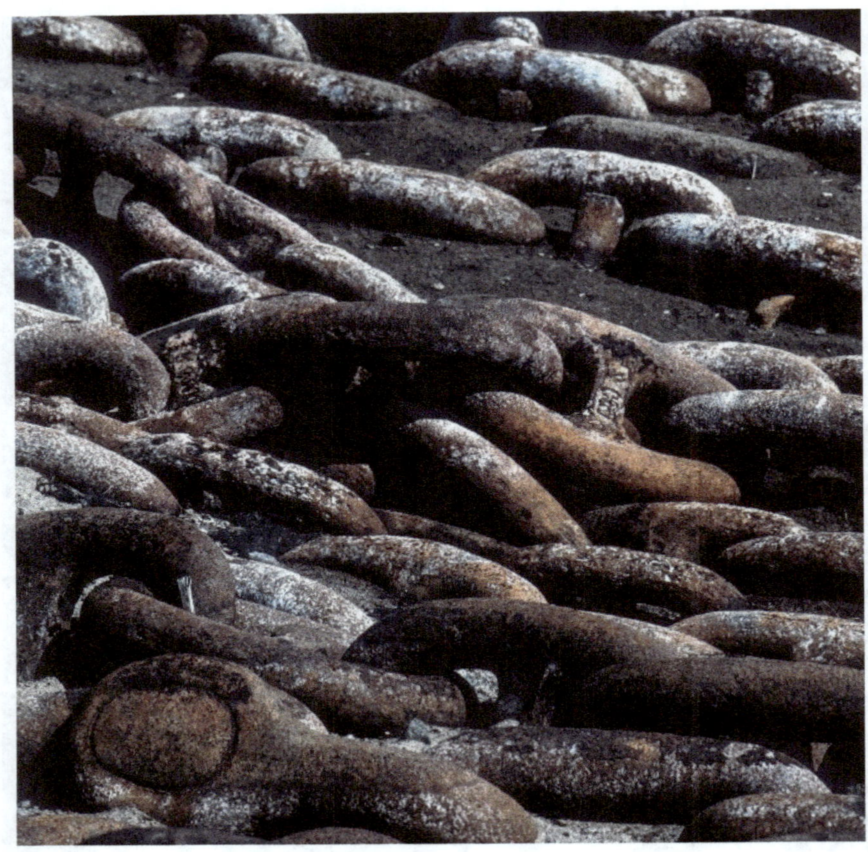

Remember Jesus Christ, raised from the dead, descended from David. This is my gospel, for which I am suffering even to the point of being chained like a criminal. But God's word is not chained.

Bible reference: 2 Timothy 2:8-9

Context: Encouragement to Be Faithful

Illustration ID (credit): fy_76 (author)

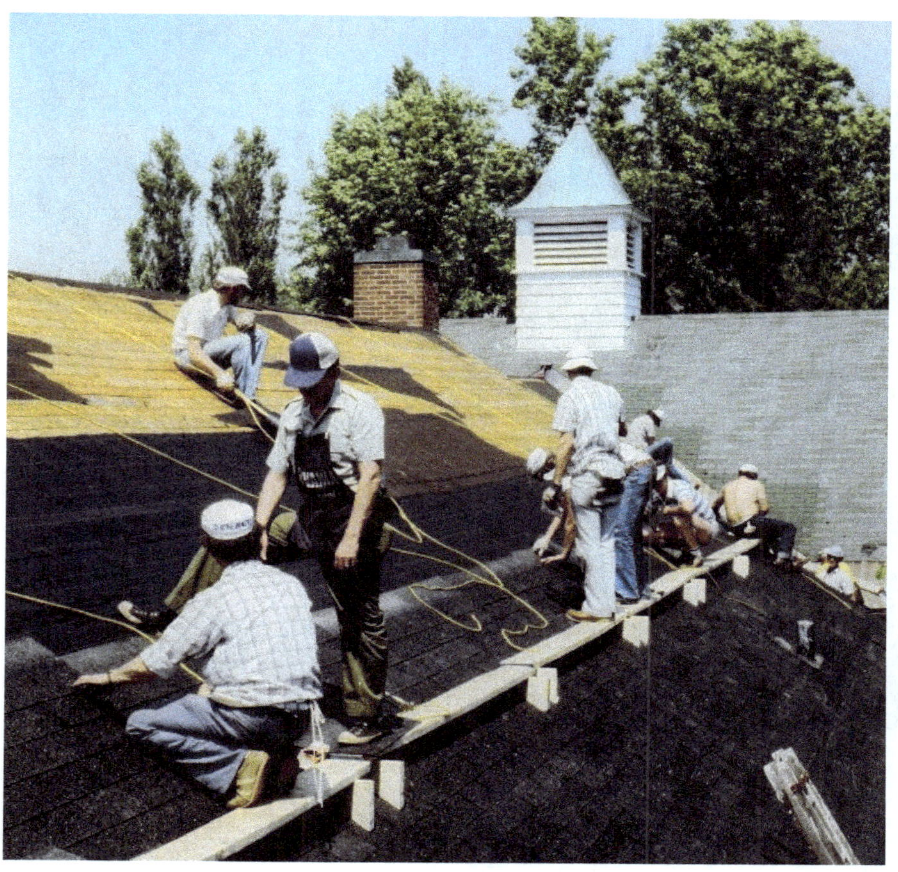

Do your best to present yourself to God as one approved, a workman who does not need to be ashamed and who correctly handles the word of truth.

Bible reference: 2 Timothy 2:15

Context: A Workman Approved by God

Illustration ID (credit): fy_04 (author)

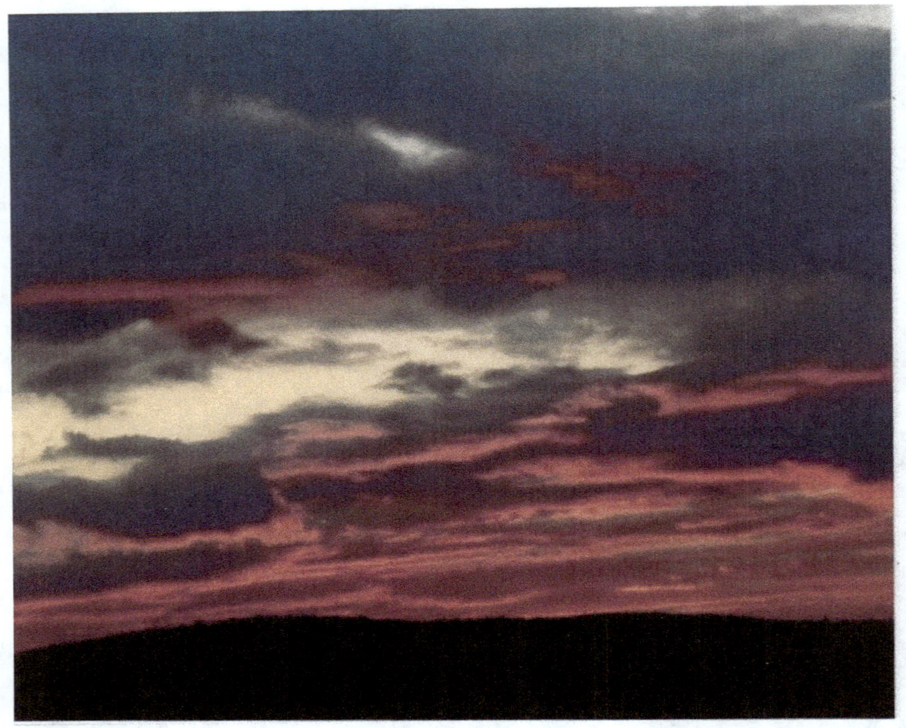

. . . he saved us, not because of righteous things we had done, but because of his mercy. He saved us through the washing of rebirth and renewal by the Holy Spirit,

Bible reference: Titus 3:5

Context: Doing What Is Good

Illustration ID (credit): fx_1000 (author)

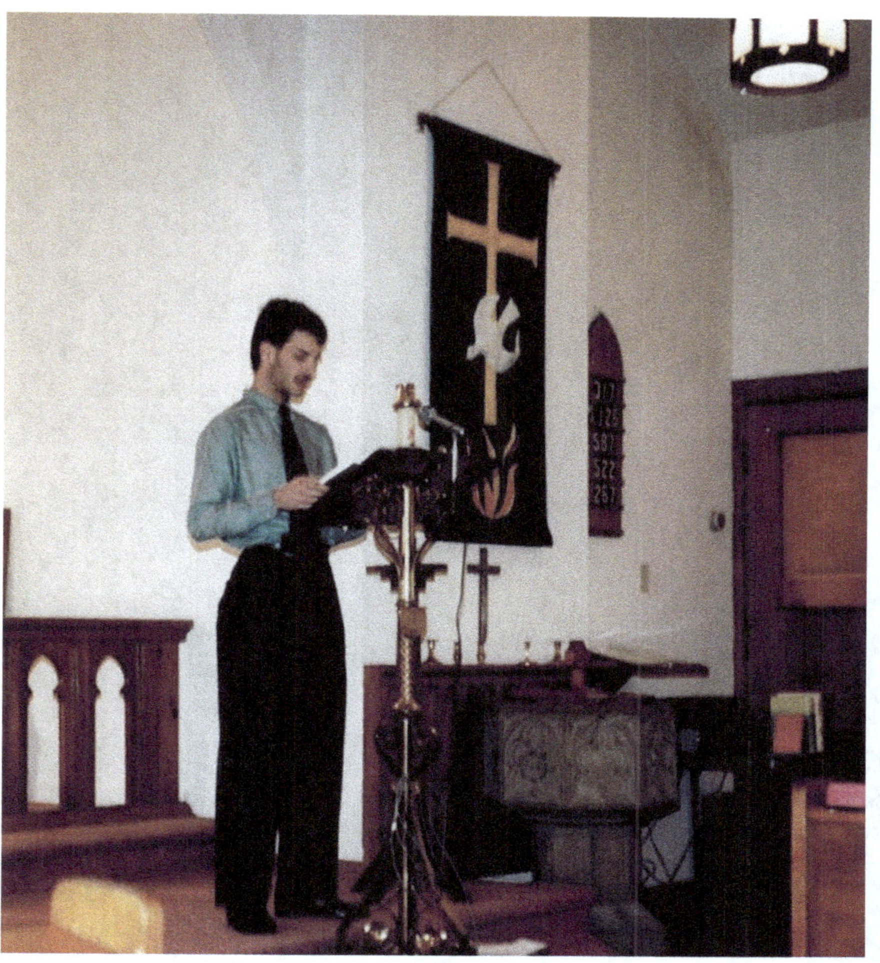

I pray that you may be active in sharing your faith, so that you will have a full understanding of every good thing we have in Christ.

Bible reference: Philemon 1:6

Context: Thanksgiving and Prayer

Illustration ID (credit): fc_1103 (author)

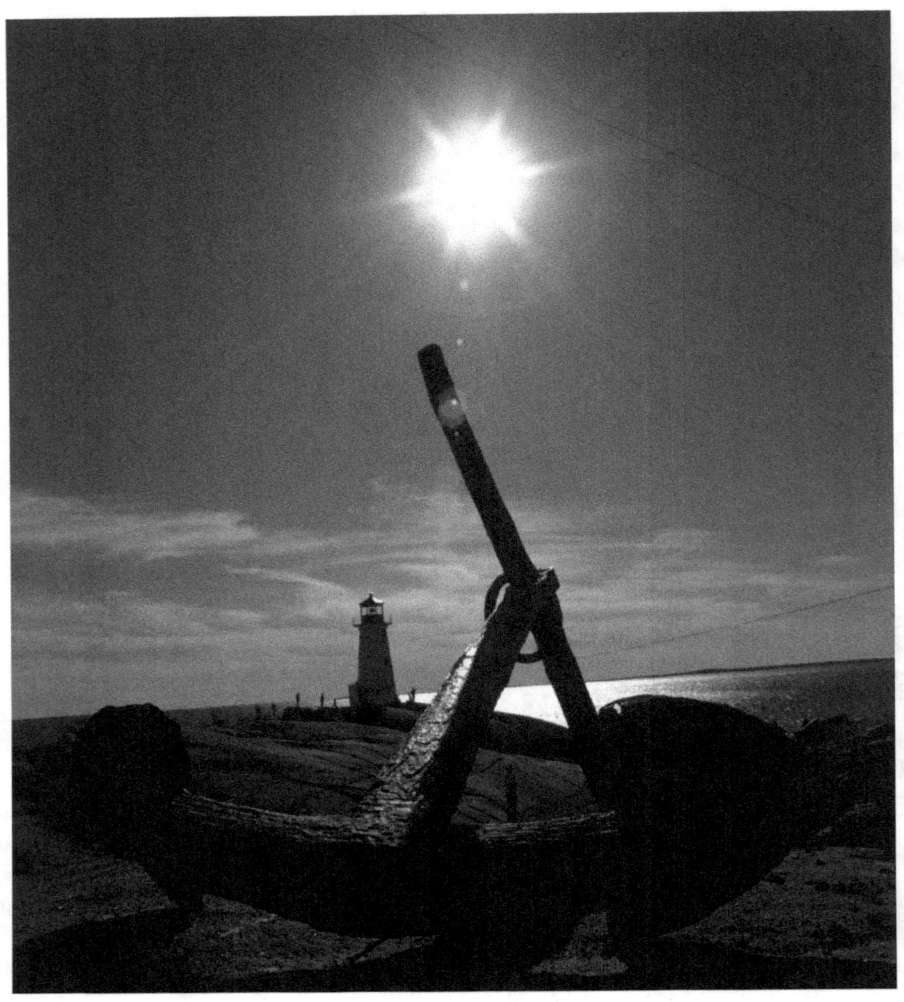

We have this hope as an anchor for the soul, firm and secure.

Bible reference: Hebrews 6:19

Context: The Certainty of God's Promise

Illustration ID (credit): fa_15 (author)

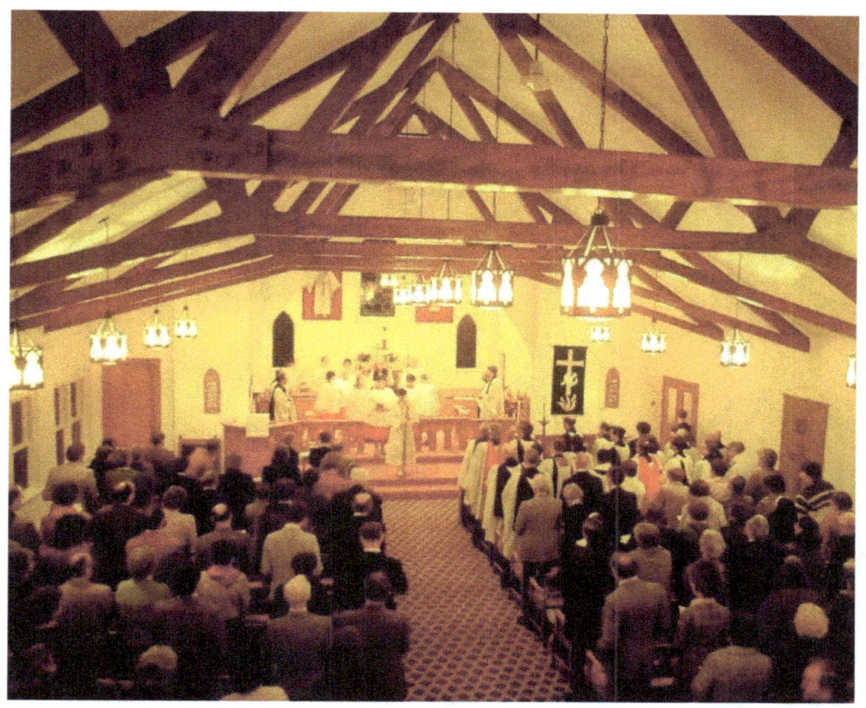

And let us consider how we may spur one another on toward love and good deeds. Let us not give up meeting together, as some are in the habit of doing, but let us encourage one another--and all the more as you see the Day approaching.

Bible reference: Hebrews 10:24-25

Context: A Call to Persevere

Illustration ID (credit): fa_43 (author)

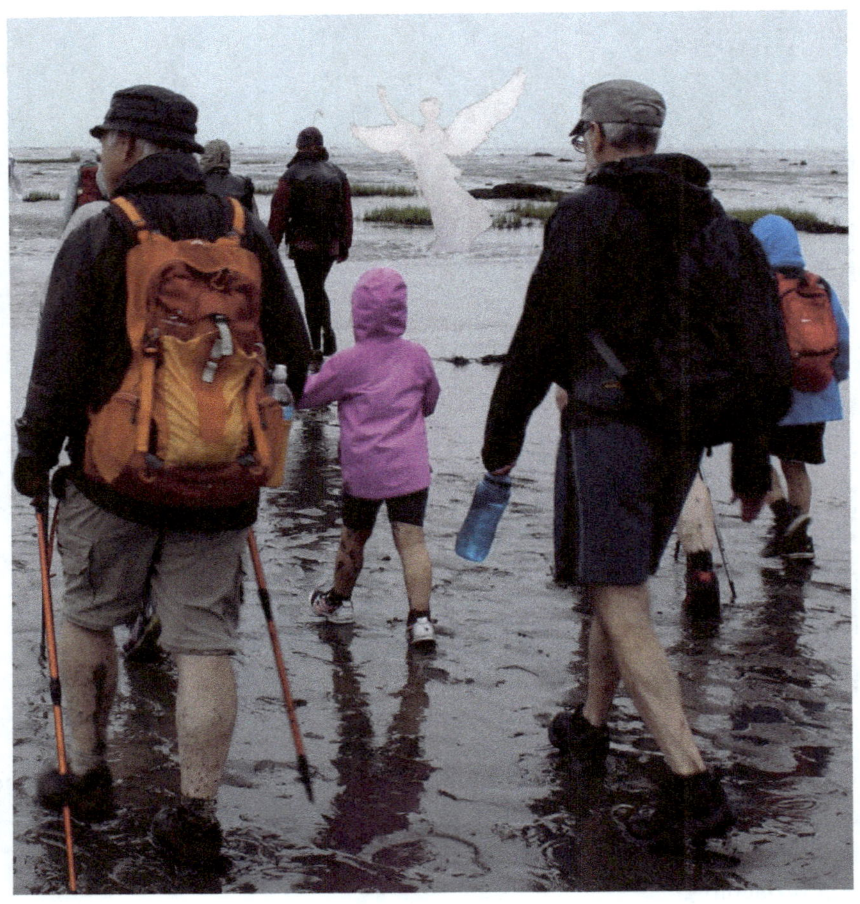

Do not forget to entertain strangers, for by so doing some people have entertained angels without knowing it.

Bible reference: Hebrews 13:2

Context: Concluding Exhortations

Illustration ID (credit): fs_444e (author, enhanced by Jim Fraser)

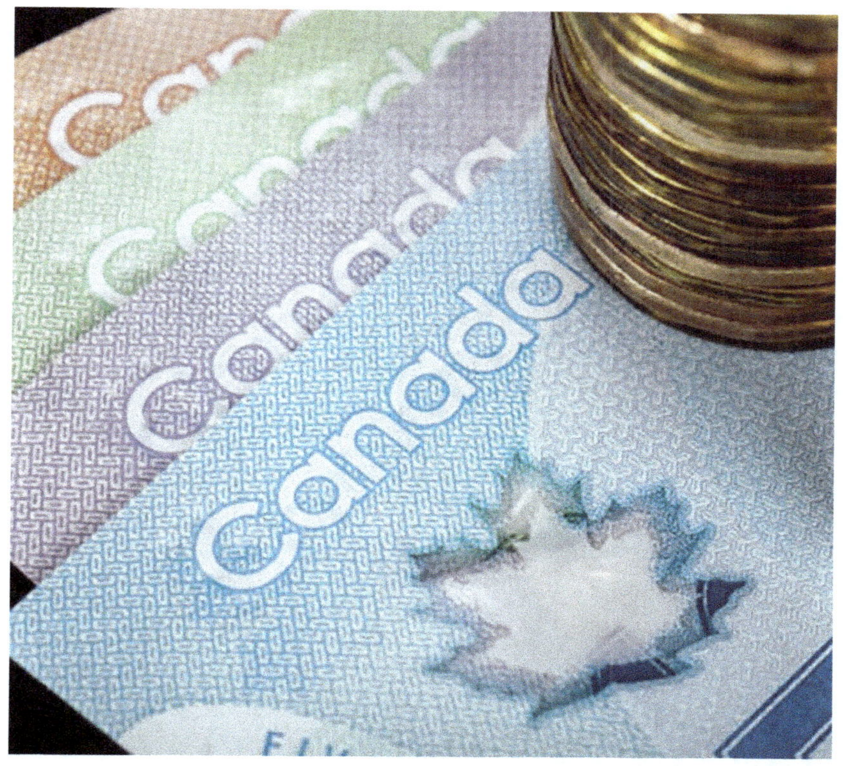

Keep your lives free from the love of money and be content with what you have, because God has said, "Never will I leave you; never will I forsake you."

Bible reference: Hebrews 13:5

Context: Concluding Exhortations

Illustration ID (credit): fs_777_1140 (istockphoto)

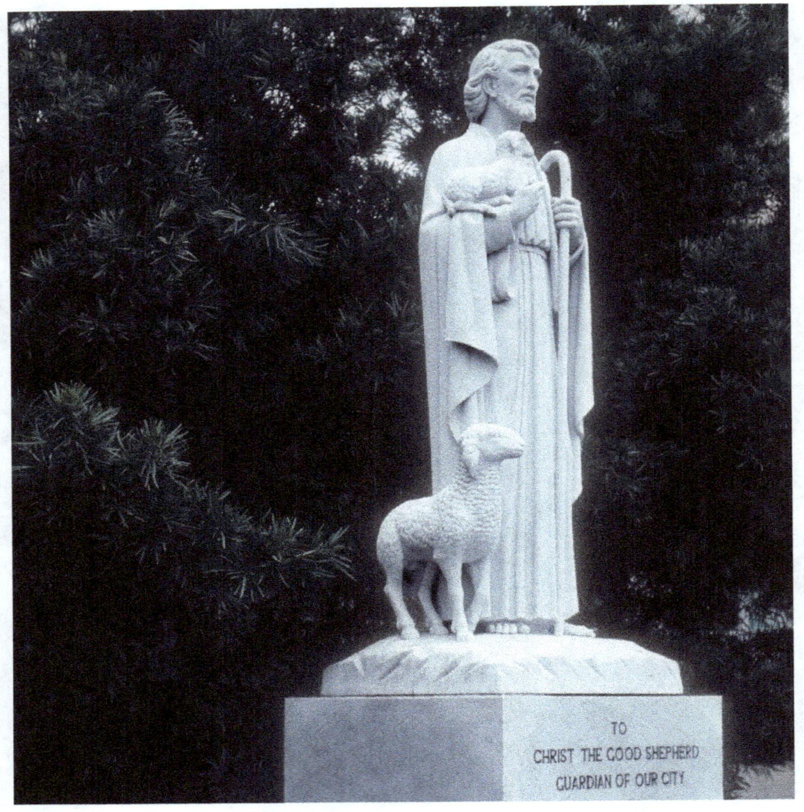

May the God of peace, who through the blood of the eternal covenant brought back from the dead our Lord Jesus, that great Shepherd of the sheep, equip you with everything good for doing his will, and may he work in us what is pleasing to him, through Jesus Christ, to whom be glory for ever and ever. Amen

Bible reference: Hebrews 13:20-21

Context: Concluding Exhortations

Illustration ID (credit): fs_347 (author)

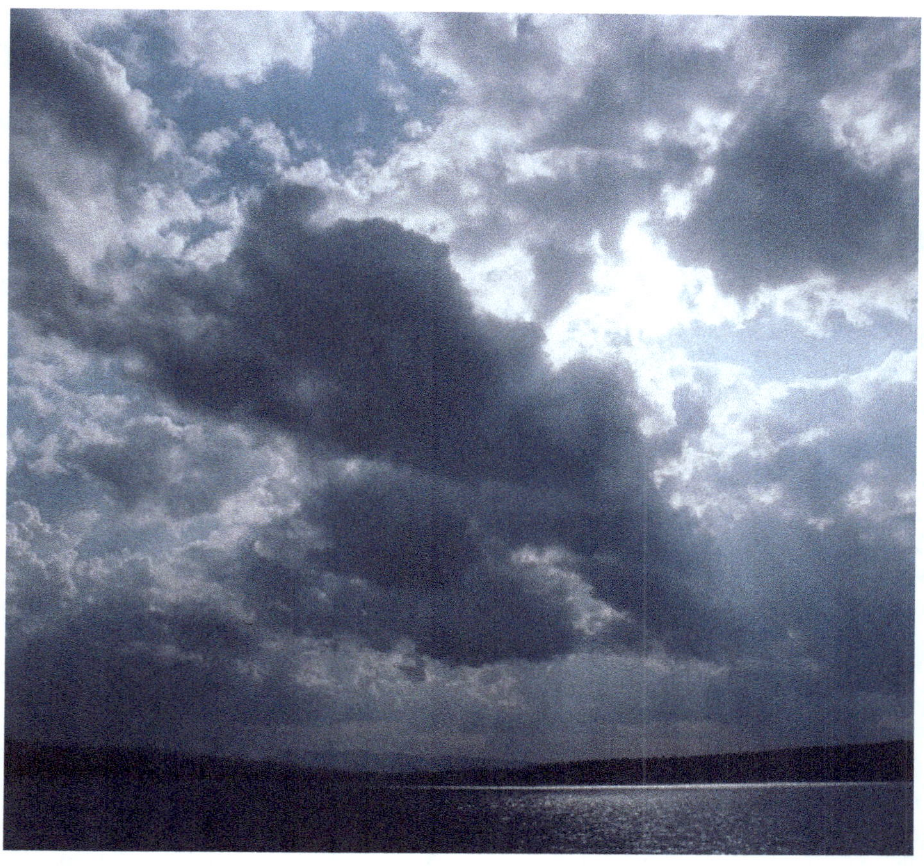

Consider it pure joy, my brothers, whenever you face trials of many kinds, because you know that the testing of your faith develops perseverance.

Bible reference: James 1:2-3

Context: Trials and Temptations

Illustration ID (credit): fy_07 (author)

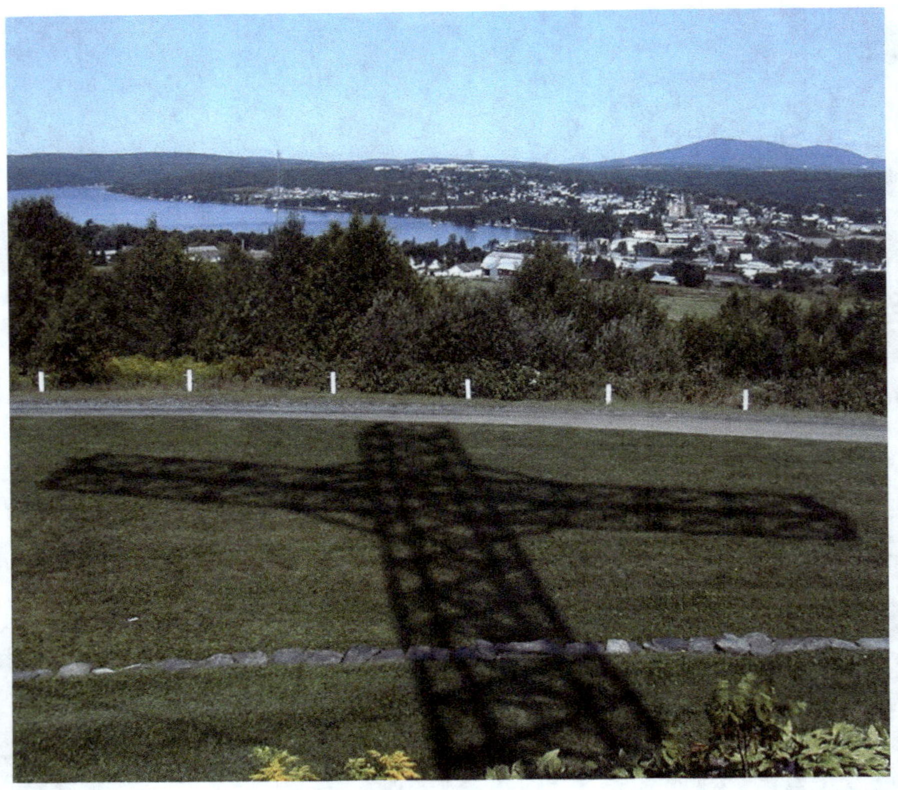

Every good and perfect gift is from above, coming down from the Father of the heavenly lights, who does not change like shifting shadows.

Bible reference: James 1:17

Context: Trials and Temptations

Illustration ID (credit): fx_7690 (author)

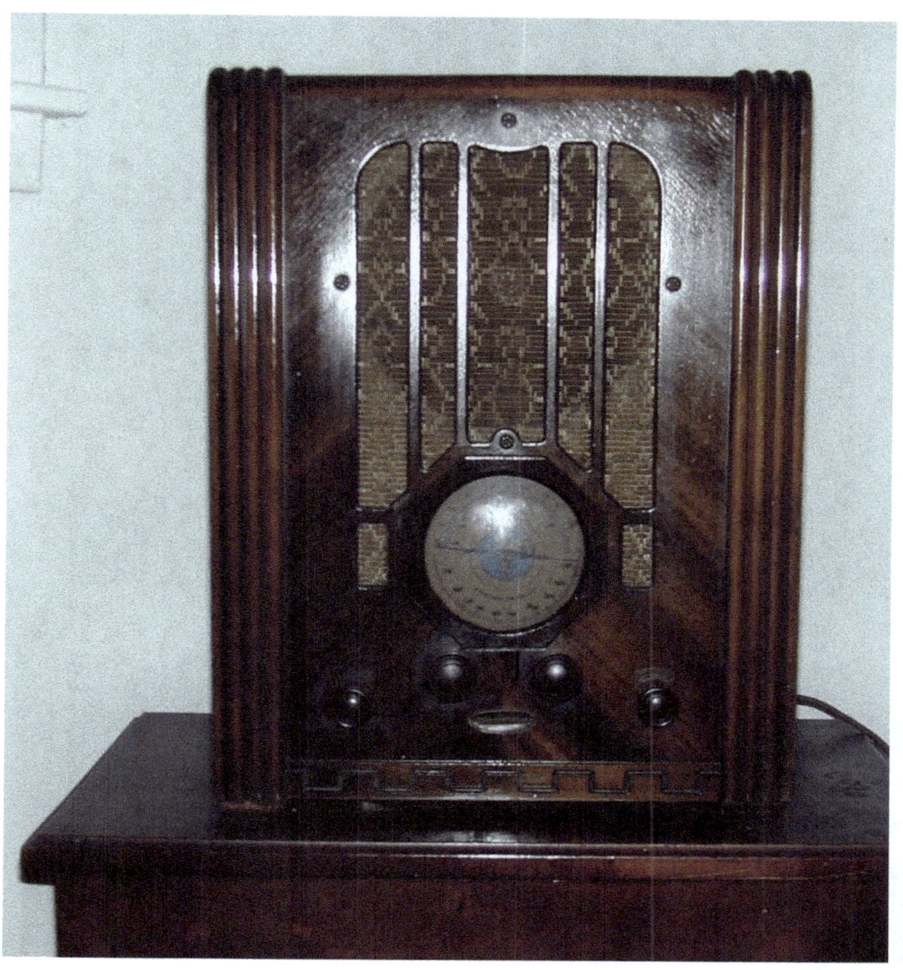

Do not merely listen to the word, and so deceive yourselves. Do what it says.

Bible reference: James 1:22

Context: Listening and Doing

Illustration ID (credit): fy_89 (author)

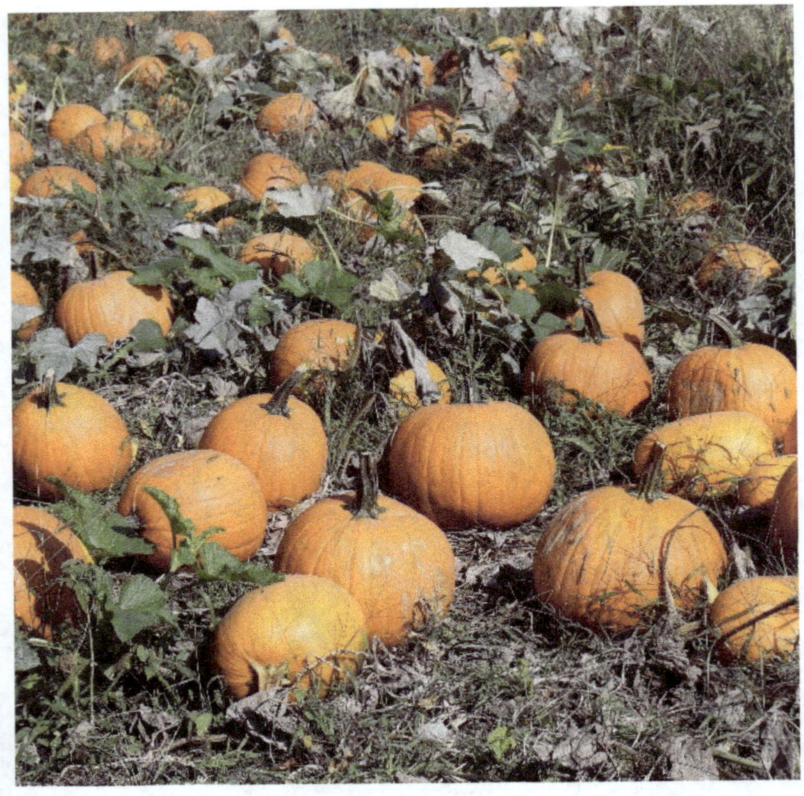

Peacemakers who sow in peace raise a harvest of righteousness.

Bible reference: James 3:18

Context: Two Kinds of Wisdom

Illustration ID (credit): fy_09 (author)

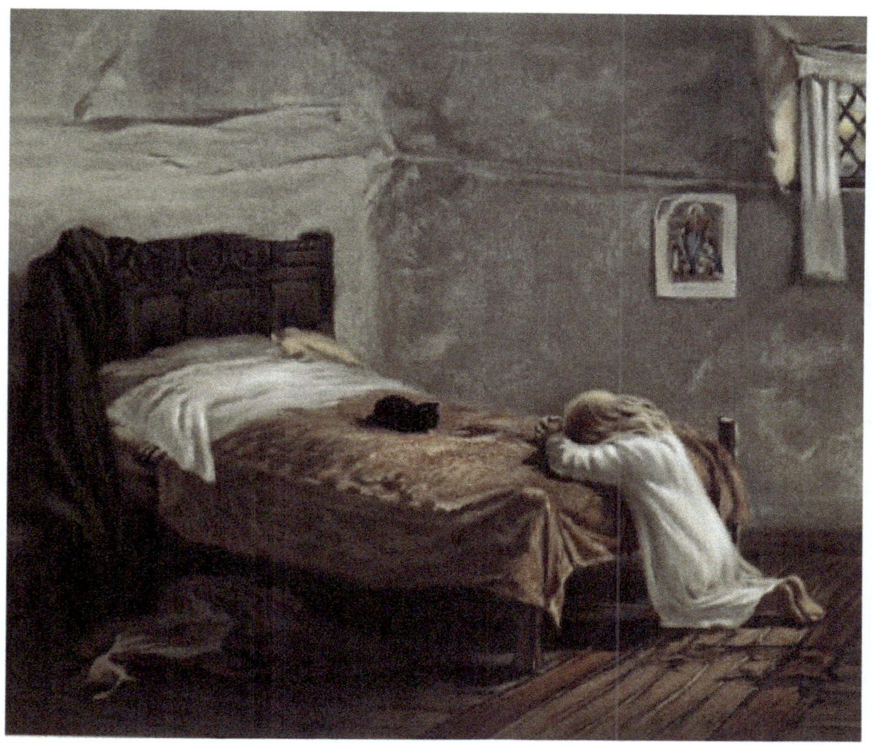

Therefore confess your sins to each other and pray for each other so that you may be healed. The prayer of a righteous man is powerful and effective.

Bible reference: James 5:16

Context: The Prayer of Faith

Illustration ID (credit): fx_318 (Humphrey family archive)

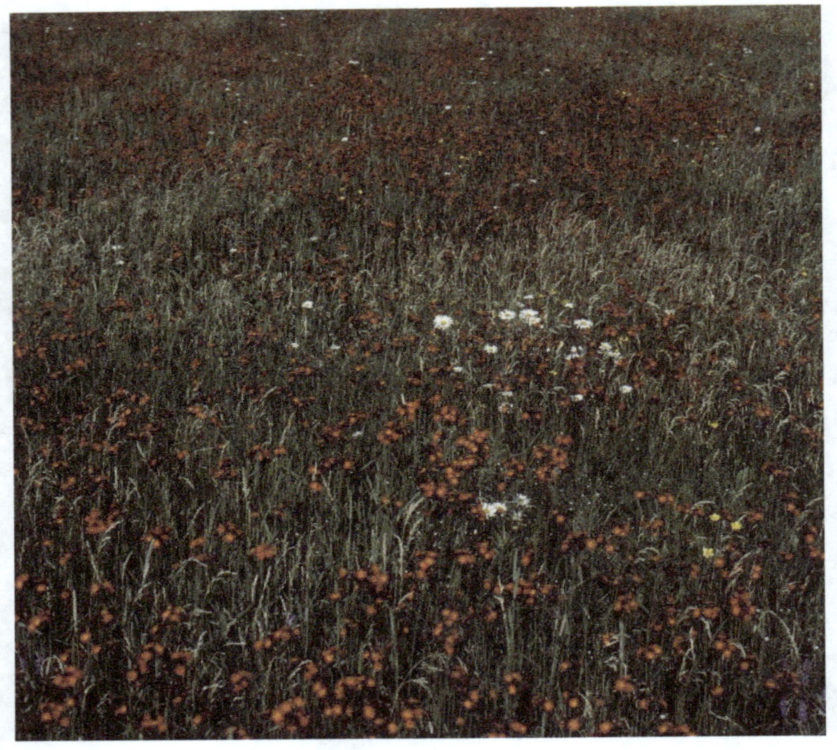

For, "All men are like grass and all their glory is like the flowers of the field; the grass withers and the flowers fall, but the word of the Lord stands forever."

Bible reference: 1 Peter 1:24-25

Context: Be Holy

Illustration ID (credit): fy_05 (author)

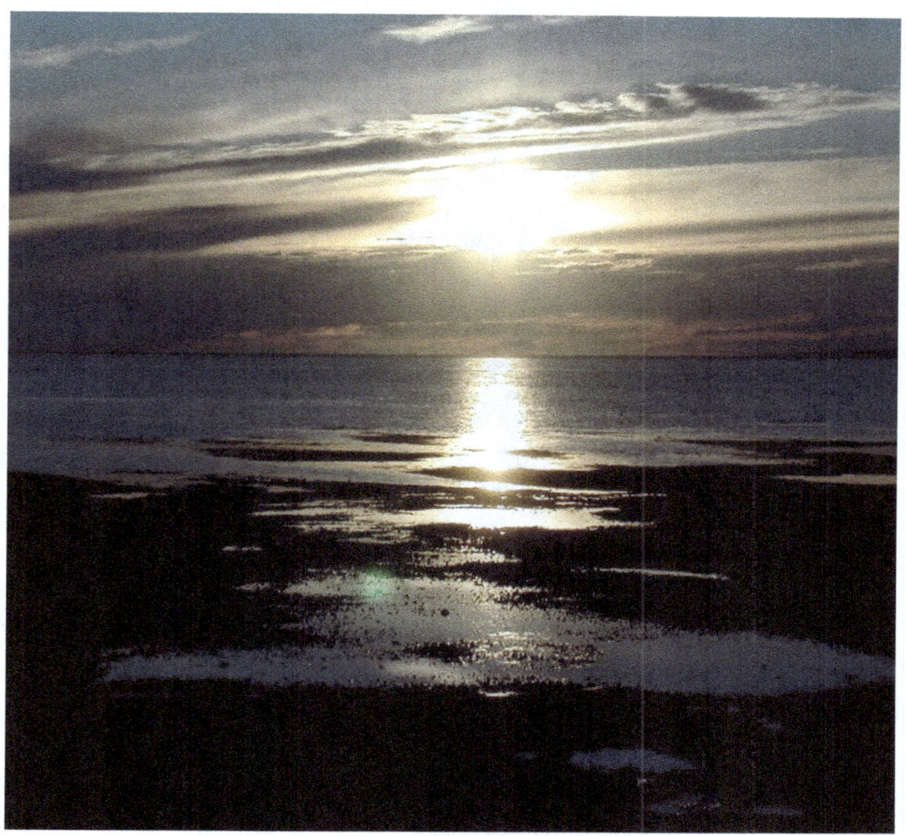

But you are a chosen people, a royal priesthood, a holy nation, a people belonging to God, that you may declare the praises of him who called you out of darkness into his wonderful light.

Bible reference: 1 Peter 2:9

Context: The Living Stone and a Chosen People

Illustration ID (credit): fx_0608 (author)

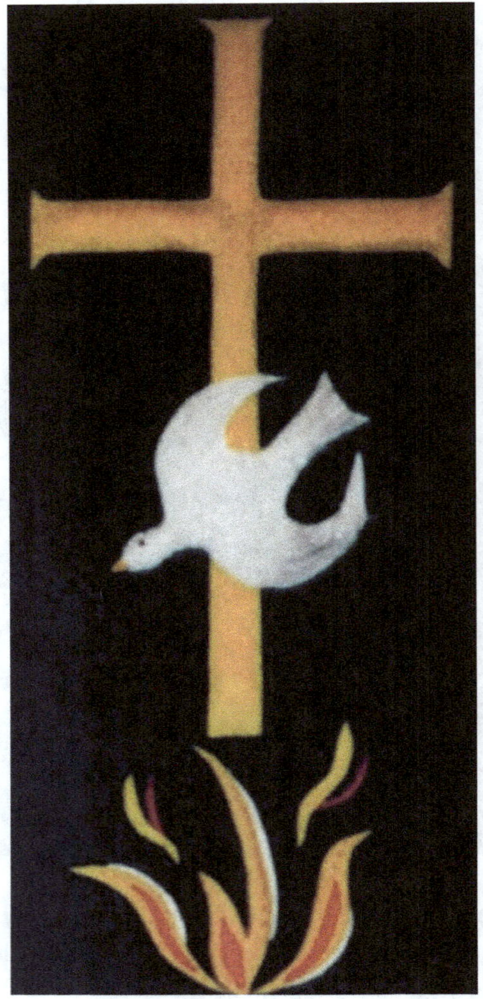

For prophecy never had its origin in the will of man, but men spoke from God as they were carried along by the Holy Spirit.

Bible reference: 2 Peter 1:21

Context: Prophecy of Scripture

Illustration ID (credit): fc_1104 (author)

How great is the love the Father has lavished on us, that we should be called children of God! And that is what we are! The reason the world does not know us is that it did not know him.

Bible reference: 1 John 3:1

Context: Children of God

Illustration ID (credit): fx_4931 (author)

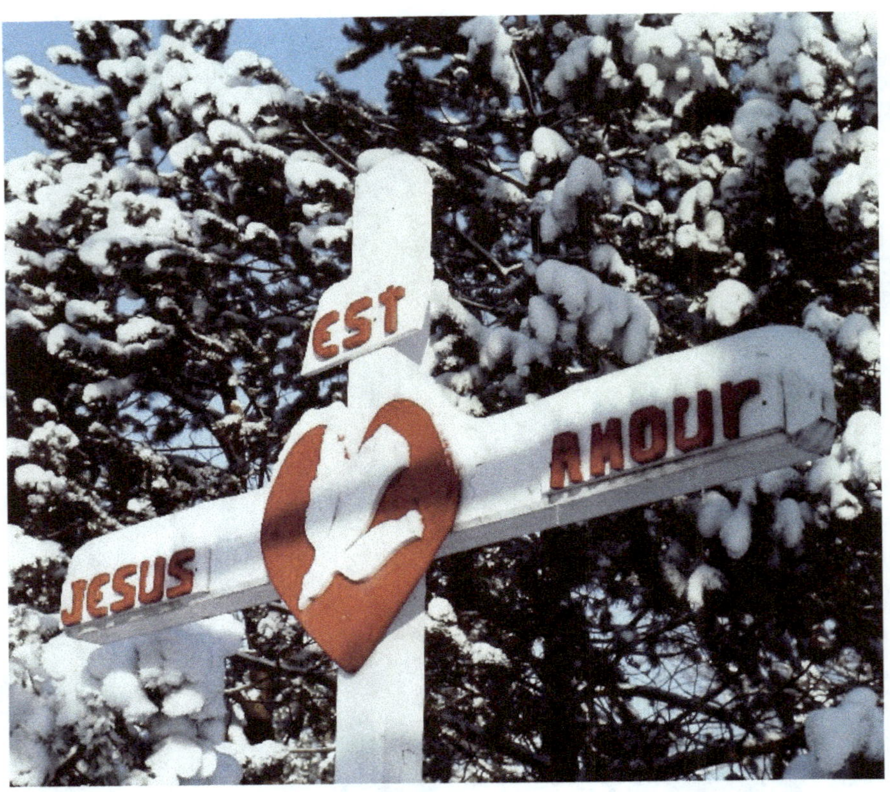

And so we know and rely on the love God has for us. God is love. Whoever lives in love lives in God, and God in him.

Bible reference: 1 John 4:16

Context: God's Love and Ours

Illustration ID (credit): fs_355 (author)

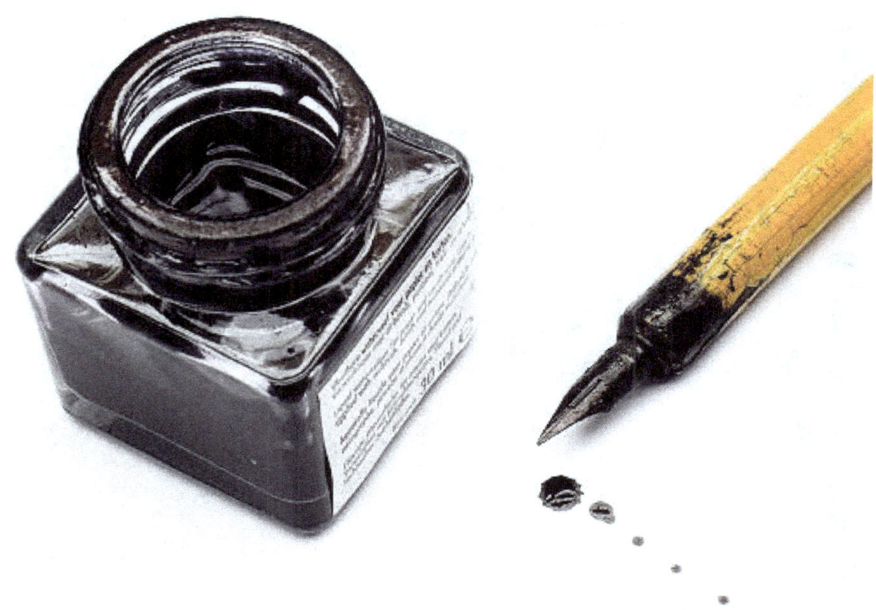

 I have much to write to you, but I do not want to use paper and ink. Instead, I hope to visit you and talk with you face to face, so that our joy may be complete.

Bible reference: 2 John 1:12

Context: (unspecified)

Illustration ID (credit): is_144334647 (istockphoto)

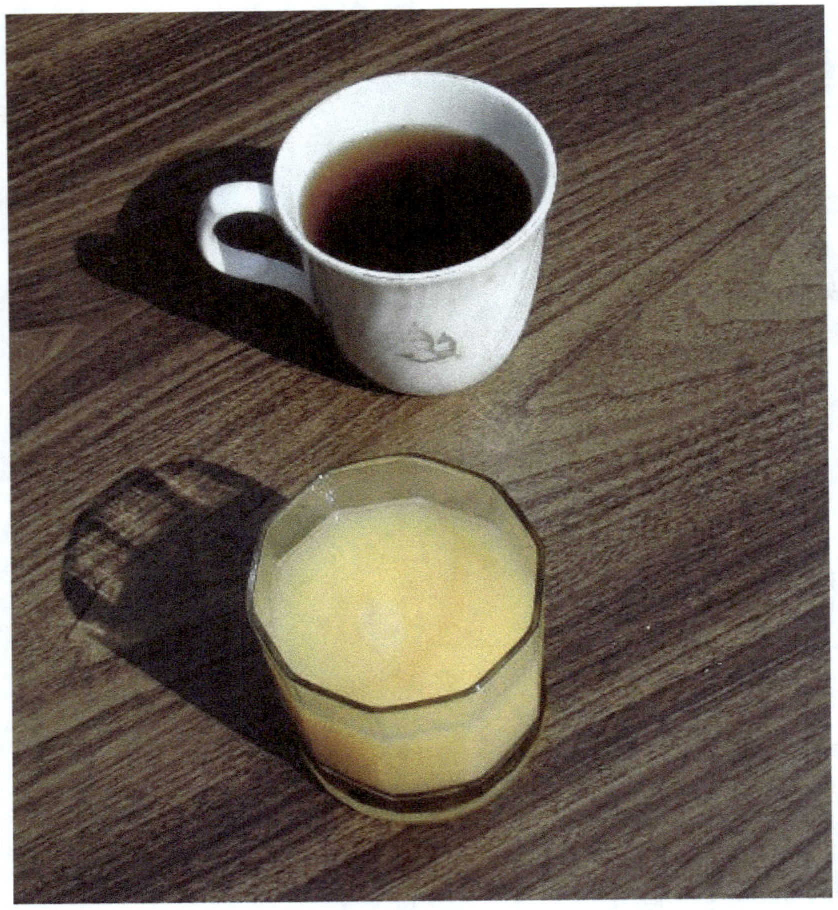

We ought therefore to show hospitality to such people so that we may work together for the truth.

Bible reference: 3 John 1:8

Context: (unspecified)

Illustration ID (credit): fx_0929 (author)

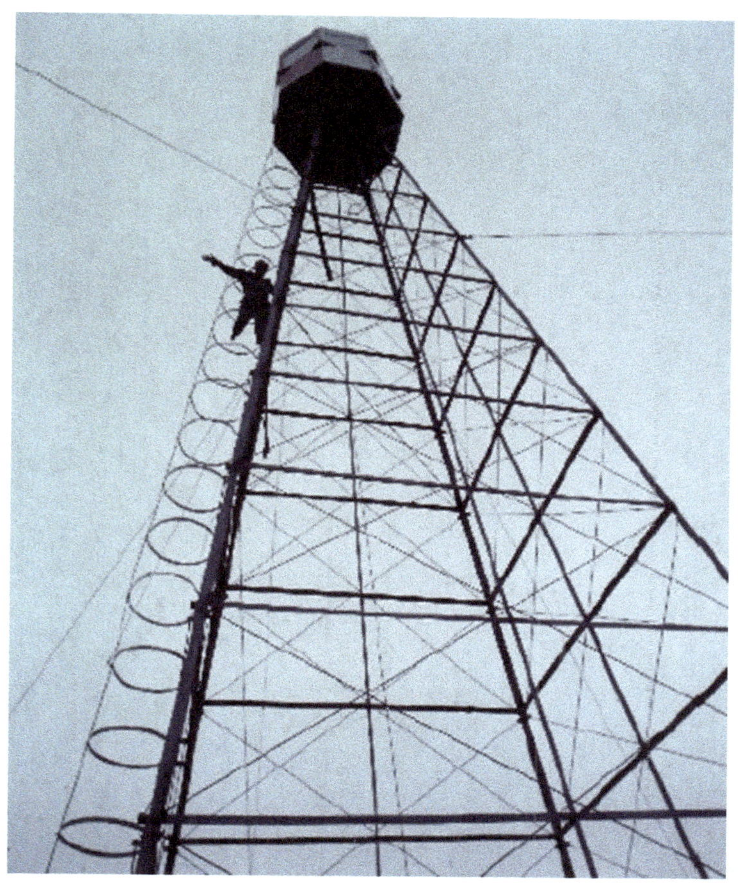

To him who is able to keep you from falling and to present you before his glorious presence without fault and with great joy -- to the only God our Savior be glory, majesty, power and authority, through Jesus Christ our Lord, before all ages, now and forevermore! Amen.

Bible reference: Jude 1:24-25

Context: Doxology

Illustration ID (credit): fz_fall (author)

Section 8: Prophetic/Apocalyptic Literature

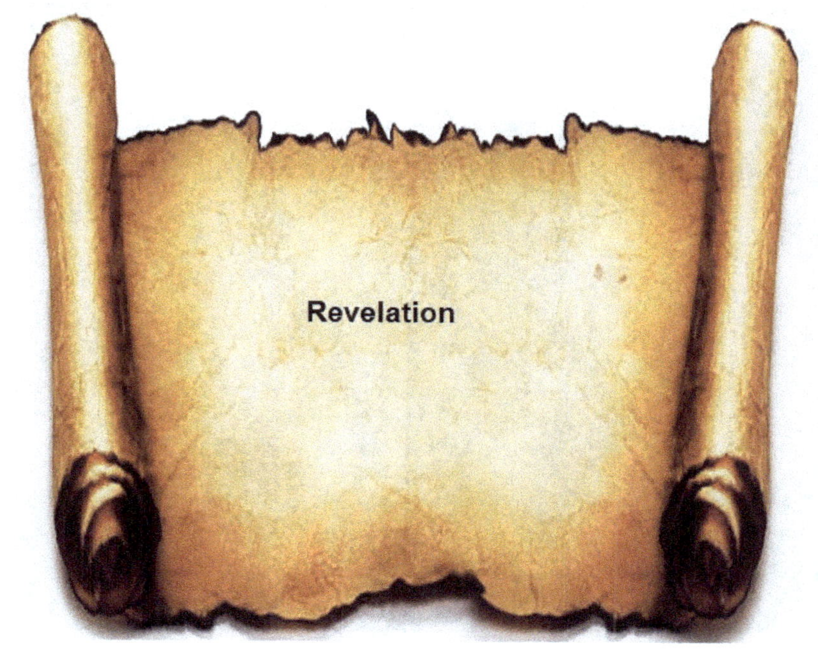

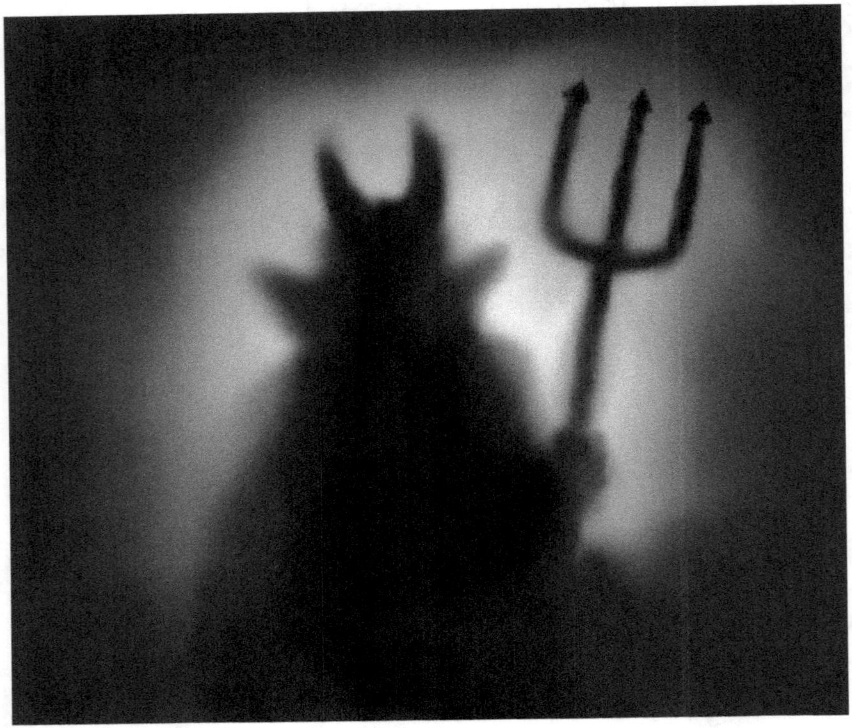

Do not be afraid of what you are about to suffer. I tell you, the devil will put some of you in prison to test you, and you will suffer persecution for ten days. Be faithful, even to the point of death, and I will give you the crown of life.

Bible reference: Revelation 2:10

Context: To the Church in Smyrna

Illustration ID (credit): is_1041968878 (istockphoto)

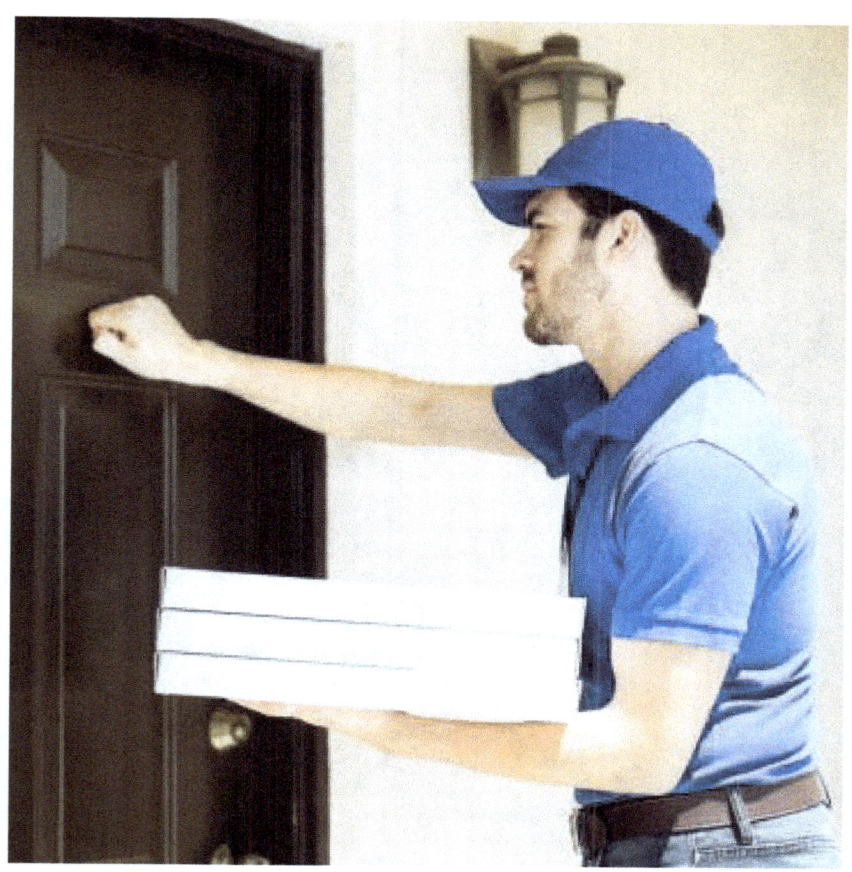

Here I am! I stand at the door and knock. If anyone hears my voice and opens the door, I will come in and eat with that person, and they with me.

Bible reference: Revelation 3:20

Context: To the Church in Laodicea

Illustration ID (credit): is_865382534 (istockphoto)

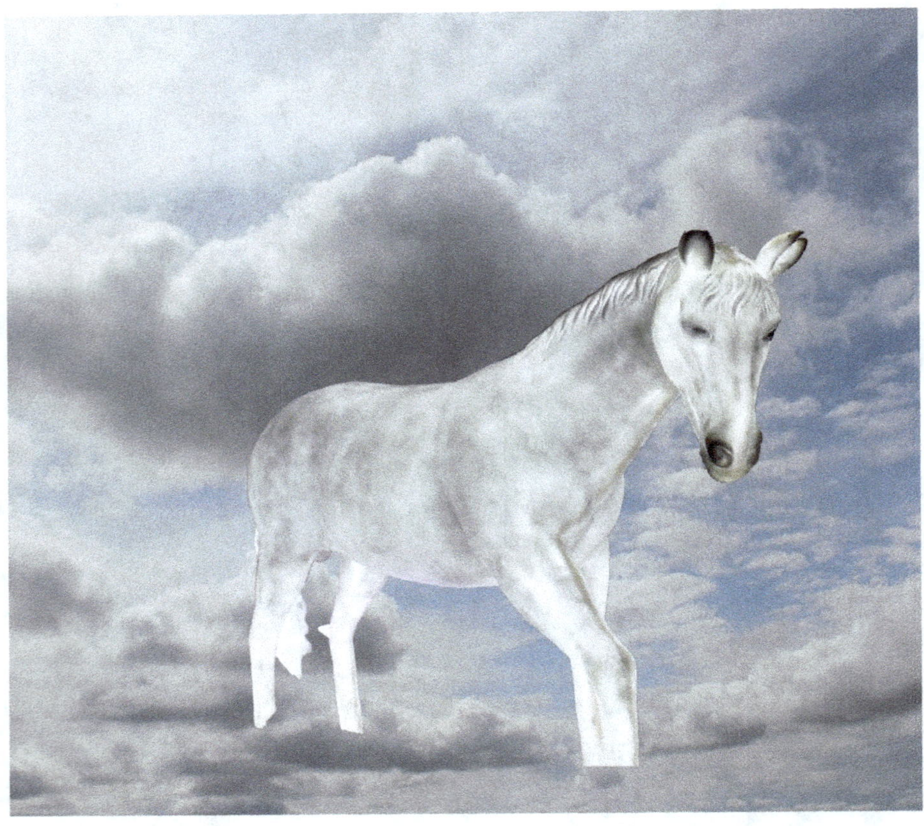

I saw heaven standing open and there before me was a white horse, whose rider is called Faithful and True. With justice he judges and wages war.

Bible reference: Revelation 19:11

Context: The Rider on the White Horse

Illustration ID (credit): fc_4511e (author, enhanced by Jim Fraser)

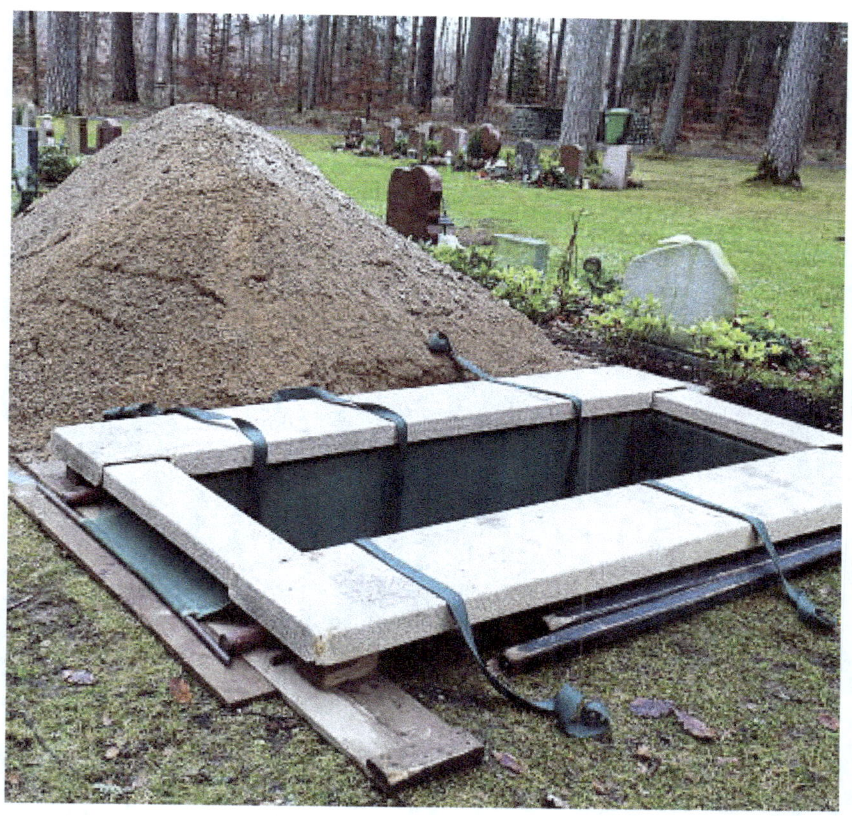

He will wipe every tear from their eyes. There will be no more death or mourning or crying or pain, for the old order of things has passed away.

Bible reference: Revelation 21:4

Context: The New Jerusalem

Illustration ID (credit): is_502635722 (istockphoto)

There will be no more night. They will not need the light of a lamp or the light of the sun, for the Lord God will give them light. And they will reign for ever and ever.

Bible reference: Revelation 22:5

Context: The River of Life

Illustration ID (credit): fx_3953 (author)

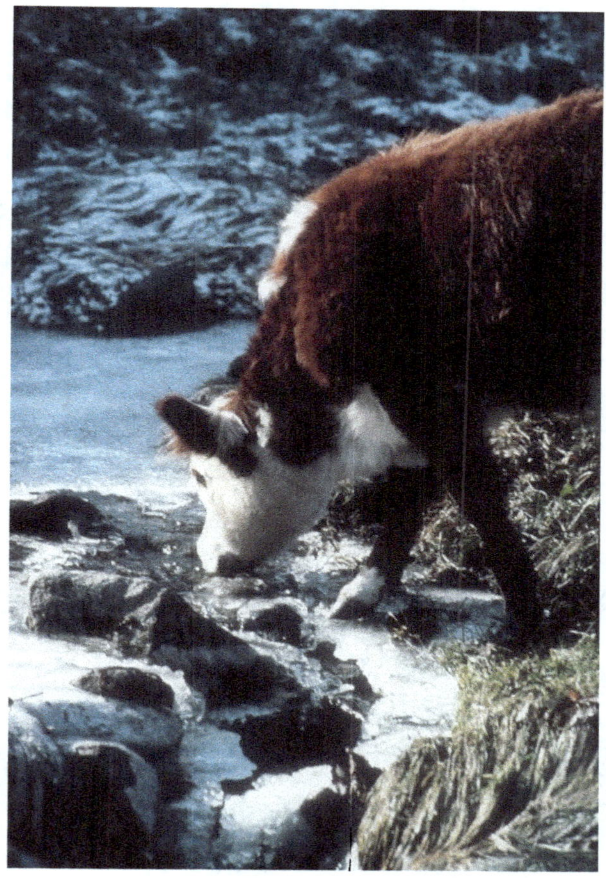

Let the one who is thirsty come; and let the one who wishes take the free gift of the water of life.

Bible reference: Revelation 22:17b

Context: Jesus Is Coming

Illustration ID (credit): fs_339 (author)

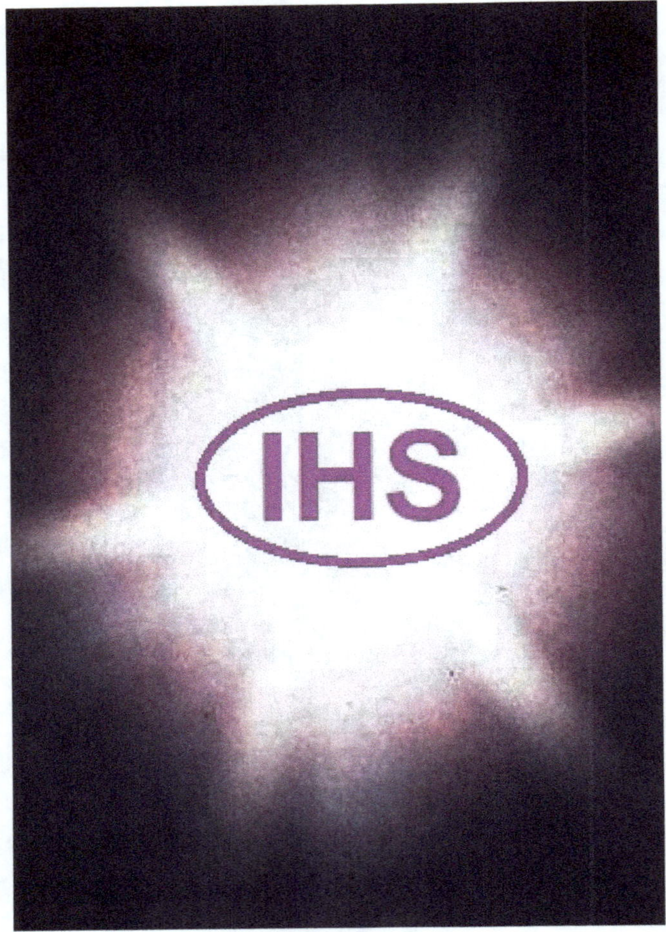

He who testifies to these things says, "Yes, I am coming soon." Amen. Come, Lord Jesus.

Bible reference: Revelation 22:20

Context: Jesus Is Coming

Illustration ID (credit): fy_666 (author)

Epilogue

You may have noticed the highlighted letters I, H and S on the book's front cover as well as on the previous page. And it may have reminded you of having seen these letters in various Christian settings such as on baptismal fonts, church lecterns or gravestones.

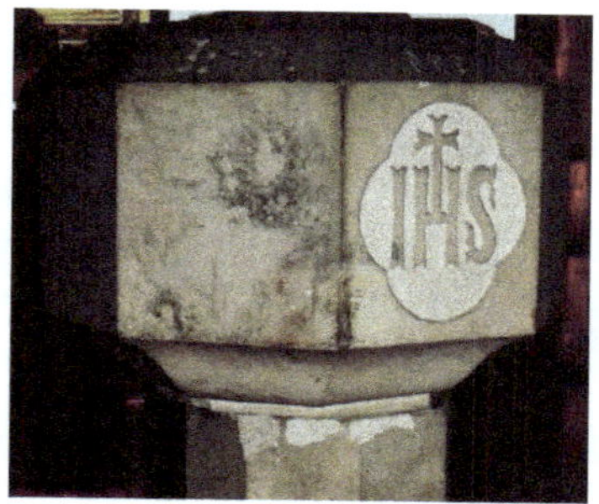

(Linda Hoy)

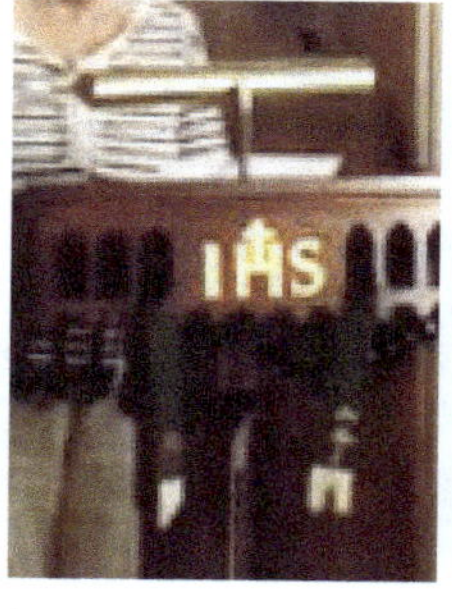

(Author)

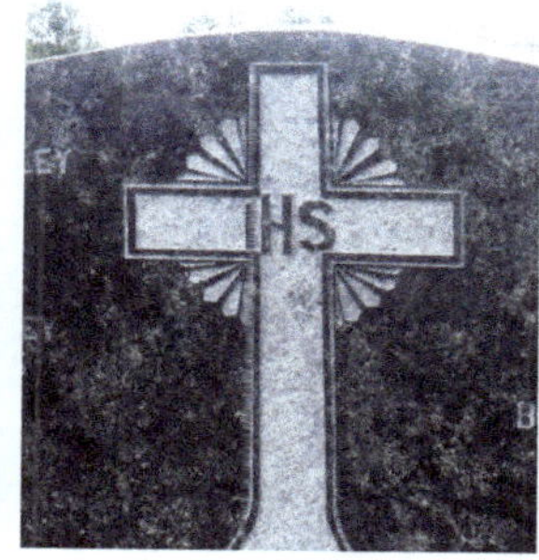

(Leslie Nutbrown)

What is the meaning and origin of IHS? Perhaps you, like many Christians, thought that the letters simply stood for "In His Service". I also shared that understanding until I investigated the term's origin in the course of research for this book. Below is a summary of what I learned.

> IHS is a Christogram. A Christogram is a monogram or combination of letters that forms an abbreviation for the name of Jesus Christ, traditionally used as a religious symbol within the Christian Church . . . In the Latin-speaking Christianity of medieval Western Europe (and so among Catholics and many Protestants today), the most common Christogram became "IHS" or "IHC", denoting the first three letters of the Greek name of Jesus, ΙΗΣΟΥΣ, iota-eta-sigma, or ΙΗΣ . . .

> "IHS" is sometimes interpreted as meaning "ΙΗΣΟΥΣ ΗΜΕΤΕΡΟΣ ēsous Hēmeteros Sōtēr, "Jesus our Saviour") or in Latin "Jesus Hominum (or Hierosolymae) Salvator", ("Jesus, Saviour of men [or: of Jerusalem]" in Latin) or connected with In Hoc Signo. English-language interpretations of "IHS" have included "In His Service". Such interpretations are known as backformed acronyms. . .

The IHS monogram with the H surmounted by a cross above three nails and surrounded by a Sun is the emblem of the Jesuits, according to tradition introduced by Ignatius of Loyola in 1541. (www.wikipedia.org)

Now, with the publication of **Illustrated Holy Scriptures**, there is another backformed IHS acronym to add to the list.